MW01031036

MINDS
and
BODIES

PHILOSOPHY OF MIND SERIES

Series Editor: Owen Flanagan, Duke University

SELF EXPRESSIONS
Mind, Morals, and the Meaning of Life
Owen Flanagan

THE CONSCIOUS MIND
In Search of a Fundamental Theory
David J. Chalmers

DECONSTRUCTING THE MIND
Stephen P. Stich

THE HUMAN ANIMAL
Personal Identity without Psychology
Eric T. Olson

MINDS AND BODIES
Philosophers and Their Ideas
Colin McGinn

MINDS
and
BODIES

Philosophers and Their Ideas

COLIN MCGINN

New York   Oxford • Oxford University Press   1997

Oxford University Press

Oxford   New York
Athens   Auckland   Bangkok   Bogota   Bombay   Buenos Aires
Calcutta   Cape Town   Dar es Salaam   Delhi   Florence   Hong Kong
Istanbul   Karachi   Kuala Lumpur   Madras   Madrid   Melbourne
Mexico City   Nairobi   Paris   Singapore   Taipei   Toyko   Toronto   Warsaw

and associated companies in
Berlin   Ibadan

Copyright © 1997 by Oxford University Press, Inc.

Published by Oxford University Press
198 Madison Avenue, New York, New York 10016

Library of Congress Cataloging-in-Publication Data
McGinn, Colin, 1950–
Minds and bodies: philosophers and their ideas / Colin McGinn.
p. cm. (Philosophy of mind series)
Includes index.
ISBN 0-19-511355-1
1. Philosophy of mind—Book reviews.   2. Ethics—Book reviews.
3. Mind and body—Book reviews.   I. Title.   II. Series.
BD418.3.M38   1997
128'.2—dc20   96-27353

1 3 5 7 9 8 6 4 2

Printed in the United States of America
on acid-free paper

Preface

I have not reprinted all my book reviews in this volume, omitting those that are more technical and of less general interest. But I have included virtually all those that have appeared in nonspecialist journals. They are reproduced here in their original form. I have not thought it worthwhile to rewrite earlier pieces in the light of later reflections, though there is in fact very little of a substantive nature I would wish to alter. The titles of the pieces were originally supplied by my editors, never by me; since these generally met with my approval I have let them stand. I am grateful to my various editors for allowing me to reprint these reviews, and for inviting me to write them in the first place. I am also grateful to Catherine McKeen for photocopying above and beyond the call of duty.

New York   *C. M.*
January 1997

Contents

III. ETHICS

MINDS
and
BODIES

Introduction

Writing a philosophy book is an arduous and exacting task. One does not emerge from the experience unscathed. The mental burden lies mainly in the necessity of keeping a complex argument, or set of arguments, in one's head for a long period of time, constantly repeating and refining them, day and night—until they come to seem either like gibberish or platitudes or both. Bertrand Russell wrote somewhere that the problems of logic are so inhumanly abstract that the philosophical logician only manages really to think about them for five minutes a year. Russellian exaggeration, no doubt, but it gives some idea of the feat of mental contortion needed to sustain the abstracted state of mind required to complete a substantial work of philosophy. It is actually rather amazing that it happens as often as it does (ballet dancing perhaps provides a distant analogy). And then there is the unpleasant sense of insecurity that comes with it—the feeling of being constitutionally inadequate to the task.

Reviewing philosophy books partakes of this arduousness. The reviewer, no less than the writer, must absorb and fully master a complex of arguments, grasping the whole they compose and appreciating how the entire structure is held in place. These arguments must then be reproduced in capsule form, so that the reader of the review can follow what the book contains. Then the arguments must be evaluated, with the weak points identified and exposed. This means that it is necessary to go one step beyond the author of the book, who presumably thinks her position sufficiently well defended and has not anticipated the criticisms made. These criticisms must be fair and accurate. All this must be done by sympathetically entering into the intellectual world of the author, not simply imposing one's own perspective on the material. One of the hardest things about reviewing philosophy books is that one must grasp the thought processes of someone else, though these may be very different from one's own. The reviewer must recapitulate the process of composing the book, and then offer a critical response to it.

I never write a philosophy review without feeling more or less crushed by the task. It is always much harder than I expect. At some point in reading the book, I wonder whether I will be able to write anything at all: the author's position refuses to come into focus, and I have no idea what I want to say about it. Then, after a sweaty few days, marked by a tension in the chest, I begin to see the shape of what I will write. I think of a workable way to expound the book's main thesis, and some response to it suggests itself to my laboring mind. I nearly always vow that this is the last review I am going to write for a good long time. But then an interesting book comes along, one that I want to read anyway, and about which I think I may have something useful to say. So here we go again. I have been doing this now for twenty years and have racked up nearly fifty of these mind-crunchers. I am disconcerted when people think these are just tossed off on a lazy wet weekend, as if reviewing were a leisure activity.

So why do I do it? It interferes with my own work; it's exhausting; and it garners very little academic credit. The reason is that I believe it is a valuable form of writing. It is valuable for me because it forces me to come to grips with someone else's ideas, instead of wallowing constantly in my own. I would recommend it to all philosophers, especially at the start of their careers. It encourages sound intellectual habits, by enforcing concision, clarity, and intellectual empathy—not to mention critical responsibility. It also discourages the kind of intellectual solipsism that afflicts so many academic philosophers. But it is valuable, too, in affording contact with thinking people who are not professionally involved in philosophy. Here I am speaking of reviews written, not for professional journals, but for publications that represent the wider intellectual culture. Most of the reviews included in this volume were written for such publications—the *Times Literary Supplement,* the *London Review of Books,* the *New Republic,* and others. The difficulty of the task is here compounded by the fact that one must write in such a way that the interested layman can follow what is being said, while doing justice to the content of the book in question. According to the editors of these magazines, not many specialists can do that. Yet such magazines are one of the only places in which academic philosophy is publicly heard. I myself believe it to be extremely important that the wider culture be informed of what is happening in academic philosophy; indeed, I believe it to be vital to the intellectual health of a community that serious philosophical work be brought before the public mind. This is because philosophical problems are part of everyone's mental landscape, so people should be made aware of the best that is being done to deal with these problems. Also, there is so much bad stuff out there competing for attention that it is important to put the good stuff across to people. In short, I believe in my subject, and I want to educate people in it as best I can.

The trouble is that book reviews in such publications tend to have a very short "shelf life"—a matter of weeks usually. They are comparatively widely read when they appear, but they soon disappear into the misty past. I have always found this dispiriting: so much effort for a result that lasts such a short time. And I often put ideas into my reviews that I do not express anywhere else, so that ideas I would like to have some permanence are quickly forgotten. I am therefore happy to be able to prolong the life of some of these pieces by resurrecting them now in book form. I hope that general readers with a taste for philosophy will find the collection useful, as providing an accessible window into what must sometimes seem like a wilfully arcane world. Since I have reviewed books by many of the leading philosophers of our time, it is to be hoped that the collection offers a picture of what has been going on in philosophy for the last twenty years or so. This book can thus be seen as a rather unorthodox introduction to contemporary philosophy.

I am sometimes charged with having an excessively acerbic reviewing style. And it is quite true that I can be severely critical of what I am reviewing. I must confess that I have a somewhat visceral reaction to work I perceive to be shoddy or dishonest, and I see no point in concealing my opinion. I have therefore made many "enemies" during the course of the last twenty years of criticism. The plain fact is that every author wants to be reviewed in terms of absolutely unqualified praise (I include myself), even though they do not want *everyone* to be so lauded. On several occasions I have been congratulated by A for having spoken the unflattering truth about B's book, only to find myself the object of an angry communication from A for having dared to criticize *his* latest effort—while the standards I have applied are precisely the same in the two cases. That, as they laughingly say, is human nature. Nevertheless, I have often felt that the cost in terms of personal enmity is not worth it. There is a constant conflict in book criticism between the urge to be truthful and awareness of the consequences of candor. And the better one is at detecting the faults in someone else's work, the greater the resentment at having done so. I see no way out of this dilemma except to cease reviewing, but that seems too cowardly a solution. I can only plead to those I have criticized that my intentions have always been to tell the truth as I see it. If I am wrong or unfair, that will ultimately reflect badly on me—not on them. The mirror image of this, and also something I have experienced more than once, is the tendency to be overgenerous in one's assessment of a book. This produces a peculiar nagging feeling, as if one has betrayed one's higher ideals. The moral risks in book reviewing are very real; any reviewer worth her salt feels them keenly. I can assure anyone whose book I have negatively reviewed (or positively reviewed!) that these risks have always been uppermost in my mind. I dislike unfairness as much as anyone, but I also dislike craven mealy-mouthed back-scratching.

This is a very mixed collection, ranging across pretty much the whole field of philosophy, as well as dipping into intellectual biography. But the majority of the pieces have to do with the mind, in one way or another. It might be helpful if I identify some the themes that have governed my treatment of the issues covered; these characterize my general approach to philosophical questions. First, and least controversially, I stoutly affirm the principles of rationality and objective truth. Dispassionate reason is the right way to deal with the questions that puzzle us, not rhetoric or political convenience. I apply this method as much to ethics as to metaphysics and philosophy of mind. Relativism and subjectivism never raise their ugly heads in these pages. Clarity and rigor of argument are the standards adhered to. But, second, I also oppose scientism—the tendency to think that all genuine questions are scientific in nature and are to be settled by empirical methods. I take philosophical questions to be a distinctive *type* of question, not to be answered by the prevailing paradigms of science. In ethics, too, I reject scientism, taking ethical questions to be *sui generis*, and not in any way inferior to scientific questions. Taking these two principles together, then, I believe in a form of rationality that is not scientific in nature. It is not that there is science on the one hand and irrationalism on the other. Rather, the notion of rationality has subvarieties, of which scientific rationality is only one. Philosophy, including ethics, exhibits its own kind of rationality, in which *argument* is the key method, not empirical investigation. To those readers who have run away with the idea that twentieth-century philosophy has done away with the notions of objective truth and universal reason, let me assert categorically that that is not the case. Such a position is the property of an irresponsible (and confused) few; it is very far from orthodox.

More substantively, I am guided in these essays by a commitment to what is sometimes called metaphysical realism. That is, I take both the external world and the world of the mind to be equally and fully real domains. I thus reject, on the one hand, all forms of idealism about the physical world: there is no sense in which the world of planets and plants and platypuses is mind-dependent, still less "socially constructed." And, on the other hand, I reject behaviorism and instrumentalism about the mind: thoughts and feelings are as real as anything else we refer to, and they are not to be reduced to mere behavior or treated as dispensable constructs. The universe thus contains two sorts of entity—physical things and mental things—neither being assimilable to the other. And this means, obviously, that there is a problem about how these equally real but distinct things are related to each other—the mind-body problem. That problem does not exist if either of the two can be analyzed in terms of the other, or if the reality of either is doubted. Many of the essays that follow deal with this problem in one form or another. My general position is to take the problem as genuine and as extremely hard. I do not believe that any current theory makes a significant dent in the mind-body problem. I thus hold that the relation between the mind and the body is a deep mystery. More than that, there are hints in these essays that I take it to be a *permanent* mystery. This is a position I have argued for elsewhere, in *The Problem of Consciousness* (Basil Blackwell, 1991) and *Problems in Philosophy* (Basil Blackwell, 1993); I mention it now because it informs my attitude to many of the books discussed here. It is a position directly related to the realism just affirmed: for there is a mystery about the relation between the physical and the mental only because both are real constituents of the world. Something can transcend our powers of understanding only if its nature is not constituted or constrained by those powers. It is because truth is not epistemic that there is room for the possibility that the nature of mind and matter might not be accessible to human thought.

Beyond these four assumptions I am guided by nothing except the particular topic at hand. I try to be as open-minded as possible, without (as some wit once said) letting my brain fall out. I hope that the virtues of forthright intellectual exchange will be evident to readers; thought thrives best when continually put to the challenge. Rational argument is still one of the most powerful forces ever to grace this little planet of ours. It deserves to be encouraged and celebrated in all its forms. This book is my tribute to the powers of human reason, as well as an acknowledgment of its limitations.

I

PHILOSOPHICAL LIVES

1

Wittgenstein: My Wicked Heart

Ludwig Wittgenstein: The Duty of Genius
by Ray Monk
Cape, 1990

Ludwig Wittgenstein: A Student's Memoir
by Theodore Redpath
Duckworth, 1990

Was Wittgenstein a spiritual as well as a philosophical genius? Ray Monk's exceptionally fine and fat biography puts us in a better position to answer this question than we have been hitherto.

Perhaps the best place to begin trying to understand Wittgenstein's character is with the photographs that exist of his face. He himself advised friends to pay more attention to people's faces and often passed remarks about the faces of others, saying (according to Theodore Redpath) of Locke that he had "a nice face," of Descartes that he had "the face of a murderer," of T. S. Eliot that he had "a modern face" (meant disapprovingly). I recommend, in particular, a striking picture of Wittgenstein, reproduced in Monk's book, which was taken in Swansea in 1945 by Ben Richards—a young man almost forty years Wittgenstein's junior, with whom he was then despairingly in love.

Even at this distance of time, and in two-dimensional monochrome, it is hard to meet Wittgenstein's gaze full on for very long. The eyes engage you immediately: they are imploring eyes, yet with an intense rage flaring just behind the iris, sending off an unnerving blend of supplication and admonition—your own eyes reflexively rebound from them. Framing the scalding ice of these eyes are the sharply scored facial lines of the orbits and brow, which have the informal exactitude of the numbered paragraphs that make up his books. The exclamatory shock of hair brings an incongruous

Reprinted with permission from the *London Review of Books* (November 22, 1990).

boyishness into the face. There is a scornful lift to the finely sculpted nose. The mouth is distancingly tight and yet minutely puckered, as if sensually restrained, bleakly kissless. A slight tilt of the head warns of a denunciatory access in the offing. The look is simultaneously delicate and military, tender and ferocious. If you stare hard at the face, it seems to shift aspect from one of these poles to the other, much as his famous duck-rabbit drawing does: from saintly to demonic and back again. You feel the excitement and peril of an encounter with the man. He seems both harsh and gentle, one of these traits replacing the other with no change of underlying form, as if an "ambiguous soul" informs the face. It is a face that sends a spear of doubt into the core of your own integrity: yet it sternly repels all incursions from outside. You might say that it is the face of an executioner—though an executioner of a very special kind.

The bare facts of Wittgenstein's life are by now fairly well known: the difficulty has been to discern in them an intelligible human being. Born into a rich and richly cultured Viennese family in 1889, a family of achievers and suicides, he took up the study of engineering, which brought him to Manchester to do research on kites. This led him to more purely mathematical interests, and thence to the foundations of mathematics, when he came across Russell's *Principles of Mathematics*. Philosophy surged through him and, at Frege's suggestion, he went to Cambridge to study with Russell. With phenomenal speed he impressed Russell with his logical talents: indeed, he virtually destroyed Russell's own philosophical confidence. The spiritual torment that marked his life was already much in evidence at this time, as was his power over others.

Abruptly he decided to go and live alone in Norway for two years so that he could work on logic in complete isolation. This plan was thwarted by World War I, which saw Wittgenstein, first, behind the lines and then, voluntarily, at the front. He was decorated for conspicuous bravery, having chosen the most dangerous position available to him, the observation post; and he also worked fitfully on the *Tractatus*. He finished that searing book soon after the war ended, but he could not find a publisher; neither was it well understood by Russell and Frege, his two great mentors. Eventually, however, Russell's influence led to its publication in German and English.

Wittgenstein then became an elementary schoolteacher in rural Austria, living in extreme poverty and declining the help of his aristocratic family. He quit this job when his punitive disciplinary methods got him into trouble with his pupils' parents, and he eventually found his way back to Cambridge, after spending a year designing a house for his sister. The *Tractatus* was by now celebrated by the logical positivists, who contrived to ignore its mystical thrust. His own attitude toward the book was one of growing retraction, and he began to work out a new philosophy.

He next made efforts to secure manual work in Russia but the authorities there would only allow him to teach philosophy, so he gave up the idea of emigration. He considered training as a doctor instead, but carried on working out his new philosophical ideas. In 1939 he was elected G. E. Moore's successor in Cambridge, which helped him avoid Nazi persecution, but he found the post stifling. He wanted to contribute to the war effort, in due course exchanging his professorial duties for those of a dispensary porter at Guy's Hospital.

After the war he reluctantly returned to Cambridge, where he worked on the material that was to become *Philosophical Investigations,* dominating the philosophical scene there. His dissatisfaction with Cambridge, academic life, and England generally ("the disintegrating and putrefying English civilisa-tion") culminated in his resigning his chair and going to live and work in solitude in Ireland. The last two years of his life he spent living as the guest of various friends, having no income and no home of his own. He died in 1951 of cancer of the prostate, not living to see the publication of the work that had occupied the second half of his life.

What kind of character was it that carved out this exceptional life? Three episodes in it are particularly telling. First, there are his acts of military valor during World War I, which are easily misconstrued. It was not a matter of patriotism or comradely solidarity—in fact, he detested and despised the other soldiers; it was rather an exercise in self-purification, a proof to himself that he could live in the right spirit. The war, he said, saved him from suicide by effecting a transformation of his soul: it enabled him to achieve the state of ethical seriousness he sought. It was in the same spirit that he gave away his vast inherited wealth to already rich members of his family. This had nothing to do with a sense of economic injustice or compassion for the poor: it was purely a matter of expelling from his life anything that might compromise the integrity of his spirit—an act more of pride than of generosity.

The third notable incident is that of his brutal treatment of children at the school in Otterthal and the court case at which he lied about the extent of the corporal punishment he administered; and, years later, the return there to apologize to the children for this violence. It should be noted here that the hair pulling and ear boxing were more often the result of Wilttgenstein's impatience with some of his dimmer pupils' slowness to make progress in algebra than they were punishment for ordinary bad behavior. In this epi-sode we see overt violence centering on intellectual impatience, accompanied by dishonesty about this violence. This incident was, it appears, the chief subject of the tortured confessions he later made to friends—again as a means to selfpurgation.

Monk narrates this life with understanding, care, industry, and exemplary impartiality. He has had full access to the material in the possession of Wittgenstein's literary executors, his knowledge of the philosophical and cultural background is deep and extensive, and he possesses exactly the right combination of censure and sympathy. After reading his book I felt that I had finally begun to grasp what kind of man Wittgenstein was, as well as learning a good deal about the relation between his life and his work. I hope the book is widely read both inside and outside academic philosophy, especially outside. It is a considerable achievement.

Russell wrote darkly of Wittgenstein: "He was a very singular man, and I doubt whether his disciples knew what manner of a man he was." Those disciples, by the way, who are said to mimic Wittgenstein's manner, might be interested to learn from Redpath that Wittgenstein told him that he had picked up mannerisms of speech and gesture from Frege—the archenemy as far as some of these disciples are concerned. Out of what ingredients was this singular man composed? Here is a summary list: he was vain, self-absorbed, emotionally solipsistic; he hated the artificiality and pretentiousness of university life, favoring the company of "ordinary people"; he had a deep love of music and rudely rigorous standards of musical quality; he relished hard-boiled American detective stories, as well as Hollywood Westerns and musicals; his sense of humor could be surprisingly puerile, though oddly endearing; he was passionate and demanding in personal relations yet often capriciously cold; he held (at least at one time) that Jews were incapable of genuine originality, here following the weird theories of Otto Weininger; and he had a difficult time dealing with his sexuality. What are we to make of these disparate ingredients? How do they hang together?

The key seems to lie in the pride for which he ceaselessly berated himself. Everything in his life seemed either to bolster this pride or to consist in an effort to dismantle it. Philosophy, essentially a prideful subject, and so a potentially humiliating one, was a chief source of the conceit he strove constantly to extirpate: hence the self-cancelling metaphilosophy of both the *Tractatus* and the *Investigations*. The ruthless domination of others, so numbingly applied to young acolytes, sprang from his conviction of his intellectual and moral superiority, and so had to be accompanied by declarations of his own lack of "decency." Even the difficulty he had in staying physically close to those he loved shows his inability to give himself up to another: nothing must encroach on the charmed region of his own spirit. Sex felt like a fall from this exalted state, as if his own body were an affront to his pride of soul. His life was thus an insoluble alternation between self-celebration and self-condemnation. The corny humor and taste for popular culture function like outposts of his psyche to which he could flee to escape his pride and the self-loathing it inevitably produced. This explains the sense one has that these pockets of his personality are curiously remote from the center of the man: they are peripheral bolt-holes from that molten core of fierce self-devotion. In this light it comes as no surprise that he found masturbating at the same time exhilarating and distressing. The image of him starchily and painfully confessing his transgressions, some major, some risibly minor, intentionally wounding his pride while simultaneously fueling it, perfectly sums him up. The idea that humor might play a role in holding his pride in check seems not to have been a possibility for him: to let jokey self-ridicule into the inner temple was more than his pride could take—too much like laughing in church. Where would the nobility of self-abasement be then?

This lifelong struggle with his pride took a form that ought to have seemed to him more doomed than it did. His method was that of direct assault: fierce self-scrutiny, merciless self-condemnation, exposure to experiences calculated to chasten and humiliate. He approached his own soul like a kind of moral engineer: there was a fault in the design and it had to be dismantled, tinkered with, reconstructed, possibly scrapped altogether. Gazing inward, poking around inside, was the way to rid the spiritual machine of its imperfections. Such directness of approach to a problem was quite alien to his announced philosophical method: for obliqueness and indirection were to be the essence of philosophical advancement. The obvious flaw in this approach to himself was that it inevitably ran the very risk it was supposed to eliminate—the narcissistic absorption in his own being that stood between himself and the outer world. Another method—if method there must be— would be to try turning a bored eye and ear away from one's own soul and toward the lives and feelings of others, hoping that one's own moral improvement will occur while one is, as it were, otherwise engaged.

One of the most shocking and revealing of Wittgenstein's remarks occurs late in his life when he is reflecting on his love for Ben Richards, which struck me as the most outward-directed affection of his life. In his late fifties now, he writes, as though the thought were new to him: "It is the mark of a *true* love that one thinks of what the *other* suffers. For he suffers too, is also a poor devil." What alarms here is the very banality of the thought, and indeed one looks in vain for any similar sentiment in his earlier romantic attachments. "Perhaps the fly had at last found its way out of the fly-bottle," Monk remarks, trenchantly and rather tragically. Not that Wittgenstein managed even in this case to translate his strong feelings into an ordinary romantic relationship with the young man in question.

This bears on the disputed question of Wittgenstein's alleged period of homosexual promiscuity, reported by William Bartley III. In a finely judged appendix Monk addresses himself to Bartley's claim that Wittgenstein used to avail himself of the sexual favors of "rough young men" in a certain park in Vienna, casting considerable doubt on the veracity of this claim. As Monk argues, Wittgenstein's obvious discomfort with his sexual nature, hetero- or homosexual, makes the idea of such freewheeling promiscuity seem quite incredible. It would, moreover, be extremely surprising if such activities had been confined to a single, short period of his life, never to resurface. Often, in the course of reading about Wittgenstein's romantic involvements, I found myself heartily wishing the he *had* been homosexually promiscuous.

That would certainly have eased the lot of the unlucky Francis Skinner, whose love for Wittgenstein clearly included a desire for sexual contact that Wittgenstein apparently did his best to avoid—though, happily, he was not totally successful in this. One such "lapse" is reported in Wittgenstein's notebooks, and incidentally shows Redpath to be wrong in his belief that there was nothing more "lurid" between Skinner and Wittgenstein that a close male friendship. The two were vacationing together in Norway and Wittgenstein reports himself as being "sensual, susceptible, indecent" with Skinner: "Lay with him two or three times. Always at first with the feeling that there was nothing wrong in it, *then* with shame. Have also been unjust, edgy and insincere towards him, and also cruel." These are disturbing words in more ways than one. Were cruelty and lovelessness his only possible response to actual human intimacy? Did his need for the affection of another always have to turn into a refusal or incapacity to lay his own heart on the line?

My impression is that sexual promiscuity was about the last thing Wittgenstein could tolerate—and also that *ethically,* it would have been a definite step in the right direction. Unfortunately, he didn't see it that way. A story is told that a close friend of his once said of him that "he never had a good fuck in his life." I cannot vouch for the truth of this story but it seems to me infinitely more probable, and infinitely more woeful, than the idea that he once indulged a taste for rough trade. It marks a real lack in his conception of the spiritual life of a human being, as well as being sad in itself.

This is of a piece with the story that is told, amusing in its way, about the one female love of his life, Marguerite Respinger, whom he at one time wished to marry and, with a proposal in mind, invited on a holiday with him. She turned up in remotest Norway only to find that her suitor's idea of a prenuptial vacation was that they should see very little of each other and spend the two weeks in prayer and meditation, for which purpose Wittgenstein had left a marked Bible in the room in which she was to stay. She decided, amazingly, that Ludwig was not the man for her. In any case, his wish was for a childless platonic marriage—though, oddly enough, he enjoyed kissing her for hours on end.

And what of the philosophy? Monk handles this expertly, seamlessly weaving it into the narrative, showing the intimate relationship between the ethical concerns of Wittgenstein's life and his philosophical ideas. There is much interesting scholarly material about Wittgenstein's reading and intellectual influences, and about the composition of his two major works. Perhaps the most striking item, from a biographical point of view, is Wittgenstein's late remark: "Nearly all my writings are private conversations with myself. Things that I say to myself tête-à-tête." Here his personal solipsism finds its natural counterpart in his philosophical style: always a turning inward, as if only his own thoughts are ultimately worth heeding. And this, of course, is part of the strength and charm of his philosophical writing, and of him as a personality: an enclosed world of numbered paragraphs, both poetic and mathematical, where no alien voice intrudes. There is beauty but also desolation in this ideal.

I began by asking whether Wittgenstein was a spiritual genius. That question really has two parts: was he the spiritually sublime individual—the "saint"—people often said he was? And did he know *how* to be such an individual, whether or not he was one himself? I think the answer must be no to both questions. His vanity, emotional solipsism, and coldness put him well outside the category of the saint; and his engineering (or surgical) approach to his spiritual condition seems to me wrongly conceived, embodying as it does a deep mistake of ethical attention. But a better question might be this: given his nature, did he live a noble and ethically distinguished life? (He clearly lived an impressive and remarkable one.) Here I think we must do him the courtesy of taking him at his word and not allow our natural sentimentality about great men to get in the way of hearing what he actually says about himself. Of Moore's reputation for saintly childlike innocence, Wittgenstein remarked: "I can't understand that, unless it's also to a *child's* credit. For you aren't talking of the innocence a man has fought for, but of an innocence which comes from a natural absence of temptation." If we take seriously Wittgenstein's own repeated assessment of himself as "rotten" and "indecent," as having a "wicked heart"—in whatever way these epithets were meant—then it becomes clear why he regarded his life as a mighty struggle with himself, and what he had to overcome to achieve the moral standing he did. His peculiar greatness comes from that agonizing battle between his natural hubris and the humility he craved, between his compulsive devotion to himself and his willed concern for others. The singularity of his spiritual achievement consists in this strained amalgamation of aggressive megalomania and abject self-mortification. Somehow this battle brought something spiritually valuable into the world that had not been there before: an ability, we might say, to attend religiously to the face of another human being—but to do so as if this were the strangest and most impossible thing in the world to achieve.

2

Wittgenstein: Soul on Fire

Philosophical Occasions, 1912–1951
by Ludwig Wittgenstein
edited by James Klagge and
Alfred Nordmann
Hackett, 1993

Wittgenstein: The Terry Eagleton Script,
The Derek Jarman Film
by Terry Eagleton and Derek Jarman
Indiana University Press, 1993

Ludwig Wittgenstein did most of his publishing after his death, leaving that sordid business to his literary executors. The modest curriculum vitae that accumulated during his lifetime—one short book, which was his doctoral dissertation, one article, one book review—has now expanded to fifteen substantial volumes. And there is more where that came from. Wittgenstein would hardly have flourished in today's academic environment. The greatest philosopher of the century would have had to fight hard for tenure. His kind of perfectionism is no longer tolerated.

Not that Wittgenstein would himself have cared, given his propensity for leaving the profession of his own free will. It is only the world that would have suffered. There is a characteristic poignancy, in any case, in the fact that his great mature work, *Philosophical Investigations,* should have been published two years after he died in 1951, thus sparing him the anguish of its instant and prolonged celebrity. So canonical is that work, indeed, that it is hard to believe that it was written by anyone. It stands there like a natural monument, the result of superlunary dictation.

Wittgenstein's philosophical legacy consists principally of the binary star formed by the *Tractatus Logico-Philosophicus,* which appeared in 1922, and the *Philosophical Investigations,* high-density objects giving off complimentary glows. The views expressed in these two works are sharply opposed in

Reprinted with permission from the *New Republic* (June 20, 1994).

content and in outlook, but there persists a single underlying preoccupation, and there are common threads. More than any philosopher before him, Wittgenstein was concerned with the link between language and reality. He wanted to understand how, by emitting sounds, we manage to say something about the world beyond language. By what mechanism or means does language, and hence thought, come to be meaningful? And what are the limits of meaning?

Wittgenstein's contribution, put in the broadest terms, is that he saw how difficult this simple question is. Talking about things is a deeply puzzling phenomenon, not the transparent act of mind-world engagement that we tend to assume. How must the world be, and how must language be, for it to be possible that the two should join in occasions of meaning? What constitutes this unlikely nexus?

In the *Tractatus* the answer was a highly abstract metaphysical system buttressed by formal logic, in which the structure of reality and the structure of thought were deduced from the requirements for any possible kind of semantic representation. This became known as the picture theory of meaning. "What any picture, of whatever form, must have in common with reality, in order to be able to depict it—correctly or incorrectly—in any way at all, is logical form, i.e., the form of reality." That is, for language to depict the world, it is necessary for these two poles to share an inner logical structure, so that facts and propositions partake of the same transcendent logical order. Language and the world are one, in their deep metaphysical essence. This ultimate monism may not be apparent on the surface of language, but it must be so beneath the surface; and there must exist an ideal language in which the necessary sameness of form with reality is made fully transparent. To construct such a language would be to devise a symbolic system in which the structure of the world would reach right through our modes of representation: a flawless metaphysical mirror, as it were. The puzzles produced by our imperfect ordinary language would be finally laid to rest once the ideal language was available.

And yet Wittgenstein did think that there is a residue of significance not covered by such an account of meaning. For there are things that cannot be said, but only shown. "There are, indeed, things that cannot be put into words. They *make themselves manifest*. They are what is mystical." This realm includes ethics, aesthetics, philosophy itself. Strictly speaking, utterances of those kinds are literal nonsense, since they cannot be brought under the picture theory of meaning, but Wittgenstein has no doubt about their importance and their legitimacy. The famous last sentence of the *Tractatus*, "What we cannot speak about we must pass over in silence," is not intended to suggest a dismissive attitude toward the unsayable. It recommends, instead, a reverential, attentive speechlessness in the face of the transcendent. What cannot be put into language can still be apprehended, in quiet obliqueness. The form of the mystical, unlike the form of reality, is not any kind of logical form. It lies outside the space of possible fact.

None of this survives in Wittgenstein's later work. In place of abstract deductions about the essential nature of language and the world, we have meticulous observations of what actually occurs in the use of language; an intense distrust of generality; an insistence on the irreducible multiplicity of our "language games"; and the introduction of the living human being at the root of what makes language work. There is no longer any such thing as "the general form of a proposition," any more than there is a general essence for what we call a game; and no longer is it the function of all words to denote a constituent of reality. The whole notion of an ideal language is riddled with error and confusion. No picture, however arcane or mental or logical, could ever confer a meaning. Rules of language, even for mathematical terms, cannot take a grip on our thought and conduct independently of our being naturally prone to make particular choices. Our justifications always run out, and we must act without appeal to foundations.

What is basic, in the later philosophy, are the language games that we actually play, and the "forms of life" into which they are woven. Meaning must be sought in those activities, not in a hidden mechanism or a sublime structure. Where once meaning seemed crystalline, unitary, and remote, now it is humdrum, multifarious, and humanly mediated. Its study is not part of formal logic or metaphysics, but of human "natural history." This is the force of Wittgenstein's celebrated dictum that the meaning of an expression is revealed in its use: there are no preexistent meanings onto which our minds magically latch. Rather, our ways of behaving with words are the sole repository of semantic significance. Wittgenstein was fond of quoting a line from Goethe: "In the beginning was the deed."

What links Wittgenstein's philosophies is a deep ambivalence about language. In the earlier work language is credited with a marvelous inner logic; yet it is also held to be inadequate to the expression of some of our most profound concerns. It is like a perfectly engineered precision tool that can work only within severe limits. Even the ideal language of Wittgenstein's first philosophy cannot say what can only be shown. And in the later work we are told that "philosophy is a battle against the bewitchment of our intelligence by means of language," though elsewhere we are assured that "philosophy may in no way interfere with the actual use of language; it can in the end only describe it." On the one hand, ordinary language is held to be perfectly in order as it is, not needing reform or censure on philosophical grounds alone. On the other hand, it is supposed to give rise to intractable confusion, because of the misleading analogies it suggests, and because its grammar fails to reflect the actual use of words. Language encourages us to talk nonsense, but it is not less than ideal because of it. It is like a perfectly adapted organism that has a regrettable tendency to turn on its owner.

Moreover, language has its limits, in the early Wittgenstein and the late, as a foundation for thought and action, since it rests upon something non-linguistic in nature. The learner of language needs more than verbal explanation if he is to latch onto what is meant, since no word is self-interpreting;

the teacher must rely on the learner's taking his instructions in a certain way and acting appropriately. For the same reason, the analysis of one sentence by means of another sentence cannot escape the circle of signs, and the slack must be taken up by modes of natural response that resist codification. Language is possible only because it is not self-reliant, because it is parasitic on a foundation of nonlinguistic abilities and dispositions. In this sense—here we see the ghost of the *Tractatus*—language cannot communicate its own presuppositions.

This ambivalence about the powers of language reveals itself in Wittgenstein's prose style. There is great confidence in the expressive capacities of language, even the pared-down, monosyllabic vernacular that he preferred; but his style is also halting and allusive, discontinuous and metaphorical. He writes as if he is determined not to ask more of language than it can deliver, not to give the reader the illusion that things are clearer and straighter than they really are. Certainly his prose requires the utmost scrutiny, as well as an ability to engage creatively with what is being said. And it strives for an intellectual effect that goes beyond discursive formulation to alter one's "way of seeing." "Say what you choose," he says at one point, "so long as it does not prevent you from seeing the facts." This can sound odd, coming from someone who ceaselessly reminds philosophers of their perilous tendency to misuse language; but it fits the deeper aim of curing distortions of vision caused by language itself. For all his obsession with language, Wittgenstein's heart was not exactly there. He was as much concerned with what language cannot do as with what it can.

In *Philosophical Occasions*, James Klagge and Alfred Nordmann have usefully and skillfully assembled various writings by Wittgenstein that have been scattered and hard to obtain. The variety is such as to permit a synoptic view of his several concerns—from comments on Frazer's *The Golden Bough*, to pieces on ethics, sense-data, cause and effect, free will, the nature of philosophy. There are also some revealing letters and an informative essay by Henrik von Wright on the writings that Wittgenstein left behind. The book is an excellent source, and it provides a nourishing supplement to the *Investigations*.

Particularly interesting are the remarks on the nature of philosophy, which expand illuminatingly on themes pursued in the *Investigations*. Philosophy, for Wittgenstein, is not to be conceived in the traditional way as a maximally general science, so that the task of the philosopher is to develop an entirely universal theory of reality. Instead, philosophical work consists in dismantling confusions and mythologies by paying careful attention to our ordinary concepts, resisting the false analogies suggested by our forms of expression. The problems are difficult, not because they concern especially deep features of reality, but rather because it is hard for us to obtain a clear view of what we already know very well. Philosophy, or the search for the ultimate theory, is over, but philosophizing must go on.

"Philosophical problems can be compared to locks on safes, which can be opened by dialing a certain word or number, so that no force can open the door until just this word has been hit upon, and once it is hit upon any child can open it." There is nothing intrinsically profound about the right combination, nor about the result it secures; the difficulty lies purely in the trouble we have in hitting upon the answer, in seeing what is before our eyes. This has the consequence that the workings of our language are as opaque to us as a secret code, even as there is nothing hidden or recondite about these workings. We fail to grasp the truth about our language precisely because it is so familiar to us. The philosopher must approach his own mastery of language like an anthropologist, striving to see it afresh. Alienation is sound method.

Wittgenstein's influence, for good or ill, has been continuous and unparalleled. Something of his own estimate of the nature of this influence can be gleaned from the lapidary preface to the *Investigations*, where he says of the "remarks" that compose that "album": "I make them public with doubtful feelings. It is not impossible that it should fall to the lot of this work, in its poverty and in the darkness of this time, to bring light into one brain or another—but, of course, it is not likely." The pessimism here is not the result of feeling that he will be ignored or underappreciated, since he goes on to admit that fear of plagiarism was a major stimulus to publication: "I was obliged to learn that my results (which I had communicated in lectures, typescripts and discussions), variously misunderstood, more or less mangled or watered-down, were in circulation. This stung my vanity and I had difficulty in quieting it." It is worth asking whether these presentiments apply also to his posthumous reverberations. How much mangling and diluting has there been? More to the point, how much projection and assimilation has there been? For it takes two to influence; and in the case of Wittgenstein the influence tends to be more of a mixing than a pouring. Cloudiness is apt to be the upshot.

From the moment he stepped into philosophy, from the not-so-adjacent field of engineering, Wittgenstein had an impact of extraordinary proportions. From the first he thrilled Bertrand Russell, no lagger in the head area, with his intensity and his brilliance, leading Russell to proclaim him the next great hope in philosophy. Later Wittgenstein's criticisms so withered Russell intellectually that he more or less gave up the kind of philosophy of which he was a main architect, turning instead to less theoretical matters. (Russell eventually turned against Wittgenstein's mature style of philosophy, declaring him to have given up serious thinking.) In Vienna in the 1930s, the logical positivists found the rationale for their own scientistic ideology in Wittgenstein's *Tractatus*, and their teachings went on to dominate philosophy for a lamentably extended period—though they grotesquely misrepresented the content of that work, notably in respect to its professed mysticism. This aspect of the *Tractatus* was totally antithetical to their own outlook.

Installed at Cambridge in the thirties, Wittgenstein dominated the scene, founding a new style of philosophy and combining torment and insouciance a way that was to become de rigueur in certain quarters. There were no genuine philosophical problems to fret over, but it was agony to philosophize all the same. ("The real discovery is the one that makes me capable of stopping doing philosophy when I want to. The one that gives philosophy peace, so that it is no longer tormented by questions which bring *itself* into question.") "Wittgensteinians" everywhere mimicked the master's mannerisms, declining to theorize, airily dismissing the exertions of earlier thinkers. Whether or not you understood him, Wittgenstein *had* to be right.

Then, in the sixties and seventies, came the backlash. Systematic philosophy reasserted itself, and Wittgenstein was eclipsed by Frege, Quine, formal semantics, cognitive science. He was too low-tech, too reactionary, too depessing. There was a new thirst for theory. During the last decade partisanship has tended to give way to scholarly exegesis, to learned detachment: the arch antiprofessional has become professionalized. Wittgenstein is now beaten down by footnotes. Much of this has been fruitful, enabling us to gain a clearer idea of what he really means, though the boldness of his thinking is apt to be obscured by the sobriety of the commentary. What still remains to be done, however, is to identify what is good and bad in the man's work. He was neither a philosophical god nor a philosophical curio. He should be engaged more than exhibited. Let's argue with him.

But the fascination with Wittgenstein is not owed only to his philosophical work. His life also has a transfixing effect. For professors especially, Wittgenstein represents an ideal of intellectual purity and worldly indifference that answers to an impulse that still throbs, however faintly, within their conventional breasts: no home, no money (he gave his fortune away), no tie. He is the rootless poetic genius they might have been in another life. But the interest has spread beyond the borders of the academy in recent years, even to those not contaminated by the philosophical disease. There have been Wittgenstein novels, Wittgenstein memoirs, Wittgenstein biographies. You hear his name on television.

Some of this interest stems, no doubt, from prurient interest in his homosexual behavior, which was actually much less extensive than one might wish. Far from indulging in vigorous promiscuity with legions of unschooled lads (as some have alleged), Wittgenstein seems to have had trouble engaging in any kind of sexual relationship with the objects of his affection. But I suspect that the current obsession with the difficult and austere Viennese-Oxbridge philosopher has a grander reason. It is that Wittgenstein exemplifies an idea of heroism.

Of flawed heroism, to be sure; but still he stands for something for which people yearn, even if they would run a mile if it tapped them on the shoulder. Wittgenstein seems like a man who twangs to his own extreme ideals, who is racked by his own integrity. His life is made up of a series of dramatic gestures in placation of a god of flint and fire. He has a clear center but not a still one, not one at peace with itself. The core rages with molten purity, scorching the human surround. You can see this white-hot demon patrolling behind his eyes, unsleeping and merciless, missing nothing. It bears down on the man, the mere man, refusing to cut him the slightest moral slack. People are stirred by this vision, but also frightened by it. They see what it might do to the usual moral mush.

Much was required of Wittgenstein by his steely god. First he must escape the comfortable embrace of his rich and cultured Viennese family and go to Manchester, where he studies engineering. Then he is called upon to abandon that career for the philosophy of mathematics, though profoundly uncertain of his capacities in this area. Having made a resounding success of this new vocation, he is obliged to remove himself from his friends and his supporters in Cambridge to live alone in a self-made hut in deepest Norway. During World War I, naturally, he has no alternitive but to enlist in active service, to put his life at serious peril with a view to self-purification. (He reads Tolstoy and Augustine at the front.) Only this proximity to death puts thoughts of suicide out of his mind.

When he completes the *Tractatus,* he feels the need to abandon altogether the field in which he has excelled, give away all his money, and become an elementary school teacher, which he quickly comes to hate. He flees again, and reluctantly returns, after a period as a monastery gardener, to Cambridge, where he develops a new philosophy, repudiating the work for which he has become famous. Then he decides that a job as a manual laborer in Communist Russia is what his soul craves. Sadly, they will employ him only as a professor, unskilled labor not being a scarce commodity, so he declines to go, glumly resuming his Cambridge professorship, which he describes as "a living death." A spell doing menial work as a hospital porter during World War II is then indicated, followed by more solitary hut-living in Ireland. Finally, he spends his last days, penniless, in the house of his doctor, working on the subject of certainty, dying of prostate cancer.

All this is interspersed with spasms of self-loathing, forced confessions of his supposed sins to friends and tireless perfectionism about his work and his moral state. Spiritual struggle is the unrelenting theme: struggle with the philosophical incubus, with his own pride, with a soiled and compromised world. No wonder he described himself as like a man glimpsed through a window in an unseen storm, appearing to walk quite normally, but in fact keeping his balance only with the greatest exertion. This is heroism of a sort, despite the invisibility of the opposing forces. It carries the idea that decency (a favorite word of Wittgenstein's) is something that comes as a hard-won achievement, and that it must fight a constant battle with the corruption of the soul. Purity costs. It hurts. It can make you do peculiar things.

The drama of Wittgenstein's life and personality makes him a uniquely suitable subject for a philosophical film. I once discussed the idea of such a film with Jonathan Miller, but we decided it would be too difficult to get right. Recently the project has been executed by the literary theorist Terry Eagleton and Derek Jarman, who died this year. They have attempted to convey Wittgenstein's life and thought in visual form. The film consists of an album of cinematic paragraphs—visual remarks, as it were—and it is an imaginative and serious attempt to render its subject's life in form and in color. Especially in color: Jarman renders the austere philosopher of language from a painterly standpoint. It is not a prism of Wittgenstein's own devising; he was interested in color for its logical grammar, not its aesthetic or expressive possibilities.

Spatially, the film is confined and claustrophobic, shot against a uniformly black background. Optical interest is supplied by the vivid hues of the clothes worn by everyone except the protagonist, who remains steadfastly gray and dowdy. He will not brighten up. (Karl Johnson's portrayal of Wittgenstein accumulates to an eerie reincarnation of the original. Johnson presents an uncanny physical resemblance to Wittgenstein, in both face and physique; he has Wittgenstein's eyes and mouth exactly right, the fragile ferocity of the gaze, the sensual rejection of the thin, inturned lips. And the voice is the perfect blend of the military, the preacherly, and the childlike.) Russell wafts about in bright red, Ottoline Morrell traverses most of the spectrum, Keynes mixes and matches like a chromatic polymath. There is even a loquacious Martian sporting the reptilian green that is standard in that community. This method of representation is quite successful, and it aptly projects an impression of floating abstractness on the characters, condensing them into conceptual beacons, animated categories. That is probably how Wittgenstein himself tended to see people, despite his advice that one should study people's faces with the utmost care. It is a mark of his personal solipsism, as well as his extreme sensitivity to the presence of others. (He always chose to live alone.) Yet he himself stands in no need of chromatic heightening, having a natural, if somewhat glacial, internal iridescence.

There is a fair amount of philosophical talk interpolated into the narrative. My unease peaked at these points. It is not that what is said is inaccurate, but it gives the impression that philosophical discussion is just a clash of portentous profundities, a duel of gnomic pronouncements; and the mordant tone of the film encourages this impression. But philosophical discourse is nothing like that: it consists of argument, counterargument, clarification, detail, restatement, recantation. Philosophy is not intrinsically incomprehensible or faintly silly. I note that no philosopher appears to have been consulted in the making of the film, which is really quite amazing. Did anybody involved in making the film actually study Wittgenstein's works, or the commentaries on them? I fear that they took the view that Wittgenstein is what you make of him. If so, they were wrong: his philosophy does *not* consist of a series of "inspired suggestions," from which the reader is invited to derive his own lessons, or to indulge his own fancy. It is a tightly constructed body of doctrine.

Eagleton's original script was substantially altered by Jarman, no doubt because of its dramatic inertia: it is all spouting heads. Apart from the amateurish way in which the philosophy is presented, the central flaw in

Eagleton's script is its inaccurate and stereotypical depiction of Russell, who appears as a shallow libertine much given to the hackneyed phrase ("Oh come on, old bean, don't be so ornery"). I suppose that, aside from not doing his homework properly, Eagleton finds it politically unacceptable that an English aristocrat could have been as intense and as passionate as any exotically accented European.

In his introduction to the script, Eagleton asserts that the *Tractatus* is "the first great work of philosophical modernism," and that "its true coordinates are not Frege and Russell or logical positivism but Joyce, Schoenberg, Picasso." This is bizarre, and it is sufficiently refuted by the pedestrian fact that Wittgenstein expresses his debt to Frege and Russell in the preface to that abstract and technical work (no mention of those other guys). This is a particularly brazen attempt by Eagleton to wrench Wittgenstein from his natural context and put him in the service of Eagleton's own purpose, which is the interpretation of the humanistic disciplines according to social theory.

It is not remotely correct to say, as Eagleton does, that "before contemporary cultural theory, Wittgenstein was teaching us that the self is a social construct," whatever that means. Wittgenstein was not concerned with such issues. The social intrudes on his thinking only as the requirement that rules of language should be open to public correction, that they not be "private." This has nothing to do with whether one's personality is a product of social determinants. It is a risible distortion to read Wittgenstein's later work as some kind of anticipation of Foucault and company. Wittgenstein never abandoned the traditional problems: knowledge, meaning, mind, mathematics, logic, explanation, analysis. He was not a literary or political theorist. He was a pure philosopher.

Understanding Wittgenstein on his own terms, however, is often the last thing that the fascinated want. They have their own needs, their own uses, for him. They seek confirmation of their own views and values by an acknowledged genius. But what really makes Wittgenstein so interesting, as a thinker and a man, is the distance that separates him from familiar ways of thinking and being. To get the most out of him, you have to see that he is nothing like yourself.

3

Wittgenstein: Seething

Ludwig Wittgenstein: Cambridge Letters
edited by Brian McGuinness and
Georg Henrik von Wright
Blackwell, 1995

Wittgenstein to John Maynard Keynes:

When I saw you *last* I was confirmed in a view which had arisen in me last
term already: you then made it very clear to me that you were tired of my
conversation etc. *Now please don't think that I mind that!* Why shouldn't you
be tired of me, I don't believe for a moment that I can be entertaining or
interesting to you. What I *did* mind was to hear through your words an un-
dertone of grudge or annoyance. Perhaps these are not exactly the right
words but it was that sort of thing. I couldn't make out for some time what
could be the cause of it all, until a thought came into my head which was by
an accident proved to be correct. It was this: I thought probably you think
that I cultivate your friendship amongst other reasons to be able to get some
financial assistance from you if I should be in need (as you imagined I might
be some day). This thought was *very* disagreeable to me.

Wittgenstein to Frank Ramsey:

A thing which is of much greater importance to me & was so on Saturday
evening, is, that I still can't understand how, being my supervisor & even—
as I thought—to some extent my friend, having been very good to me you
couldn't care two pins whether I got my degree or not. So much so, that you
didn't even think of telling Braithwaite that you had told me my book would
count as a dissertation. (I afterwards remembered one day talking to you
about it in hall & and you saying 'it would be absurd to write another thesis

Reprinted with permission from the *London Review of Books* (March 21, 1996).

now straightaway,')—Now you'll want to know why I write you all this. It is not to reproach you nor to make fuss about nothing but to explain why I was upset on Saturday & couldn't have supper with you. It is always very hard for a fellow in my situation to see that he can't rely on the people he would like to rely on.

Wittgenstein to G. E. Moore:

> Your letter annoyed me. *When I wrote Logik I didn't consult the regulations,* and therefore I think it would only be fair if you gave me my degree without consulting them so much either! As to a Preface and Notes; I think my examiners will easily see how much I have cribbed from Bosanquet.—If I'm not worth your making an exception for me *even in some STUPID details* then I may as well go to Hell directly, and if I *am* worth it and you don't do it then—*you* might go there.
>
> The whole business is too stupid and too beastly to go on writing about it so—L. W.

Wittgenstein to Bertrand Russell:

> During the last week I have thought a lot about our relationship and I have come to the conclusion that we really don't suit one another. THIS IS NOT MEANT AS A REPROACH! either for you or for me. But it is a fact. We've often had uncomfortable conversations with one another when certain subjects came up. And the uncomfortableness was not a consequence of ill humour on one side or the other but of enormous differences in our natures. I beg you most earnestly not to think I want to reproach you in anyway or to preach you a sermon. I only want to put our relationship in clear terms *in order to draw a conclusion.* . . . Now, as I'm writing this in complete calm, I can see perfectly well that your value-judgments are just as good and just as deep-seated in you as mine in me, and that I have no right to catechise you. But I see equally clearly, now, that for that very reason there cannot be any real relation of friendship between us. *I shall be grateful to you and devoted to you WITH ALL MY HEART for the whole of my life, but I shall not write to you again and you will not see me again either.* Now that I am once again reconciled with you I want to part from you *in peace* so that we shan't sometimes get annoyed with one another again and then perhaps part as enemies.

And these were his best friends.

In none of these cases did a permanent rift open up between Wittgenstein and his correspondent. He relented in the case of Russell, suggesting that they limit their relationship to areas in which their constitutional differences would not show up; and the other three cases were based on misapprehensions that were cleared up by the object of Wittgenstein's wrath. What is remarkable, indeed, is the great fondness that Wittgenstein elsewhere shows for these men; a fondness clearly accompanied by a dread of betrayal and emotional compromise. It must have been at least as painful for him to write these letters as it was for their recipients to read them. They are love letters of a sort—tormented, distrustful, angry, pleading, prideful. And they obviously represent a standard of purity in personal relations that few people would be willing to live by.

The love between Wittgenstein and Russell is the most evident, and touching, especially in the earlier days of their friendship, when Wittgenstein was engaged on the logical work to which Russell had devoted so much of his early life. Their postwar meeting at The Hague, in order to discuss logic, set up after much effort and anguish, and following many years of separation, is like nothing so much as a romantic tryst. Russell breathlessly writes: "I have got here without misadventure and I hope you will. Come on here straight the moment you arrive. It *will* be a joy to see you again." After the weeklong meeting Wittgenstein writes: "I enjoyed our time together *very* much and I have the feeling (haven't you, too?) that we did a great deal of real work together during that week."

I don't mean to suggest that this was a homosexual relationship in any straightforward sense, but it was certainly romantically tinged (if not drenched). Their shared infatuation with logic, so evident in these letters, is refracted through the medium of fraternal collaboration and mutual dependence. There is a strong sense that they found in each other just what they needed: Russell certified Wittgenstein's passionate genius and tolerated his eccentricities, while Wittgenstein echoed and amplified Russell's own yearning for perfect rigor and mental intensity. With so much riding on each other it is not surprising that their relationship was so charged. It is sad that in later years their friendship soured, with Wittgenstein writing to Moore: "Russell was there"—at the Moral Sciences Club—"and most disagreeable. Glib and superficial, though, as always, *astonishingly* quick." Russell, for his part, took the view that Wittgenstein had given up serious thinking. Their mutual disillusionment has all the flavor of sundered lovers.

Aside from these interpersonal frictions and fruitions, the letters provide evidence of Wittgenstein's sense of his own mental instability. "Sometimes things inside me are in such a ferment that I think I'm going mad: then the next day I am totally apathetic again. But deep inside me there's a perpetual seething, like the bottom of a geyser, and I keep on hoping that things will come to an eruption once and for all, so that I can turn into a different person." And again:

> Every day I was tormented by a frightful *Angst* and by depression in turns and even in the intervals I was so exhausted that I wasn't able to think of doing a bit of work. It's terrifying beyond all description the kinds of mental torment that there can be! It wasn't until two days ago that I could hear the voice of reason over the howls of the damned and I began to work again. And *perhaps* I'll get better now and be able to produce something decent. But I *never* knew what it meant to feel only *one* step away from madness.

He does not appear to have ever sought psychiatric help, and was sceptical of Freudian theory, but these words clearly signify mental suffering of an extreme degree. Nor is it clear quite what it was that caused him such agony of mind. He seems to have found refuge in his work, if it was going well, and in certain intense friendships; and if these failed him, there was always solitude and isolation, which he sought at different periods of his life.

We also learn something of Wittgenstein's conception of genius, in two stray remarks. Of one of Schubert's works he says that it has "a *fantastic* kind of greatness"; and speaking of the bizarre Otto Weininger he says: "It is true that he is fantastic but he is *great* and fantastic." I take Wittgenstein to mean that true genius—or at least one species of it—consists in wrenches of the imagination, journeys into the phantasmagoric. There must be something shocking in the work, something that bursts the bounds of the orderly and controlled and familiar. And his own work displays this: the *Tractatus* rigorously declares its own meaninglessness in granite-like sentences, while the *Investigations* profoundly rejects philosophical profundity as just "a house of cards." Both books take fantastic journeys in their own way: they conjure alien worlds that lurk within the obvious and mundane; they stir the imagination as much as the intellect. Even while celebrating the ordinary, they strike a fantastic note. Indeed, Wittgenstein himself has a kind of fantastic greatness: he is hard to believe in, and would be impossible to invent.

It is clear from these letters how close the *Tractatus* came to not being published. Without Russell's generous backing it would not have been. At one point Wittgenstein feels compelled to write, after having the book rejected:

> I've already comforted myself on that score, by means of the following argument, which seems to me unanswerable. Either my piece is a work of the highest rank, or it is not a work of the highest rank. In the latter (and more probable) case I myself am in favour of its not being printed. And in the former case it's a matter of indifference whether it's printed twenty or a hundred years sooner or later. After all, who asks whether the *Critique of Pure Reason,* for example, was written in 17x or y. So really in the former case too my treatise wouldn't need to be printed.

When it was eventually published it became a classic, its more fantastic aspects studiously ignored by its positivistic devotees. It is interesting to speculate what he would have felt about its publication in view of his later repudiation of the entire approach of the book. Perhaps he would have favored his recommendation about reading Weininger: put a negation sign in front of the whole thing and read it anyway.

His need for isolation could reach peaks of austerity not usually countenanced by those "who want to be alone." In remote Norway he would live for many months in a tiny hut of his own construction, cut off even from the nearest village by a lake he had to row across for provisions. We can be sure that his accommodations were sparsely furnished and poorly heated. His eating habits were notably spartan. This stripped-down environment seems to have served some deep need for spiritual purification, as well as permitting the concentration he needed to push his thinking to its furthest reaches.

Since he had a strong need for people, one can only assume that the loneliness he must have endured was intentionally inflicted. Perhaps he disdained his dependence on other people, feeling it to be a weakness that had to be purged by cold, deprivation, and isolation. Or perhaps they were a too tempting distraction from dealing with his own spiritual difficulties.

As I was reading these letters I also happened to be reading a fine new study by Robert Norton, *The Beautiful Soul: Aesthetic Morality in the 18th Century*. The book traces the history of the concept of moral beauty from Plato and Plotinus, through Shaftesbury and Hutcheson, and into Kant, Schiller, and Goethe. Norton explores the way this concept merged with Pietist religious traditions in German-speaking countries and suffused their moral culture. Simply put, the idea was that each person should be engaged on the task of radical self-transformation in the direction of a "beautiful soul," this being thought tantamount to moral perfection. Given Wittgenstein's own heritage, it is very tempting to place him in this tradition. Certainly he often speaks as if his soul exists in some state of ugliness—"my life is FULL of the ugliest and pettiest thoughts and actions imaginable (this is not an exaggeration)," he writes to Russell—and was clearly engaged on a lifelong project of spiritual reconstruction. When in the *Tractatus* he writes that "ethics and aesthetics are one and the same" it is possible to hear him expressing the identity of inner beauty and moral goodness that was such a dominant part of the ethical tradition in which he grew up. This makes sense of what must seem to many British observers to be an eccentricity of Wittgenstein alone: he is here simply being true to his cultural origins. Morally speaking, he is a mixture of Pietist German moral aestheticism and Cambridge-style male Hellenism (if I may be excused these weighty isms). His aesthetic tastes tended toward the austere and unadorned, as with the house he designed for his sister and his own spare prose style; and that seems to have been the kind of aesthetic object he wanted his soul to be, too. The danger of this approach to virtue is, of course, the temptation toward spiritual narcissism and moral inaction—and these, too, seem to be traits of which he was not wholly innocent.

Wittgenstein was famous for his abrasive honesty, his reckless truthfulness. In a striking early letter to Russell he states his opinion of a work highly esteemed by the Cambridge community:

> I have just been reading a part of Moore's *Principia Ethica:* (now please don't be shocked) I do not like it at all. (Mind you, quite *apart* from disagreeing with most of it.) I don't believe—or rather I am sure—that it cannot dream of comparing with Frege's or your own works (except perhaps with some the *Philosophical Essays*). Moore repeats himself dozens of times, what he says in 3 pages could—I believe—easily be expressed in half a page. *Unclear* statuements don't get a bit clearer by being repeated!!

It is not that what he says here isn't true, but I doubt that many other people at the time would have had the courage to say so—still less a new postgradu-

ate student, as Wittgenstein then was. What is also notable, though less salient, is the oblique negative evaluation of some of Russell's own work, which
Wittgenstein plainly implies is of the same low quality as Moore's book.

Why this compulsion to express opinions he knew would wound their
object and might lead to his own rejection? Intellectual honesty is one
answer, but it seems a more pointed thing than that. In *Wittgenstein: The Duty
of Genius* Ray Monk reports that as a child Wittgenstein was unusually com-
pliant and solicitous of other people's affection, even at the expense of the
truth. Perhaps he was aware of this tendency in himself and felt compelled to
resist it on every possible occasion. It was an act of purification—a deliberate
mortification of his desire to be liked. Unwelcome truthfulness was a means
of beautifying his own soul. The damage done to others was presumably
their own affair.

These letters provide a fascinating glimpse of Wittgenstein and his friends
at an intimate and revealing level. I am sure their publication would have
horrified him.

4

Russell: Loftily Earthy and Earthily Lofty . . .

The Life of Bertrand Russell
by Ronald W. Clark
Jonathan Cape and Weidenfeld
and Nicolson, 1975

This first full-scale, sedulously researched and copiously documented biography of Russell conducts us unhurriedly from his childhood at Pembroke Lodge, Richmond, up through his early Cambridge years. Thence we are led to his first marriage and its pathetic demise, his opposition to World War I, via his passionate and enduring attachments to Lady Ottoline Morrell and Lady Constance Malleson (Colette), to his later marriages, American sojourns, and steady emergence into the public eye, culminating in his efforts to secure a safe nuclear arms policy. En route we are treated to a chronicle of British intellectual and political life from 1872 to 1970, with illuminating sidelights on such notables as D. H. Lawrence, Wittgenstein, and the Webbs. The result is a thoroughly workmanlike and well-rounded portrait of Russell.

Mr. Clark succeeds in conveying, amid the welter of detail, a strong sense of the man: compounded of a dominating (of others as well as himself) and aristocratic intellect, a passionate and romantic nature, tempered (one might almost say civilized) by ironic humor and a fair measure of ordinary human kindness. The style and stance adopted by Mr Clark are greatly unobtrusive, the story unfolded with a minimum of psychological probing and authorial judgment. Particularly revealing are the contemporary letters and journal entries, which suggest an immediacy of feeling sometimes lacking in the retrospections of Russell's own *Autobiography*. New light is thrown on epi-

Reprinted with permission from the *New Scientist* (October 30, 1975).

sodes cursorily treated, if at all, by Russell himself. A totally unreciprocated love for Mrs. Whitehead is plausibly conjectured, while his own account of his affair with Helen Dudley emerges as a bit of a whitewash. The history of his troubled association with Ralph Schoenman is painstakingly dissected, and to Russell's credit. If there abides a residual impression of enigma over Russell, it is the enigma of the man—at once loftily earthy and earthily lofty. What is clear is that his outlook on human life never fundamentally changed.

In the prologue to his *Autobiography* Russell tells us that "three passions, simple but overwhelmingly strong, have governed my life: the longing for love, the search for knowledge, and unbearable pity for the suffering of mankind." In each of these it may be said that he experienced failure and disillusion. His emotional life was in almost perpetual turmoil, much of it self-inflicted; and he never lived with either of the women who dominated his life—Ottoline and Colette. Nor was he, contrary to a popular view, a mere philanderer, but was impelled by a deep and conscious need to alleviate spiritual solitude through love—the less elevated amorous adventures notwithstanding. As to his intellectual achievement, considerable as it was, his main desire—to found mathematical knowledge on a bedrock of logical certainty—was thwarted by the discovery (in which, ironically, he played the leading part) of the set-theoretic paradoxes. Russell's "logic" turned out to be epistemologically shakier than classical mathematics. And his other philosophical work is now, with whatever justice, largely neglected. His political activities on behalf of mankind, despite the indefatigable energy and transparent integrity with which he invested them, were dubiously effective—whatever one might think of their purely notional merits.

But it is not on account of this or that achievement that we primarily revere Russell. What distinguished him was the purity of purpose, sincerity of spirit, and sheer humanity that informed everything he did. This impression of Russell, irresistibly engendered by the *Autobiography*, is not dimmed by Mr. Clark's candid and unflinching portrait.

5

Russell: You Would Not Want to Be Him

Bertrand Russell: A Life
by Caroline Moorehead
Sinclair-Stevenson, 1992

Bertrand Russell's first and formative love affair was with symbolic logic. But the relationship, though fertile, was troubled. Beginning in rapture, as he molded and extended the new concepts and techniques, sweeping away the barren detritus of two millennia, the affair eventually foundered on a stinging paradox, unexpected and intractable, which abruptly took the shine off the whole thing. His devotion crumbled, and he was driven to seek comfort elsewhere, never quite regaining his former idealism. It must have been very disillusioning, and no doubt tainted his other romantic involvements, which also began in ecstasy and then became mired in refractoriness of one kind or another. For the antinomial is not adorable. And if logic can't be trusted, what can?

Along with Frege, Peano, and others, Russell constructed the basic machinery of modern mathematical logic, clearing up the defects of the older syllogistic logic, and putting the new logic to use in the analysis of mathematics itself. The program was to provide a rigorous demonstration of classical mathematics in purely logical (including set-theoretic) terms, thus setting mathematics on a transparently secure foundation. Russell also applied his bright new tool to ordinary language, notably in the Theory of Descriptions, which enabled him to keep meaning denotational while avoiding ontological inflation, and in the treatment of epistemological and metaphysical questions, where he thought it could be used to reconstruct our empirical knowl-

Reprinted with permission from the *London Review of Books* (November 19, 1992).

edge on a rational basis and to dissolve some ancient puzzles about substances and properties. The logic of relations, in particular, played a key part in releasing him from a youthful infatuation with Hegelian monism. Mathematical logic was going to be the basis for an entire new philosophy, in which traditional quandaries would be replaced by systematic advances. With logic by his side there was nothing Russell could not do.

During the composition of *Principia Mathematica,* aided by Whitehead, his old teacher, Russell spent ten hours a day for ten years in the most intimate communion with the forms and relations of predicate calculus and set theory, defining and deducing, covering thousands of pages with dense symbolism, wearing out (as he later said) his intellectual vigor. He gave logic the best years of his life and the purest part of his soul. What a nasty shock, then, to discover that a relatively simple logical manipulation issues in outright inconsistency. Consider all the classes that are not members of themselves, such as the class of dogs, which is not itself a dog, and try to combine them into a big class of their own, the class of classes that are not self-members: then you have the result that this class is a member of itself only if it is not and is not only if it is. Contradiction! Red alert! The concept of a class reveals itself as intrinsically paradoxical, hardly a solid basis for mathematical truth. Surely there must be some mistake, some slip of reasoning: at least that is what Russell thought when he first stumbled on the problem. Unfortunately, the reasoning is sound, and it shows that our naive understanding of the principles of class formation, heretofore adopted by Frege and Russell, is flawed. Nor did Russell succeed in producing a cogent resolution of the problem, the Theory of Types looking too much like an ad hoc stipulation to prohibit us from trying to talk about the offending class. The self-evident had self-destructed. "Arithmetic totters," as Frege famously wrote when Russell sent him the bad news. So, we must presume, did Russell's adulation of his now not-so-perfect Significant Other. Formal logic did not have the beauty and virtue Russell fondly supposed; and its excellence in other respects could only heighten his sense that the holy was corrupt at the core. The simultaneous disenchantment with his first wife, Alys, must have felt minor in comparison with this intellectual trauma, Russell's theoretical passions running a good bit deeper than his personal ones. No wonder he spent three thwarted years struggling to patch things up, fretting over a blank sheet of paper for days on end, settling in the end for a messy compromise. Not surprisingly, too, he lost interest in the further developments in formal logic that followed *Principia.* The magic, as they say, had gone. (Gödel's incompleteness result could only salt the wound.)

I dramatize all this because the biography of a great thinker like Russell must make some attempt, however ham-fisted, to reconstruct the role of ideas in the thinker's life—the *living* role of ideas. Russell's relations with purely intellective objects are at least as significant, emotionally and otherwise, as his movements, marriages, finances, and what not. Some language must be found to confer color on these inner adventures and disappointments, to compensate for the invisibility of the events. And we need some understanding of how the life of the pure intellect intersects with the overt life of practical action. How do those abstract journeys bear upon more worldly concerns? Russell's pained adherence to rationality in social and political matters, for example, must have been influenced by his experiences with formal logic. The power of the new logic in theoretical areas would naturally fuel a belief in the political benefits of rationally driven progress; first the pure science, then the ameliorative practical applications. Logic, after all, is about the rules of correct reasoning, how to derive only truths from other truths. On the other hand, the discovery of the paradoxes would sound a note of caution about excessive reliance on abstract principles, encouraging pragmatism over foundationalism. It might, indeed, undermine faith in the competence of pure reason to encompass every human concern: beyond the rim of coherence, clarity, and certainty there yawns an abyss of chaos, obscurity, and doubt—the place where religions traditionally step in. Russell's yearning for a religious creed compatible with his atheism has its counterpart in his logicism and its limitations: a solid core of rigorous truth surrounded by a murky penumbra of unruly forces. (Wittgenstein's distinction between saying and showing has a similar architecture.)

If this sounds romantic or pretentious, it is entirely in keeping with Russell's own attitude to his life. High-flown, intense, earnest, idealistic, tragic—this was the quotidian language of Russell's official self-conception. Caroline Moorehead's biography is at its least comfortable in dealing with this aspect of its subject: it is as if she can't quite see where all this is coming from and is mildly embarrassed by it. Nor does she make any real effort to relate Russell's theoretical convictions to his general outlook. She is much happier detailing the superficial facts of Russell's life—which she presents with efficiency and balance. Her narrative flows smoothly along, with places, people, and books each assigned their proper slot, but venturing little in the way of character analysis or critical judgment. There are potted summaries of Russell's main ideas, which are generally accurate but rather wooden, more fact-checked than felt, and a good deal of solid documentation, some of it new. The women in Russell's life, in particular, are roundly and sympathetically represented, though their faults are by no means glossed over. There is nothing much wrong with the book, as far as it goes: but it is left to the reader to try to fit the pieces together into an intelligible whole. Ray Monk's biography of Wittgenstein succeeds in bringing an enigmatic character to life, but Moorehead's book leaves the real Russell just out of reach—a mere compilation of deeds and words. She seems not to be able to enter into Russell's anguished cerebral psychodrama in the way Monk did with Wittgenstein—perhaps because Monk is himself a philosopher. And without a more serious attempt to reconstruct Russell's inner life much of the reportage makes him look at best hyperbolic and at worst silly (which is not to say that he was never either of these things).

The book is the most successful in conveying the man when Russell and his intimates are able to speak for themselves. Fortunately, the two pivotal people in Russell's life—Ottoline Morrell and Ludwig Wittgenstein—gave rise to a revealing quantity of writing, mostly in the form of letters. Here is a typical passage from Bertie's love letters to Ottoline: "How can you ask if your love can be anything to me? It can be everything to me. You can give me happiness, and what I want even more—peace. All my life, except a short time after my marriage, I have been driven on by restless inward furies, flogging me on to activity and never letting me rest. . . . You can give me inward joy and expel the demons." Or again: "Life is like a mountain top in a mist, at most times cold and blank, with aimless hurry—then suddenly the world opens out, and gives visions of unbelievable beauty." This exalted tone changes, sadly, as the affair wears on and Ottoline's refusal to leave her husband has its inevitable effects: "It is your gradual and inexorable withdrawal—like the ebbing tide—that keeps me over and over again at the very last point of agony. You flatter yourself in thinking that you can imagine passionate love; as far as I have observed, you can't imagine it a bit." Then, a week later: "I always bring great misery to anyone who has anything to do with me; I can't help communicating the inward misery which I carry about like the plague." And: "Forgive me dearest—I will try to love you with more moderation. . . . [I]t is like a child crying because its parents have left it in the dark all alone." The last sentence may show more psychological penetration than Russell knew: the death of both his parents before he was five was undoubtedly a large factor in determining his lifelong feeling of loneliness and isolation.

Russell speaks often of the good effects Ottoline had on him, opening him up to less cerebral concerns, but is is pretty clear that his disappointment in this affair went very deep, and when it foundered he seems to have become a different person. He had passed from an emotionally deprived childhood to a barren first marriage, and was clearly in desperate emotional shape when, at the age of thirty-seven, he fell in love with Ottoline. She was not, by her own admission, much interested is sex in general and did not find the sexually needy Bertie attractive in that way; nor did they get to spend much time together. Russell obviously found the whole thing excruciatingly painful, and never seems to have got over it.

At the same time Russell's friendship with Wittgenstein was having its own exhilarating and devastating impact on him. He writes: "Wittgenstein has been a great event in my life. . . . I think he has *genius*. In discussion with him I put out *all* my force and only just equal his. . . . I love him and feel he will solve the problems that are raised by my work, but want a fresh mind and the vigour of youth. He is *the* young man one hopes for." But when Wittgenstein pointed out some fundamental defects in Russell's nascent *Theory of Knowledge* he told Ottoline he was ready for suicide, saying later: "My impulse was shattered, like a wave dashed to pieces against a breakwater." The episode caused him to conclude grimly: "I saw that I could not hope ever again to do fundamental work in philosophy." These words should not be taken lightly: what had sustained him for so many years—his logical and philosophical power—was now shown to be wanting. And it could not have helped that Wittgenstein openly disapproved of so much in Russell's character. Like Ottoline, Wittgenstein first offered Russell hope and passion, but then promptly stomped him into the ground. Together the two of them extinguished something deep and good in Bertie's character. Thereafter he becomes a less sympathetic figure, more publicly directed, more cynical, less pure, worldlier. Perhaps neither of them realized how vulnerable the towering intellect who wrote *Principia Mathematica* was; in any case, they made a mess out of the man—however inadvertently.

There are suggestons in Moorehead's book that Russell did not find his own brilliance easy to live with. This strikes me as true and important; we should not underestimate the burdens imposed by Russell's exceptional degree of brain power. Many of his most troublesome traits—troublesome to others and to himself—stem from this central fact: his obsessiveness, perfectionism, self-absorption, censoriousness, abstractedness, morbidity, coldness, loneliness, extremity. With great powers of concentration and mental capaciousness come many unhappy side-effects: everything gets magnified and nothing is forgotten; the mental volume is always set too high; life becomes a ceaseless effort to cure restlessness; overexertion alternates with boredom; an alienating impatience infects every human dealing. When Virginia Woolf expressed admiration for what she called Russell's "headpiece" she used a telling expression: his intellect was a kind of appendage or incubus, inharmoniously attached, and too great a weight for a mere mortal to bear. He was like one of those people described by Oliver Sacks—someone with an abnormally enhanced mental faculty who must somehow find a way to accommodate their affliction of riches. In pictures of him you can see it raging uncontrollably behind his eyes, as if he were a man possessed. He was top-heavy with brains.

Two contrasing impressions emerge from Moorehead's account of Russell's life, more strongly than from his own autobiography. The first is the sheer abundance of the man: the enormous number and range of things written, the strenuous and varied political activity, the roll-call of top-notch friends, the many love affairs, the sheer quantity of packed years. It all seems exemplary and enviable, the perfect intellectual life. Who now has Russell's intellectual and moral authority? He was presciently on the right side, politically and morally, nearly all the time, and he made fundamental contributions to human thought. But there is another impression, scarcely less evident: that of an appalling emotional bleakness, both personal and doctrinal. Some of this is traceable to overt difficulties, like the failure of his marriage to Alys or his experiences during World War I; but some of it is harder to explain, and requires a deeper account. No doubt, as remarked, his early orphaning contributed to the feeling of desolation, but his brother Frank did not share Bertie's arctic temperament. There was, by many accounts, a chilly charmlessness to him, despite the humor and love of children, a dry awkwardness of body and soul, which repelled the kind of natural affection he craved.

My guess is that this was the natural consequence of a certain childlikeness combined with a searing and ruthless intellect. His mind simply would not permit him the kind of looseness necessary in dealing with ordinary human relations; he was always held in its exacting grip. Every sentence uttered had to be perfectly formed, and every personal encounter slotted into some wider theoretical vision of what Life was about. It was all part of some *Principia Russellia,* axiomatically laid out, fully articulated. The stern intellect was for ever vigilant. Even his strictly philosophical work sometimes reads as if it would have benefited from less scorching brilliance and more bemused plodding; for everything is required to submit to the ominpotent Russell intellect. He commended Wittgenstein for his commitment to the edict "understand or die," but in Russell's case, unlike that of Wittgenstein, this took the form of a systematizing reductive urge that does not always suit the topic. His mind, he said, was like a searchlight, sharp and focused—but it was a searchlight that burned as well as illuminated, consumed as well as created. Russell was a victim of his own particular form of genius. You would not want to be him.

6

Russell: The Machine in the Ghost

Bertrand Russell: The Spirit of Solitude
by Ray Monk
Jonathan Cape, 1996

Reading a biography is always at the same time an act of autobiography—an act of self-reflection and self-evaluation. As one absorbs the life of the subject, one is forced to go over the events and themes of one's own life, making comparisons and drawing lessons. This can be an uncomfortable experience. In the case of Bertrand Russell and me there is a special edginess to the process. Although I never met him, I read Russell with great fervor and fire at around the age of twenty, devouring as many of his books as I could. His autobiography was a particularly potent influence upon me, with its mixture of extreme intellectualism and emotional idealism. I let myself be thoroughly Russellized. He has been a voice in my head ever since. (How many others have been indelibly marked by the Russell persona?) I admit that I idolized the man.

It is not that this callow worshipfulness has remained constant. There has been the small matter of my own life to live, and reading (and reviewing) two earlier biographies of Russell—by Ronald Clark and Caroline Moorehead—did much to dampen my idolatry. But ploughing through Ray Monk's massive, thorough, and probing first volume has been an especially chastening experience, as it will be for all Russell worshippers. This is not because, as might be expected, I find my admiration for Russell seriously dented—though it is certainly qualified; rather, it is the sheer unhappiness of the man that is so disturbing. It is hard to accept that one has modeled oneself on a

Reprinted with permission from the *Times Higher Education Supplement* (May 24, 1996).

person whose experience of life was so chronically and sharply painful—
a person who felt himself to be so emotionally unhinged, so malformed,
so deranged, so desperate. This is not the kind of inner life one wants
to duplicate. In later life Russell wrote a book entitled *The Conquest of
Happiness*—and somehow the very title tells it all: happiness never simply
came for Russell, it (or some simulacrum) had to be fought for, acquired by
main force. All human idols have feet of clay, but Russell seems also to have
existed in a state of living hell.

You think I exaggerate: how could this world-famous, titled, healthy,
long-lived, stunningly brilliant, witty, womanizing figure be that miserable?
The answer lies in the very constitution of his personality, the texture of the
Russell self. A recurring image in Russell's self-descriptions, sensitively
picked up by Monk, is that of being a ghost. Here is a characteristic burst,
from a letter to his lover Colette O'Niel:

> The centre of me is always and eternally a terrible pain, a curious wild
> pain—a searching beyond what the world contains, something transfigured
> and infinite—the beatific vision—God—I do not find it, I do not think it is to
> be found—but the love of it is my life—it's—like passionate love for a ghost.
> At times it fills me with rage, at times with wild despair, it is the source of
> gentleness and cruelty and work, it fills every passion that I have—it is the
> actual spring of life within me.

Or again, speaking further of his search for the sublime:

> The outcome is that one is a ghost, floating throgh the world without any
> real contact. . . . I am haunted—some ghost, from some extra-mundane
> region, seems always trying to tell me something. . . . But it is from listen-
> ing to the ghost that one comes to feel oneself a ghost.

So much for the coolly rationalistic atheist, or the jovially sybaritic aristocrat,
that Russell is sometimes represented as being. The real Russell feels himself
to be a wispy specter from the grave, subhuman, removed, seeking futilely
for a religion that will still his torments.

This image has a number of aspects: the ghost is shadowy, bloodless,
inhuman, insubstantial, invisible, disembodied, alien, cut-off, feared, lost,
unloved, dank, disgusting, dead. Each of these adjectives captures some
aspect of Russell's personality, his mode of being. Above all, there is the sense
of radical isolation and otherness that Russell so often cries out against.
Monk reports a dream Russell had in old age: "I imagine myself behind plate
glass, like a fish in an aquarium, or turned into a ghost whom no one sees;
agonisingly, I try to make some sort of human contact but it is impossible & I
know myself doomed forever to lonely impotence." This is a shockingly
disturbing image: to feel oneself so removed from others that one exists in a
separate insulated sphere in the shape of an unseen wraith. It is the barest
kind of existence, and the logical limit to human loneliness.

Why should Russell have felt like this? Monk suggests, with great plausibility, that the roots of Russell's sense of ghostlike isolation go back to

his wretched infancy. His mother and sister died of diphtheria in quick succession when Bertie was two; then his father died, apparently of grief, two years later, staying alive just long enough to complete a mediocre book about religion. He was raised by his grandparents, against the will of his deceased parents, until his grandfather died when he was six, leaving the child in the clammy and tenacious embrace of his domineering Presbyterian grandmother. In this repressive puritanical atmosphere of mindless Protestant devotion, full of reproachful sighs and soul-cramping discipline, the boy Russell developed habits of solitude, concealment, and intensely pensive bookishness. He withdrew into his own ethereal world of mathematics, haunted by his dead parents, cut off from those nearest to him. His more boisterous elder brother, Frank, rebelled outwardly from all this and summarily detested Pembroke Lodge and all that it stood for; while Bertie, more timid, younger, more eager to please, rendered his real nature invisible to those around him, sealing himself into an airtight container, alone with his grief and loss. He became a wandering ghost early on.

The personality that grew from these tragic beginnings also had its explosive and toxic side. Hatred, murder, and insanity became part of Russell's mental landscape. Monk is particularly good on the last of these, tearing aside the mask of rationalism to reveal the molten soul beneath. Writing to Ottoline Morrell, Russell himself declares: "I doubt if even you know how nearly I am to a raving madman. It is only intellect that keeps me sane; perhaps this makes me overvalue intellect as against feeling." He seems to have been continually haunted by the fear of madness, of which there was indeed some in his family; and his extremes of emotion are certainly akin to madness. Associated with this came murderous impulses:

> I remember when I wanted to commit murder, the beginning was a sudden picture (I hardly ever have pictures at ordinary times) of a certain way of doing it, quite vivid, with the act vivid before my eyes. . . . I took to reading about murders and thinking about them. . . . It was only hard thinking that kept me straight at the time—the impulse was not amenable to morals, but it was amenable to reasoning that this was madness.

He did in his youth try actually to strangle his friend Edward Fitzgerald, and had murderous impulses at other times too. Some of the sudden callousness he could show to people must have had a similar source.

Monk's thesis is that the fear of madness was a controlling theme in Russell's life, causing him to restrain and flagellate his deepest emotions, and to retreat into cloistered abstractions. Part of the appeal of Joseph Conrad's work for Russell lay in his understanding of madness, as well as his acute sense of human loneliness.

Russell's love life veered exhaustingly from fleeting ecstacy to deep despair. To be loved by Russell was no picnic. He was clearly starved of normal female affection as a child and thereafter sought it with a ferocity that could only backfire. In the case of his first wife, Alys, he moved swiftly from joy-ously kissing her breasts in a treehouse to something close to smouldering disgust, though he stayed with her for nine long years in a sexless and loveless marital prison. His next love, of Ottoline, was powerful and sus-tained, but (a) she was happily married, (b) she had other lovers, (c) she found Russell physically unattractive. For Russell, the relationship was mostly pain and sexual frustration, with some ecstatic interludes, and an inability to free himself from his feelings for her. With Colette the problem was her itinerant acting career and her affairs with other men, which left Russell ravaged by jealousy. He wanted marriage and children, not the odd weekend with someone with dispersed romantic interests. His affair with Helen Dudley was a sudden flop: having asked her to England to marry him, he lost interest as soon as Ottoline manifested her rivalry with Helen by stepping up her sexual interest in poor Bertie. He undoubtedly treated Helen shabbily, especially in not explaining to her the seriousness of his prior affection for Ottoline. Meanwhile Helen told Ottoline everything that had happened between her and Russell, which was not quite what he had admit-ted to Ottoline; the result was that Ottoline lost her affection for Russell. Etc., etc.

In all this mess, Monk finds Russell culpable on many counts. But I think he underestimates the emotional desperation that led Russell to these tan-gled relationships. He did not manage to have a halfway satisfactory love life till his forties. Sex was a powerful force in his life, but it was granted very restricted outlet, leaving him emotionally starved to the point of near-insanity. It is also exceedingly difficult to have any confidence in one's judg-ments about such matters, the human heart being a mysterious organ, and the realities of romance so complex and impenetrable. I do not myself find Russell's behavior in this respect particularly low or extraordinary. Nor did Russell fare much better with his male friends; and here I think he really does come out badly. On a pair of occasions he coldly smiles as two of his closest friends—G. E. Moore and Wittgenstein—suffer from his insensitivity and lack of human sympathy. He evidently found their very real distress amusing, and it is hard to escape an impression of unsavory sadism in his responses. Moore ended up wanting to avoid his company whenever possi-ble, and Wittgenstein became remote and condemnatory. His relationship with Conrad was much better, as Monk insightfully explains, but then Russell hardly ever saw him and they were not in the same game. D. H. Lawrence wrote him a stingingly critical letter, pointing out his latent violence and dishonesty, which caused Russell to contemplate suicide momentarily; but he solved the problem by severing his relationship with the writer and with-drawing ever deeper under his intellectual carapace. There is little evi-dence in Monk's book of good and close friendships between Russell and other men; his loneliness was not to be relieved by ordinary human com-panionship. All the intensity and need is there, but somehow he lacked the humanity to covert it into the balm of friendship.

Russell did an enormous amount of work, of course, some of it of heroic proportions. *Principia Mathematica,* ten solid years in the writing, two thousand pages, probably never fully read by anyone, was a stupendous achievement, and came at considerable personal cost. Seventy-odd books, numberless articles, thousands of letters—Russell was a prodigious thinker and writer. That is the reason, after all, why biographies of his life exist. What emerges from Monk's account, perhaps surprisingly, is how much of this work was motivated by religious impulses—the need to find a substitute for the orthodox Christianity he had so painfully abandoned at age fifteen. If he could not relieve his loneliness by communion with God, then he would do it by communion with mathematical reality, or with nature, or with women, or anything else that looked suitable. His pen turned to whatever seemed to promise an alternative to traditional theism.

Connected with this, he was also obsessed with achieving intellectual certainty, and much of his philosophical work is shaped by this Cartesian concern. He had doubted God, but was there anything that could not be doubted? He was unable to achive the kind of Wittgensteinian insouciance about certainty that is characteristic of contemporary philosophy. He just could not emotionally accept that our destiny is to be uncertain, to be prey to scepticism; he felt in his bones that we ought to be certain, and were somehow falling down in our duty when certainty could not be secured.

Russell more than once comments on the dehumanizing effect of abstract work. Hence his desire to achieve something in the way of imaginative writing, about which he harbored serious ambitions in his thirties. Perhaps not very surprisingly, he had little talent in this direction—indeed some antitalent—being unable to convey anything but thought and argument. Ottoline always found this hard to take, referring to his stiffness and lack of physical and emotional charm. He was logical through and through—the machine in the ghost. He was a man of pure intellect, tinged with flippancy, and ultimately lacking a human shape. Nothing seems to have been recorded about his bedroom style, but the question merits some thinking about: for ghosts do not make the best lovers. Russell's finest hour, at least during the first half of his life, which is the period this book covers, was his opposition to World War I. Here he showed real courage, great independence of mind, boundless compassion, and a sincere concern for things other than his own mental development. One wonders how he would have turned out if this wrenching event had never occurred. The suffering of others seems to be about the only thing that connected him to other people in any deep way. Suffering and mathematics were the real things of the universe; the world of ordinary objects and people was flimsy and conjectural by comparison (his philosophy never did quite manage to find a place for the tangible and perceptible). The war at least made some dent in his instinctive solipsism.

Monk's biography, which awaits its second volume, is an exceptionally skillful and well-documented account of its subject's life, told very largely in Russell's own words, with a minimum of interpretative intrusion. It is perhaps less arresting than his earlier biography of Wittgenstein, but that is principally because Russell's life has already been well chronicled by himself and others. What Monk has achieved, aside from assembling a wealth of material in a smooth narrative form, is an articulation of the central emotional axes in Russell's life—his sense of isolation, his fear of insanity, the raging forces that propelled him in good directions and bad. Russell was a colossal fiery intellect atop a narrow human stalk, a paradoxical being who could not be a member of himself, a ghost with earthly yearnings. This biography tells us as much as we shall ever want to know about a man described by his second wife as "enchantingly ugly."

7

Peirce: Logic and Sadness

Charles Sanders Peirce: A Life
by Joseph Brent
Indiana University Press, 1993

"The opinion which is fated to be ultimately agreed to by all who investigate is what we mean by truth and the object represented by this opinion is the real." In that famous sentence, Charles Sanders Peirce (1839–1914) enunciated the doctrine for which he is most celebrated, and showed the heart of his philosophical position.

The view of truth and reality that he proposed in that sentence, and in his many writings, inverts the conception that has some claim to be regarded as standard: that inquiry indeed aims at discovering truth, and hence at uncovering reality, but that there is always a logical gap, capable of provoking skepticism, between the beliefs that inquiry yields and the facts that it aims to represent. No matter how hard you try to be right, you might always be wrong, however plural "you" are. The truth of a belief can never consist in its being believed, even when it is arrived at by the utmost diligence. But Peirce closes this ominous gap between belief and truth by defining truth in terms of the eschatology of inquiry: truth simply is that which competent inquirers will eventually come to agree it is. It follows that when doubt and disagreement cease, truth will be the inevitable result.

Peirce's notion of truth does not permit a situation in which belief reaches a steady state but fails to match the way things are, since there is no more to truth than communally accepted belief. When we say that inquiry aims at truth, we mean that it aims at socially certified agreement. We do not con-

Reprinted with permission from the *New Republic* (June 28, 1993).

47

verge on the same beliefs because they are true; they are true because we converge on them. Once inquiry has reached its end, reality is ours. Indeed, there is no distinguishing any longer between us and it. In the limit, thought and reality merge.

If truth is to be defined in terms of inquiry, then we need to understand the nature of inquiry. That was Peirce's lifelong preoccupation. He sought to elicit the processes and the procedures of reasoning, the means by which the fixation of belief occurs. In particular, he wanted to understand that peculiar way of forming beliefs known as "scientific method," which he took to be the best way of forming beliefs yet invented. The study of reasoning in general he called Logic; and he distinguished three branches of the subject: deduction, induction, abduction.

His own distinctive contribution, later advocated by Karl Popper and others, was to recognize the importance and the peculiarities of what he called abduction: the process by which the mind generates, in a kind of guessing, or in an imaginative leap, hypotheses that attempt to explain the data while going radically beyond the data, but are still testable in their light. Such hypotheses, which occur not only in science but also, for Peirce, even in our most basic perceptual judgments, are not deduced from the evidential premises; nor are they inductive generalizations from them. They are creative efforts to represent how the world has to be in order for the data to be rendered explicable. Without this method of reasoning, which is now known as "inference to the best explanation," human thought would be crippled.

But such a procedure also raises profound puzzles. How can mere guessing ever yield objective knowledge, and what is it that guides our guesses? The method of abduction looks workable only if there is a deep affinity between what the human mind naturally generates and the nature of reality; only if, that is, reality is somehow constituted by the operations of mind. And that was indeed Peirce's master view: science can be rational only if truth consists in what human inquirers converge on. Abduction reliably produces truth for Peirce because truth is to be defined as that which abduction produces. In the last analysis, then, inquiry is all there is, the persistent pursuit of stable belief. There is no question of belief corresponding, or failing to correspond, to something outside of it.

This doctrine is the essence of pragmatism, the philosophical position for which Peirce is most renowned. It is, as he was well aware (though others have not been), a form of idealism. Yet it differs from other forms of idealism, from Berkeley or Hegel, by taking method—not ideas or sense data or souls or beliefs in themselves—to be metaphysically basic. Objectivity is achieved by way of the interpersonal and dynamic corrections that method allows; and reality is established as the essentially evaluative norms of correct reasoning by which the mind is governed, plus the mental items to which these norms apply. The content of any conception is given by the method of inquiry we would use in order to investigate the object of that conception. In thus marrying idealism to logic, Peirce hoped to secure the objectivity of knowledge and its possibility.

Peirce's work on logic itself, as distinct from his insistence on its philosophical centrality, was also original and prescient. He did ground-breaking
work in formal logic, most notably in devising a logic of relations and quantification, later developed by Kurt Schroder; and he noticed more clearly
than any one before him that an adequate logic had to be grounded in an
account of representation, in what he called "semiotic." For reasoning proceeds by courtesy of signs, outer or inner, and these signs must have meaning
if the beliefs produced are to have content. Thus Peirce was led to focus
systematically on the relation between a sign, its object, and the person for
whom the sign has meaning. To understand science, Peirce had to do linguis-
tics. (Chomsky has acknowledged a large debt.) The theory of meaning becomes the basis of epistemology, and epistemology, or the theory of inquiry,
is the ultimate subject of metaphysics; here is the "linguistic turn" that became so characteristic of twentieth-century philosophy.

Signs, moreover, are shared between people, between those who cooper-
ate in inquiry; and so the idea of a community of sign-using inquirers
emerges as central to philosophical understanding. The community that
Peirce prized so highly was essentially a linguistic community. Solipsism or
individualism, which had marked so many earlier philosophies, rationalist or
empiricist, idealist or realist, is thus abandoned. In place of the image of a
solitary spectator or a cogitator seeking truth in hermetic isolation, Peirce
proposes to inject a community of inquirers into his account of what makes
knowledge possible. Thus knowledge has a sociology as well as a psychology.
Each inquirer is subject to the communal standard supplied by logic, and
expressed in a system of public signs, so that in the long run convergence of
opinion is accomplished.

All these ideas, right or wrong, have a remarkably modern ring, though
they were the work of a nineteenth-century thinker. Peirce must be counted
with his almost exact contemporary Frege as a progenitor of contemporary
philosophical thought, though he cannot be said to rival Frege's clarity, rigor,
or economy. Both men saw that traditional logic was inadequate, and appreciated the need for a more systematic understanding of language and meaning. Both were mathematicians of note, whose approaches to logic were
mathematically inspired. Frege was interested in deductive logic and its relevance to mathematical reasoning, and so his results were cleaner and
sharper. Peirce's chief interests were in the much messier area of natural
science and the logic appropriate to it. It is he who has a fair claim to
have anticipated, for good or for ill, more of the course of twentieth-
century philosophy, especially in epistemology and the philosophy of science. He was onto the right things before almost anyone else, and he deserves the routine recognition that he now receives. He was the greatest
American philosopher.

So what kind of life did he have? Absolutely awful, I'm afraid. Really
dreadful. Peirce's story bleeds with irony. It began promisingly, which makes
the end even more depressing. His father, Benjamin Peirce, was a powerful
and distinguished scientist at Harvard, and he was keen to instill in his

precocious son the characteristics of genius, which he did with considerable success. Little personal discipline was imposed; superiority was assumed; arrogance was excused; the value of intellect, and not much else, was extolled. All little Charles had to do was be brilliant, which did not come hard to him.

The result of this education, however, was that Peirce was remarkably bad at everything except brilliance, especially everything practical or cooperative. Nor did he have much respect for those in authority, including his teachers. His unconventionality, his hubris, and his lack of concern for consequences soon caught up with him. He was dismissed from every post he ever held, worked in a university for only a short time, spent his money recklessly and ended his life in poverty, virtual starvation, and uneasy relations with the law. He had few friends and was shunned by the respectable. He never managed to complete the work on which he toiled for so long. Added to all this, he suffered from trigeminal neuralgia throughout his life, a condition that involves bouts of excruciating pain in the face, which he treated with morphine and cocaine, with predictably unsettling results. (His second wife was a virtual invalid, too.) He announced impending suicide with some regularity, and not without reason. He was tenaciously persecuted by men of academic power, whom he misguidedly trusted. He lived for much of his life in a state of anxiety and overwork, on the brink of emotional collapse.

Joseph Brent's biography, the first serious account of Peirce's life, tells the sad and harrowing story with sympathy and understanding, as well as exasperation. His book is thoroughly researched, amply documented and ably written. It is gripping, in a sober way. Quoting often from Peirce's letters and other writings, Brent allows us to understand more of this strange character than we might reasonably expect to understand. The follies and the misadventures begin to form a consistent pattern, though their underlying cause remains enigmatic.

Brent's account of Peirce's friendships, notably with his supporter William James, and of his enmities, of which there were several, are particularly well handled. Peirce's fortunes were largely determined by the esteem and the affection of some, offset by the hostility and the dislike of others, who often had all the power—the most odious among them being Charles Norton Eliot and Simon Newcomb, pillars of the academic establishment. That Peirce's life and career were damaged, indeed ruined, by the intellectual ineptitude and the stuffed-shirt mediocrity of men such as these is made sufficiently clear, as are the adverse effects of the prim conformism of the society in which Peirce lived. Peirce's adulterous relation with the woman who would become his second wife was much held against him. His peers and his superiors seemed to have felt that his character and behavior would be corrupting to the young—where have we heard that before?—and so a university teaching position was not to be entrusted to him. Johns Hopkins even went to the extreme of firing all its untenured faculty and then promptly reinstating them except for Peirce, as a way of getting rid of him. He never secured another academic position, despite many efforts. And all the while he was generally acknowledged to be a genius.

What strikes me now about Peirce's career, reading Brent's account of it, is the amount of time that he spent *not* doing philosophy. As a young man he trained in chemistry and physics, and his first day job was in geodesy, working for the United States Coast Survey. His specialty there was gravimetrics, and he spent enormous amounts of time in the company of pendulums, to the study of which he made important contributions. He also worked in astronomy and photometry, publishing a book in the latter field. He was an internationally renowned scientist before he reached his forties. Recognition he had, and solid achievement, too; but employment he could not sustain, and eventually could not even secure.

He was fired from the Coast survey, it seems, because of delays in the production of his scientific reports, backed up by the malign blindness of some supposed experts who were invited to comment on his work. The nadir came when, despite a recommendation from President Roosevelt himself, and strong support from leading scientists and philosophers, he was refused a Carnegie grant to complete his work in logic. Thereafter he scratched a living from writing reviews, mainly for *The Nation,* and relied upon the charity of friends and relatives. For periods he had to sleep rough in New York, having lost his house, and he often went for days without food. Naturally his already precarious health was ruined, not to speak of his sensitive spirit. But he carried on, as best he could, with his logic.

The ironies of Peirce's life are of a numbingly predictable kind. The great pragmatist, stressing the practical instrumental character of thought, proved unable to realize his own most cherished goals through the exercise of his own practical reason. He was a procrastinator, an evader of ugly realities, a reckless spender of money. He once characterized perception, arrestingly, as the "outward clash," castigating Hegel for excessive inwardness; but his own brushes with the external world were abrupt collisions, his own perception of reality being minimal.

For all his obsession with methodology, his own schemes tended to be high on madness and low on method. Some of his awkwardness in the world Peirce put down to the cerebral consequences of left-handedness, including his convolutions of speech (he was not, to put it mildly, a clear writer), and some may have come from drugs, but the quixotic and impulsive side of his character goes far beyond such causes. He seemed often to connive in his own undermining, as if challenging the world to take a swipe at him. And for all his championing of the cooperative in intellectual inquiry, his own work was largely solitary and idiosyncratic; his group instincts were not well-developed. The idea of community was pretty notional as far as Peirce's actual practice was concerned. One might be forgiven for suspecting, if it does not sound too pop-psychological, that his emphasis on method and agreement was a form of compensation for the opposite qualities in himself.

The most salient fact about Peirce as a thinker is his early and persistent fascination with logic, formal and informal. He ranked himself at the level of Leibniz and often said he was put on Earth by God in order to do logic. In this fascination he resembles the pioneers of twentieth-century philosophy—Frege, Russell, Wittgenstein, and others. Much of this work, however, has now been done. It is hard to see how anyone today could be gripped in such a fanatical manner by a desire to set logic straight. Now logic *is* straight, thanks to these earlier obsessives.

I suspect that a large part of Peirce's career problem was simply that he was constantly preoccupied by something that cried out for preoccupation—the discoveries in logic were ripe for plucking, beckoning him to them. Instead of laboring over his tedious pendulum calculations, he was straining to think about logical matters; but he never found the time or the peace of mind to put in the effort needed to bring his ideas to fruition. He was thus continually thwarted in his own strongest inclinations, always setting up a kind of split or instability in his own activities. (How hard it would have been on the young Russell if he had been prevented from writing *Principia Mathematica*.) Only during the short period of teaching logic at Johns Hopkins do the signs of strain recede, resulting in an important and collaborative treatise on his deepest interest.

Speaking of the thwarting of work, Brent's account of the troubled history of his own book is a case in point. Written thirty years ago as a doctoral thesis in history, it took the efforts of the noted linguist Thomas Sebeok to track down the author and arrange for the original version to be revised for publication. This is a strange business, for the book is excellent in every way, and Peirce is a subject of extraordinary interest. The explanation, as Brent gives it, would appear to be that the philosophy department at Harvard University denied access to certain papers of Peirce's contained in the Houghton Library, and would not permit Brent to quote from Peirce's letters. He did not obtain persmission until 1991. Brent says:

> While the delay in publishing Peirce's philosophical manuscripts can be attributed almost entirely to skepticism or disinterest [*sic*] on the one hand, and lack of funds on the other, the delay in producing a biography was directly caused by the inaccessibility of the biographical portion of the Harvard Peirce collection. This suppression was justified by its owners, the Harvard department of philosophy, on the grounds that there was information in the letters that would seriously damage Peirce's reputation and that must, therefore, be withheld in order to protect his reputation and the sensibilities of his family (and perhaps those of Harvard University) . . . The restrictive policy led to rumors about homosexuality, sexual promiscuity, chronic drunkenness, violence and drug addiction, and since there was no published evidence to either support or disprove such accusations, Peirce's reputation has varied according to rumor about the contents of his letters and the tastes of the persons concerned with it. In fact, many of the rumors were true, but because of the decision to deny access, the research which would have put his life into its true light, that of the dignity of deep tragedy, was discouraged or forbidden.

It is clear, after reading Brent's valuable book, that whoever it was at Harvard who made the decision to impede a biographical study of Peirce made a grave mistake. And it is a sad irony that this misguided policy should come from the very institution that did so much to ruin Peirce's life and career—even to the point of forbidding him for decades from lecturing to Harvard students, despite William James's recommendations. Was he really so difficult and controversial a man that he deserves this double blow to his reputation? It is hard not to feel the force of Sebeok's comment that Brent's book reveals "a seamy side to American academic polity, its sometime brutality and mendacity, and the often cruelly corrupt machinations of higher political authority." Yes, Peirce was a wayward and singular man, who played a leading part in engineering his own downfall: but he was also the victim of some mean-spirited and merciless individuals. He ended miserably, while they prospered and no doubt congratulated themselves. Reading this biography leaves one with a bad taste in the mouth; and it is the more worth reading because of it. That pain in Peirce's face sums it up.

8

Ayer: Old Scores

The Meaning of Life, and Other Essays
by A. J. Ayer
Weidenfeld, 1990

When I was a quivering graduate student at Oxford in 1973, fresh from the northern provinces, I sat for the John Locke Prize, a voluntary two-day examination for Oxford postgraduates in philosophy. As I had hitherto been a psychology student at Manchester, I thought this would be good practice for my upcoming B. Phil. philosophy exams. It was quite an ordeal (I nearly gave up at one point), and afterward I felt I had a long way to go philosophically. A few days later Professor Ayer, who was one of the examiners, informed me that he had been obliged to require that my papers be typed, on account of their extreme illegibility: I would have to dictate them to a typist in the presence of an invigilator, both of whom I would have to pay. I apologized to him for my calligraphic delinquency and expressed some mumbled misgivings about going to all that trouble and expense, in view of my poor performance. To my surprise, he said he thought I was "worth it," on what basis I am not sure. I therefore did as I was told, spending a couple of wincing days reading out my script to be converted into cold type. I really must improve my handwriting, I thought.

Two or three weeks later Professor Ayer told me that I had been awarded the prize. He seemed almost as pleased as I was, clapping me warmly on the back and congratulating himself on his former perspicacity. As a result of this, I was enabled to pursue a career in philosophy, which I doubt would have been possible otherwise, given my educational background. Thus I owe

Reprinted with permission from the *London Review of Books* (August 30, 1990).

a considerable debt to A. J. Ayer for giving me a break when it would have been easy to allow my bad hand to count against me. Since I later became a John Locke Prize examiner myself, I know what an unusual step this was for him to authorize.

Some years later, when I was teaching at University College London, in the department Ayer had done so much to create, I met him before some lecture or other. I had just published a review in *Mind* of a collection of essays dedicated to him, which included his replies to these essays, and in the course of this review I described his remarks on the subject of *de re* necessity as "wholly worthless," a phrase I had hesitated over but felt was literally correct. As I feared, he raised the topic of this review. I steeled myself for his rebuke for dismissing his view so summarily, but he made no mention of the phrase or the verdict it enshrined, which indeed was only the most recent instalment of a long-standing disagreement between us. Instead, he took me to task over another word I had used. I had commented in the review that his present assessment of metaphysics was far more tolerant than that of his "callower years," i.e., the years of *Language, Truth and Logic*, written when he was a mere twenty-six. His complaint was not, as might be expected, that I was here implying that his earlier rejection of metaphysics was merely callow: no, his objection was to what he took to be the suggestion that he was *now* callow. I was puzzled at first that he could read the offending locution in that way, and I assured him that I had not intended it thus, pointing out that it did not logically bear that entailment, any more than use of the phrase "younger days" would imply that he was now young. In fact, I had chosen the comparative form precisely to avoid implying that he was positively callow when young, not even imagining that it might be taken to imply septuagenarian puerility. But my protests went unheeded: the elderly man of distinction was determined to interpret me as accusing him of advanced immaturity. It was not a comfortable encounter, I can tell you. On reflection, it seemed to me that I had unwittingly twanged a raw nerve in him, which revealed more about his own estimate of himself than about my verbal sloppiness: he was less sensitive to being convicted outright of having "wholly worthless" philosophical views than to there being even a hint (however subtextual or unintended) that he was in some respect intellectually unripe.

It must have been fairly soon after this that he came to read a paper at UCL, which again touched on the topic of *de re* necessity. He had flu and had lost his voice, but he didn't let that put him off. He arranged to have Richard Wollheim read his paper out for him. As the paper was mellifluously read, in cadences quite unlike Freddie's own clipped and headlong mode of speech ("prshn" for "proposition"), he nodded his vigorous assent to the arguments that were being advanced, as if congratulating an esteemed colleague on his remarkable probity, and occasionally fixing me with a beady stare where he imagined I might disagree. He was not to be deterred from fighting his corner.

The last time I saw Freddie was in the autumn of 1988, when we were both attending an Oxford discussion group he had formed well before my time.

He was suffering badly from emphysema and could only walk a few paces before losing his breath. He greeted me in the friendliest way and said half-apologetically, "I am not the man I was." I found this difficult to reply to. During the ensuing discussion of a colleague's paper he made strenuous interventions of a wholly characteristic kind: amusing, petulant, a bit axe-grinding, exuberantly deflationary. Afterward he needed a taxi to take him the hundred yards from University College to New College. A member of the group remarked to me that it would have been good to have tape-recorded that session.

I hope these personal reminiscences succeed in revealing various facets of Freddie Ayer's character, at least as it appeared to a former student of his and junior colleague: kind and decent to young aspirants, unstuffy, with an upfront vanity and vulnerability, a streak of intellectual insecurity wider than might be expected, personal directness, and a strong need never to be in the shade. I always liked him, and was sadder at his death than I expected.

In this posthumous collection of essays Ayer's strengths and weaknesses as a philosopher show forth clearly. The essays range from a 1944 piece for Cyril Connolly's *Horizon* on the concept of freedom to an article written for the *Sunday Telegraph* in 1988 on the subject of his four-minute "death" and what he experienced while in that suspended state. Between these are essays on the nature of philosophy, transcribed broadcast dialogues with Father Copleston and Arne Naess, a summary of Russell's work, an introduction to J. S. Mill, a statement of humanism, and a lecture on the meaning of life. There is the accustomed fluency of style and air of lucidity, and the sense that philosophy is an enjoyable subject: but also the impression of a man in a hurry, talking and thinking too fast for his subject matter, skidding over difficulties, curiously closed to philosophical perplexity, keener sometimes to score points than to win them. You never get the feeling, reading Ayer, that philosophy is painful—that thinking seriously about it *hurts*. Neither do you get much of a sense of the nature of philosophical creativity. Indeed, he always seems to me to be writing as if philosophy is essentially over, as if there are no more new ideas to be had. Certainly he was less than fully receptive to many of the ideas that philosophers of my generation take for granted, especially those emanating from America. Original theories were almost invariably referred to as "fashions." His was the world of Russell and Moore, Peirce and James, a bit of Carnap here, the odd mention of Quine there.

The famous radio dialogue with Copleston provides some choice moments. In it Ayer undertakes the difficult task of defending logical positivism against a shrewd philosopher, and historian of philosophy, of the despised old school. It is clear now, as it may not have been then, that Copleston roundly refutes Ayer's position, doing so with courtesy, clarity, and intellectual discipline. At times Ayer flails wildly, as his astute tormentor drives him from one uninhabitable corner to another—though it is not clear that Ayer sees it that way. The antipositivist points that Copleston fastens on are basically four. First, the verifiability criterion of meaningfulness simply has built into it, by stipulation, the very rejection of metaphysics it is intended to motivate, since on anybody's view metaphysical propositions are not going to be verifiable by means of sensory observation: their acceptance will depend upon considerations of rational coherence, economy, systematicity, and so forth. The traditional problem of the status of universals, for example, will not be decided by checking the world out experimentally: it will be decided, if it is, well, philosophically. Second, no cogent argument has ever been offered for the verificationist criterion. It is simply a dogma designed to do preset polemical work: why *should* meaningfulness consist in what can be perceptually verified? Third, the principle is open to obvious counterexamples: not merely statements from ethics, aesthetics, and metaphysics, but also such homely remarks as that there will come a time when there are no human beings—for who will verify that? Fourth, and most embarrassing, the principle of verifiability is self-refuting: for either it is itself empirically verifiable, or it is "merely formal" (whatever that may mean), or it is meaningless. Since it cannot claim to belong to either of the first two categories, it seems condemned to belong to the third, in which case it says of itself that it is gobbledygook. In fact, or course, it is just an ordinary piece of philosophy, as meaningful as any, though wildly implausible. The problem is that it is a piece of philosophy that denies its own meaningfulness—which is not a good way to get yourself accepted. Copleston also, *en passant,* makes mincemeat of Ayer's crude conventionalism about logical truth, forcing him to assert that the law of noncontradiction has no deeper status than the arbitrary rules of a game. The only area of weakness in Copleston's defense of traditional philosophy is his reliance on theological examples: he would have been wiser to choose a less controversial field of battle.

Ayer was always interested in perception and its relation to our knowledge of the external world. He was worried that what we perceive of the world (if anything) does not seem to justify what we believe about it—the problem of skepticism. This is indeed a legitimate concern, but I do not think Ayer handles it at all satisfactorily. He remarks here, as he often does elsewhere, that the causal theory of perception is inconsistent with naive realism. This is a peculiar claim, for why should the fact that the table causes me to have perceptual experiences imply that I do not really *see* the table? That is like saying that a causal theory of collision implies that objects never touch! He seems not to have been able to rid himself of the idea that what lies outside the mind, causing events in us and other bodies, is somehow cut off from the mind's direct apprehension. And perhaps that underlies his desire to find a description of experience that is neutral as to the way the world stands—a sense-datum language. There are interpretations of this project that make sense, but I have never been convinced that Ayer's is one of them. The central difficulty, over which Ayer's prose is apt to lose its usual limpidity, is what kind of vocabulary should be employed (or invented) to capture this neutral experiential content. It is not supposed to consist of words for qualities of objects, apparently, since these "go beyond" what is "immediately given," but then we are never quite told what other words we might use. Nor is it clear how his own account of how we move inferentially from perceptual data to the world is supposed to quell the sceptic's doubts. Okay, we can think of our ordinary beliefs as constituting a theory in respect of the sensory evidence, but what is to exclude the claims of rival theories—the ones we have no tendency to believe? For example, what is it about the evidence that rules out the theory that we are all brains in vats being fed these very sensory inputs by a godlike Martian physiologist? We are not told, so the common-sense theory has not yet been vindicated.

Philosophers are often rebuked for not asking what the meaning of life is or for failing to offer an answer. In his 1988 lecture Ayer both asks and answers this question. Predictably enough, he denies that life has meaning in virtue of a presiding deity, and he locates its meaning in the actual projects and fulfilments of mortal existence. He says a number of sensible and familiar things, but I do not think he quite puts his finger on the essential considerations, which I take to be as follows. To begin with, we need to scrutinize that little phrase "the meaning of life": what kind of meaning is being envisaged here? It cannot be what Paul Grice called natural meaning—as when clouds mean rain—since the question is not what causal or lawlike relations our lives stand in to other occurrences. Neither can it be a question of semantic meaning—as when a certain English sentence means that it is raining—since my life clearly does not express any kind of proposition. What must be intended is probably best put by dropping the word "meaning" altogether and substituting a word like "point" or "purpose": the question then is what point or purpose there is to human life.

It seems to be very tempting to feel, as a matter of metaphysical exigency, that it must have some point—that there must be something external to it that gives it a point. And here religious ideas are commonly invoked: it is either the existence of God that gives human life a point, or the fact of some more or less supernatural previous or subsequent life. These extramortal entities are supposed to inject a point into our life that it would otherwise wholly lack. Now the essential thing to notice about these point-conferring beings is that they are themselves instances of kinds of life, either divine or supernatural in some other way. And the idea is that they are in some way "unmeant meaners": they give point to our lives without themselves needing to have point conferred upon theirs. But now the flaw should be apparent: why should *these* lives be allowed to have meaning intrinsically while *our* lives are required to have meaning conferred extrinsically upon them? If the lives of some beings must carry meaning within themselves, as God's is supposed to, or the selves of the afterlife, then why can't our lives achieve that now? Clearly it is no use to postulate further lives—a God for God or an afterlife for our afterlife—on pain of an infinite regress. So if there is a genuine metaphysical problem about what gives human life meaning, the religious answers do not solve it; they just push it back a stage. The logical position here is precisely parallel to Wittgenstein's argument against the tempting idea that linguistic signs get their meaning from other (possibly super-natural) signs. As he saw, since this process has to terminate somewhere, why not halt it at the first stage? The only legitimate sense in which supernatural lives could give natural lives a point is the trivial sense in which the existence of other mortal lives gives point to my life: but then we have that already. There is no metaphysical problem of the meaning of human life that could be solved by multiplying lives, however supernatural those other lives may be.

Once this logical point has been clearly grasped, the only point that human life could have is to be found in what is internal to it. Ayer takes this view too, but I think he only partially locates the internal facts in question. He tends, though he is not entirely consistent in the matter, to locate the value of life in the kinds of fulfilment available to a person leading the kind of life he leads—which brings him to deny, or underestimate, the value of life for people not belonging to what he calls a "privileged minority." "The vast majority of the human race," he says, "in Asia, in Latin America, in Africa, in the so-called underclasses of the more affluent Western societies, are far too fully occupied in waging a losing struggle to achieve a tolerable standard of living for it to be rational for them to wish their miseries prolonged." And presumably, for much the same reasons, he would deny value to the lives of animals, on account of the poverty of their life projects.

Now it is not that I dispute the miseries and limitations in question, but I suggest that Ayer's inference from them betrays a lopsided conception of what makes life worthwhile. In a word, he ignores, or downplays, the impor-tance of what might be called "basic experiences": enjoying a cool drink, hearing a friend's voice, even taking a shit. These experiences constitute what life most primitively is—for Oxford dons, Amazonian bushmen, chil-dren, dogs and snakes—and it stays that way even when your novel doesn't get published or your favorite team loses the World Cup. And doesn't every-one at some time feel, especially when their life has been threatened, that these basic experiences are infinitely precious, that it will be a terrible day when you can feel them no more? The film *Robocop,* about a man who survives comprehensive violence by being made mainly robot, is precisely an exploration of this theme: the metallic man longs for the days when ordinary experiences were available to him; he wants his "lower nature" back, because without it life is hollow. What we need, I think, is a kind of two-layer theory of the value of life: on top we have the projects and satisfactions we think mostly about; beneath that, the foundation of biological consciousness we tend to take for granted. For a man not averse to the offerings of the senses, it is surprising that Ayer neglects this latter source of value. Was there a repressed ascetic lurking beneath the frankly sybaritic exterior?

The book ends with two pieces recounting his experience of four minutes of heart failure, caused by a piece of smoked salmon going down the wrong way. It seems that during these four minutes he had an experience as of being confronted by an exceedingly bright red light which he was somehow aware governed the universe. This light had two ministers who were in charge of space, which they periodically inspected. They had recently fallen down on the job because space had become slightly out of joint and the laws of nature had gone awry. It was up to Ayer to rectify matters, which he sought to do by operating on time. However, the ministers of space took no notice of him as he walked up and down waving his watch at them. He became desperate, and then the experience came to an end.

At the time this episode was reported there was some question as to whether Ayer took himself to have, or even really had, "crossed to the other side." As he makes clear in a postscript, however, no such thing is implied: by far the most likely explanation is that his brain was still functioning to generate experiences while his heart had temporarily stopped. I can see, though, why some readers may have been misled by what he wrote immediately after describing the experience in queston: "This experience could well have been delusive. . . . [A] slight indication that it may have been veridical has been supplied by my French friend. . . . [T]hese experiences, on the assumption that the last one was veridical, are rather strong evidence that death does not put an end to consciousness." The problem here comes from unclarity about what exactly Ayer means by "delusive" and "veridical." From the context it seems pretty clear to me that he means to be discussing whether he had such experiences *during* the four minutes he was heart-dead, not whether in having those experiences he was *really* seeing a red light, its ministers, disjointed space, and so on. He is not doubting that it was all some kind of dream; the doubt attaches only to its time of occurrence. The trouble is that the words he chooses mean the opposite of what he means: to ask whether an experience is veridical is to ask whether the world was really the way the experience made it seem, not whether one really *had* the experience. Here, I fear, his faulty philosophy of perception let him down, causing him to utter words that would naturally be seized upon as an abnegation of his lifelong opposition to the supernatural. This was very unfortunate, and it is not adequately cleared up in the postscript. It is clear to me, however, that he was not in any way taking seriously the idea that he had temporarily "crossed to the other side." The sober truth is simply that he had a rather strange dream during the time his heart had stopped beating.

Freddie Ayer was a man who liked three sorts of scoring: goals in football, points in philosophy, women in life. Of these three impulses I would speculate that the first represented the deepest part of his nature. His enthusiasm for sport while at Eton is stressed in his autobiography and his passion for football was obviously totally genuine. He belongs to a type abundantly exemplified on the American side of the Atlantic, referred to by the cognoscenti as the jock nerd: men of thwarted sporting ambition who sublimate their sporting instincts into intellectual pursuits. This type is to be firmly distinguished from the nerd jock: the kind of man who finds himself good at sports and has to conceal his intellectual abilities from his fellow sportsmen (it was tough being a nerd jock). Quite different intellectual styles may be expected of these two types of person: compulsive competitiveness from the former, its absence from the latter (he got all that out of his system on the sports field). The jock nerd is alway trying to score goals against his intellectual opponents. For obvious reasons this type is far commoner in academic life than the nerd jock, and he is generally found more acceptable there—especially if he has a "Sir" in front of his name. Freddie Ayer tended to do philosophy as if it were a sport, as his fondness for the metaphor of playing a game indicates. The trouble is, it is not a sport.

The Meaning of Life has an introduction by Ted Honderich that is ill-written, plodding, and faintly nauseating in places. It adds nothing to the essays that follow; and the book itself is poorly edited.

II
MIND

9

Penrose: Past Computation

Shadows of the Mind: A Search for
the Missing Science of Consciousness
by Roger Penrose
Oxford University Press, 1994

Consciousness has recently come to be cast as the fairground coconut of contemporary thought: everyone wants a crack at knocking it from its pedestal and then splitting it open to reveal the secret inner gleam. Book upon book, theory upon theory, has been hurled at the tough bristly nut of consciousness, with the hope of at least grazing the big prize—the missiles invariably falling limply at the thrower's feet or splashing wildly into some nearby goldfish bowl. The target has proved exasperatingly elusive. There has been much gleeful jeering at the form of other contestants and manly displays of theoretical bravado. Some fret pessimistically over whether the balls supplied are even capable of the appropriate trajectory. But there is always someone out there who believes that he has just the right arm for the job. And think of the glory!

Shadows of the Mind is Roger Penrose's second major shy at the stubborn coconut, the first being *The Emperor's New Mind,* which was a huge popular success. Despite the presence of the word "mind" in both titles, the bulk of both books is taken up with discussions of logic, mathematics, quantum theory, and relativity theory. There is a reason for this: Penrose believes that in those areas lie our best hopes for a scientific theory of consciousness. The new book is a systematic and lengthy presentation of an argument that purports to tell us both what consciousness is not and what it might be. As with the previous book, the reader admires and appreciates the patience, clarity,

Reprinted with permission from the *Times Literary Supplement* (January 6, 1996).

and thoroughness of the treatment, especially in difficult matters of contemporary physics. There is never any fudging or wide-eyed metaphor-mongering in Penrose; he knows his stuff inside out and he does his level best to communicate it to the lay reader. That is not to say the book is all smooth sledding: some of it is forbiddingly technical and complex, and I find it hard to imagine that the typical nonspecialist reader will make much of some sections of it. Still, the main line of argument does not require a high degree of technical sophistication for its comprehension, though it certainly demands very careful attention. Indeed, as I shall argue, the central flaw in Penrose's position can be appreciated simply by maintaining clarity about certain key conceptual distinctions. Here is where a bit more *philosophical* skill would have usefully supplemented the formidable scientific expertise on display.

The first half of the book has a negative intent, namely to show that mathematical understanding—one manifestation of human consciousness—cannot be reduced to the following of formal algorithmic procedures. That is, when a mathematician recognizes the truth of an arithmetical statement he cannot be doing so by applying a set of purely formal rules in a mechanical manner. Mathematical understanding transcends the application of formal rules to an axiomatic system. Accordingly, writes Penrose, it is not possible to simulate mathematical understanding by programming a computer to carry out purely algorithmic procedures; such a computer would be unable to appreciate the mathematical truths accessible to human mathematicians. Thus consciousness possesses a power not available in principle to a computer.

Penrose argues for this conclusion by appeal to Gödel's second incompleteness theorem, which demonstrates that no consistent formal system strong enough to formulate arithmetic can be complete, that is, generate all mathematical truths. There will always be true mathematical statements that cannot be formally derived from any system of axioms and rules. Penrose's thesis is that the Gödel result shows that mathematical truth, as we recognize it, is not accessible to a computer programmed to instantiate a consistent formal system. Gödel shows us that "human mathematicians are not using a knowably sound algorithm in order to ascertain mathematical truth," and since computers have nothing to go on except algorithms, it follows that the project of simulating human intelligence by means of a computer must be doomed. All computers can do is mechanically execute a Turing table, while Gödel tells us that human thought can get beyond the limits inherent in this method of ascertaining truth.

Thus, Penrose asserts, we have a mathematical theorem that effectively shows that our minds are not computers. The dream of artificial intelligence (AI) cannot then be fulfilled, for hard mathematical reasons. (The argument, if correct, also cuts against the dominant paradigm of contemporary cognitive science, though Penrose does not note this explicitly, since that paradigm conceives the mind as a symbol-manipulating algorithmic engine.) In order, then, to gain an understanding of what underlies our actual intellectual capacities we must undertake a search for nonalgorithmic mental principles—which is where the second, positive half of the book comes in.

Penrose expounds the Gödel argument with great care and rigor; and he patiently examines twenty potential objections to the argument, concluding that it survives all criticism. It is indeed an argument that has been much criticized since a version of it was propounded by John Lucas over thirty years ago. I myself am willing to accept the argument, so far as it goes; my objections have to do with its significance, rather than its internal validity.

Let me begin by indicating why the conclusion of the argument is not actually very surprising. It is because there are several other reasons why the algorithmic picture of human thought is implausible. First, there is every reason to doubt that our nonmathematical understanding of the world is algorithmically based. Outside of formal disciplines, our modes of reasoning are not susceptible to modeling in terms of mechanical Turing-style procedures. We do not form beliefs about the weather or novels or other people's actions or morality or even chemistry by grinding through the subroutines of a universal Turing machine. Mathematics is about the only area in which such a formalistic conception could even seem appropriate, because of the presence of the notion of formal proof in that domain.

Second, an algorithm is by definition a procedure that can be carried out *mechanically,* that is, without understanding; so it is hardly surprising that understanding itself does not admit of reduction to purely algorithmic processes. Algorithms *substitute* for understanding when used in a computer simulation; they do not reproduce it. That is precisely why we have done so well in mimicking certain aspects of human intelligence (think of the pocket calculator).

Third, algorithms are essentially syntactic procedures that operate independently of any semantic features the manipulated "symbols" might possess. (This is the basic point of John Searle's well-known "Chinese Room" argument, which sets out to show that you cannot derive the meaning of a symbol from its physical properties.) Therefore human mathematical *intentionality* cannot be modeled simply by installing a syntactic algorithmic procedure in a machine. Finally, since the demise of the formalist philosophy of mathematics, partly under the impact of Gödel's theorem, we no longer take very seriously the idea that mathematical truth can be explained purely in terms of the consistency of a formal system. Mathematical truth is no more "formal" than any other kind of truth. Modern computationalism about the mind, insofar as it is a holdover from formalist philosophy of mathematics, is as discredited as that philosophy. Both views seek, futilely, to disregard content, hoping that form alone will capture all the reality there is.

Assume, then, at least for the sake of argument, that Penrose has established the following conclusion: it cannot be in virtue of enacting an algorithm that we know mathematics, so that this knowledge cannot be simulated on a computer solely by dint of its algorithmic program. The problem is that he wishes to draw a pair of related consequences from this that simply do not follow: first, that present-day computing machines do not understand mathematics; second, that we need a radically new "noncomputable" physics if we are to explain conscious understanding. Let me be clear that I am not disagreeing with the *truth* of these two contentions: I too believe that present-day computers do not know mathematics, and also that consciousness requires a revolution in our view of the physical universe. My objection has to do with the *reasons* Penrose gives for asserting these two truths.

What the Gödel argument shows, assuming it to be valid, is that no system—a computing machine or a human brain—could know mathematics *in virtue of following formal algorithmic procedures;* but from this it does *not* follow that an ordinary computer is incapable of duplicating human mathematical understanding. The reason is simple: the computing machine *also* has further properties not equivalent to the properties that constitute its program. For example, it contains chips made of silicon; it has a certain color and weight; it has electronic impulses traveling through it; it was bought at a certain shop. And now the point is this: for all the Gödel-Penrose argument shows, it might be in virtue of these *other* properties that the system has mathematical understanding. Agreed, program properties cannot constitute or underlie mathematical understanding; but that is perfectly compatible with insisting—however implausibly—that it is (say) the *color* of the computer that gives it such understanding! For Gödel's proof says *nothing* about whether mathematical understanding can be derived from color properties or any other noncomputational property of a system. Not that the properties mentioned are remotely sensible candidates for what underlies conscious understanding; but they do serve to make the *logical* point I am after—that Penrose has not ruled out a form of noncomputational physicalism. (I myself reject all such theories; but that is another story.) Similarly, we can agree that the algorithms the brain uses will not suffice for mathematical understanding, while maintaining that it is (say) the *chemical* properties of neurons that do suffice.

To put the point differently: Gödel's theorem concerns the limits of a certain abstract entity—a formal system—to yield mathematical truth; it says nothing about whether, once that entity is instantiated in a physical object, the object can have this or that capacity. This will depend on what other properties the object has. It is not that I am saying we know what those other understanding-conferring properties are; my point is just that there is a whopping non sequitur in Penrose's argument. He forgets, in effect, that there is more to a computer than its software. The Gödel argument concerns the insufficiency of algorithmic software to yield understanding; it is silent on the powers of hardware, however conventional that may be. For all the argument shows, the computer on which I am writing might have conscious understanding of mathematics—though not indeed in virtue of its program.

This gap in the argument has a large impact on Penrose's second main thesis, namely that we need a new physics in order to explain consciousness.

PENROSE: PAST COMPUTATION

For, in view of the non sequitur just identified, he now has no argument for that thesis: any old standby property of current physics might do the job, so long as it is not a programming property. The Gödel argument by itself cannot motivate the search for a new physics, since it has no implications for the powers of currently recognized physical properties to confer understanding on a system.

It might be retorted that Penrose has a way around this criticism, which is at least implicit in his discussion. He might say that everything in current physics is itself computable and hence can be simulated on a Turing machine; so any physical property that is now ascribed to machines or brains can be *represented* as an algorithmic property. And if that is so, then we can just repeat the Gödel argument with respect to that simulating algorithm: it, too, will necessarily fail to yield mathematical truth.

This countermove is, however, irrelevant to the point at issue. It might have been relevant, if the claim had been that mathematical understanding actually consists in the algorithmic simulation that is alleged to hold for the physical properties of the system; then we might have been able to apply the Gödel argument to show that mathematical truth must reach beyond the capacities of this simulating algorithm. But that was not the claim; the claim was that the physical property itself is what confers understanding on the device in question. We should not confuse a physical system with its corresponding Turing simulation: the color of an object, say, is not the *same* property as the internal state of some computer that *simulates* the colors of things, say with zeros and ones. Only a kind of bizarre pancomputationalism could blur this distinction. But we must always distinguish clearly between following a program and being simulable by a program. My computer runs a word-processing program specified in its software; it may or may not be such that its myriad hardware properties can be simulated by some further program, say one that simulates its behavior when dropped from a bridge. I cannot rid myself of the impression that Penrose has tacitly conflated these two relations to an algorithm, which is what enables him to jump from the Gödelian limits of programs to what the physical world itself can bring about. He must somehow be thinking of the ordinary physical world as itself a formal system that is bounded by the Gödel result. But, of course, it is no such thing.

The notion of simulation can be mischievous in this regard. If I simulate the weather on a computer, I do not, of course, create a system in which winds howl and rain falls; rather, I create formal analogues of those physical phenomena. To claim that the wind blows things over in virtue of disturbances of air molecules is, therefore, not to claim that the *simulation* of these disturbances is what blows things over. In the same way, to claim that it is the neural structure of the brain that produces consciousness is not to claim that a formal simulation of that neural structure is what produces it. The reason for this is just that simulation is merely isomorphism in a specific respect; it is not total duplication of the system simulated. So from the fact that brain processes have algorithmic simulations we cannot infer that they have no productive powers beyond those of the simulating algorithm.

Accordingly there is no way out for Penrose, along these lines, in spanning the logical gap I have alleged. Besides, a simulation of the physical basis of mathematical understanding could hardly play the role of a formal system as that occurs in Gödel's proof, since it will not consist (like, say, Peano's axioms) of a set of axioms and rules of inference *concerning arithmetic*. In addition, the Penrose argument requires that the algorithm used be knowably sound and be employed *as* a proof procedure for mathematical truth; and this will not be true of a putative algorithm that merely simulates the physical properties of the system we are considering. The upshot is that, while the Gödel argument might disprove computationalism, it is made of the wrong stuff to disprove orthodox materialism. Such materialism has its own problems, of course; my point is just that Penrose is overreaching in deploying the Gödel result against it. He has thus not *shown* that consciousness requires a new physics.

There is a less technical worry about the first half of the book. As Penrose is well aware, mathematical understanding is not the only kind of consciousness there is; there are also sensations, emotions, perceptions, thoughts of many kinds. Yet his argument applies only to the mathematical case; he offers no argument against computationalism for those other areas. It is not that he thinks computationalism is *true* for nonmathematical consciousness; but nothing he says counts against its being true. This is surely very odd: should not the underlying failure of the computational approach to consciousness apply quite generally and not merely to this one specific (and peculiar) area? Penrose cannot, by invoking the Gödel result, have got to the root of what makes the mind generally insusceptible to computational treatment. It is the property of consciousness that is the nemesis of computationalism, but that property crops up all over the place, not just in mathematical reasoning.

Further, I think Penrose underestimates the difficulty for his approach occasioned by the phenomenon of *sub*conscious mathematical reasoning. He assumes that consciousness and mathematical understanding are inseparably connected, so that results concerning the latter necessarily bear on the former. But, as is well known, mathematicians often achieve their results by means of subconscious mentation, and this must involve a recognition of genuine mathematical truth—which the Gödel argument shows must exceed computational resources. Thus nonalgorithmic mathematical understanding can proceed without benefit of consciousness, which suggests that it is not consciousness itself that is responsible for the failure of the formalistic reconstruction of mathematical understanding. One suspects that, even for his chosen best case, Penrose has not put his finger on why it is that consciousness per se poses a special problem for artificial intelligence. Couple this with the fact that he offers no positive suggestions concerning *what* it is about conscious understanding that enables it to outstrip formal procedures, and we are left with a very partial picture of the terrain.

As I have suggested, the search for a new physics in the second half of the book is unmotivated by the negative contentions of the first half, but that does not mean that it is not interesting and worthwhile in itself. Admittedly, if I am right, it is a mistake to think that radical noncomputability has to be the appropriate way to formulate the goal, where this alludes to a type of physics not susceptible to the usual kinds of computable mathematics. But let us follow Penrose on the path he has chosen to see where it might lead. The central thesis now is that the problem of consciousness is integrally linked to problems in the theory of quantum mechanics, specifically to the nature of "state vector reduction"—how "measurements" collapse quantum superpositions to yield a classical world of uniquely characterized states of things. To understand consciousness we need to understand such things as why it is that Schrödinger's cat is not found to be simultaneously alive and dead, despite the existence of comparable superpositions at the quantum level. Noncomputability in the vicinity of quantum theory is what Penrose thinks might underlie the noncomputability of mathematical thought.

To pursue this conjecture, he takes us through the many oddities of quantum theory, providing a clear (though demanding) exposition of the key principles. His objectivism and realism are refreshing, and his criticisms of the standard approaches, such as that of the "many worlds" hypothesis, seem to my amateur eye pretty devastating. As an advanced introduction, it is exemplary, though there are many pages composed of such sentences as "The vector $z|\alpha\rangle$ is the orthogonal projection of $|\psi\rangle$ on the ray determined by $|\alpha\rangle$, and $|\chi\rangle$ is the orthogonal projection of $|\psi\rangle$ into the *orthogonal complement* space of $|\alpha\rangle$ (i.e. the space of all vectors orthogonal to $|\alpha\rangle$)."

But the question is whether all this yields any dividends when it comes to understanding the mind. Does Penrose forge any convincing link between quantum reduction and consciousness? Well, his eventual proposal is nothing if not ingenious. Searching for a noncomputable element in state vector reduction that will bear upon brain function, he is led to postulate a gravitational theory of quantum action that operates within tiny components of neurons called "microtubules." The idea is that at this location quantum effects may be magnified into a classical level effect that could influence the growth of synaptic connections. Thus consciousness turns out to depend upon the global superpositions of quantum states that occur inside the microtubules that exist in the cytoskeletons of neurons. The microtubules function as the conduit from the strange quantum world to revealed consciousness, and a proper theory of the transition from quantum to classical levels will have to incorporate noncomputable elements. Thus it is that our minds can know mathematical truths that we cannot prove from any formal system. We get input, so to speak, from the noncomputable antics of those marvelous quantum-sensitive microtubules in our heads.

What are we to make of all this? I would certainly not fault Penrose on

grounds of mere theoretical extravagance, since I too believe that a fundamental revision of physical theory is needed in order to make consciousness
fit into the physical world (though I would locate the problematic nexus in
the anomalous relation between consciousness and space). But I think this
particular proposal has very little to be said for it; despite the heavy artillery,
the coconut of consciousness isn't even wobbling. As we have already noted,
the search for noncomputable physical processes is otiose, resulting from an
inflated interpretation of the Gödel argument. It is in any case very hard to
see how the kind of noncomputability Penrose contemplates, operating at
the level of state vector reduction, could possibly yield an explanation of our
conscious mathematical understanding. No genuine explanatory link is suggested, and noncomputability cannot be the key to consciousness in general
anyway. And, obviously enough, the theory is hopelessly insufficient as an
account of what confers consciousness, since (as Penrose acknowledges) if it
were taken to supply sufficient conditions, then superconductors and para-
mecia would be conscious. He thus weakens the theory to suggesting only a
necessary condition of consciousness. But this softens it beyond the point of
real interest, since what needs to be added is clearly going to constitute the
vast bulk of the final theory. It will, indeed, be precisely that which makes a
system genuinely *conscious*. After all, *lots* of things about the brain are necessary conditions for consciousness—such as the proximity of neurons to one
another, or the temperature of brain tissue—but to say this is not to provide a
theory of consciousness. Microtubules are in fact everywhere in the biological
world, being part of virtually all cells, so why is it that they produce consciousness only in certain biological environments—such as brains? Presumably because the brain has some property, not itself microtubular, that permits consciousness to arise. But that is exactly the question we started with.

Among the possible positions Penrose describes is the view that consciousness is not amenable to treatment by science. He rejects this position on the
ground that it is "the viewpoint of the mystic." But I think he misses an
important distinction here. One version of the position is indeed religiously
tinged, picturing the mind as a supernatural something. But there is another
version of the position, which queries the meaning of "science" in the formulation of the thesis. If it means a body of thought potentially available to the
human intellect, then there is room for the view that the problem of consciousness might not be solvable in terms of the human science-forming
cognitive system. But if it means any theory of nature, whether or not humans can grasp that theory, then we might readily agree that the problem
has some solution in this wider cognitive space. This distinction allows us to
contemplate the possibility that inaccessibility to humanly constructed science is no mark of the mystical; it is simply a result of the limitations of
human mentality. Such a position needs to be considered along with the
others Penrose identifies (it is, in fact, my position). He thinks that we need a
new physics in order to understand consciousness; my point would be that to
get the new physics we need we would have to acquire a new mind—not

something to hold your breath for. In other words, consciousness is a mystery for the human intellect, given our mental architecture, but it does not thereby betoken anything contranatural. The mind indeed casts a shadow, and inside that shadow it itself falls.

I have made a number of serious criticisms of *Shadows of the Mind*, but I do not want to give too negative an impression of the book. It is a deeply serious and honest attempt to understand one of the hardest things there is to understand. It is full of fascinating discussions on a wide variety of topics. Much of it is eminently sensible. The science is beautifully presented. It is clearly the product of a brilliant mind. Unfortunately, however, the subject of consciousness calls for more than all these excellent qualities combined. It must have caused more broken-backed theories than any other phenomenon in nature.

10

Humphrey: Getting the Wiggle into the Act

A History of the Mind
by Nicholas Humphrey
Chatto, 1992

Consciousness is not sempiternal, it has a history, a natural genesis. Once upon a time the universe contained no consciousness; then it sprang up here and there; and now the planet is flooded with the stuff. This is not to make the trivial observation that what people think and feel changes over time and generations, sometimes quite radically; it is a point about the deep biological roots of consciousness. Just as animal bodies are products of a long evolutionary process, in which chance variation is rigorously winnowed by natural selection, so animal minds must have a remote genesis in the mechanisms of differential survival as they worked on the available materials. Eyes gradually emerged as engines for exploiting the information contained in light, relying on the given chemical and optical properties of matter; and consciousness likewise must have emerged for some good biological reason, building on the prior properties of organisms. The question is how and why this happened: how did mentality arise from cell tissue? Answering this question would tell us not merely about the etiology of consciousness; it would also help us to understand the nature of consciousness—particularly its relation to its physical substrate. If we knew the history of mind, then we would have effectively solved the mind-body problem, since we would understand how consciousness arises from matter.

Nicholas Humphrey's book is a bold and speculative attempt to reconstruct mental history and hence to develop a theory of consciousness. He has

Reprinted with permission from the *London Review of Books* (September 10, 1992).

a good project, and he is bracingly undaunted by its difficulty. He has a number of interesting and sensible things to say about a variety of topics, from the affective dimensions of color to the nature of blindsight. And he writes in a fresh (if jaunty) style. But in the end, I fear, the theory he proposes is a dismal failure: it doesn't work at all. Don't blame the author, though; blame the problem—it is just so *hard*. Like most attempted theories of consciousness, Humphrey's looks like a contender only by trading on a mixture of obscurity and circularity. What is instructive about it are the manifest contortions needed to offer something with even the appearance of a decent theory. You see Humphrey being driven from pillar to post, alternating confidence with *aporia*, in a doomed attempt to lasso his quarry. Consciousness still swims out of reach, flaunting its mysterious gleam.

The books starts encouragingly enough, by locating the problem in the nature of basic first-order sentience. Humphrey tells us, disarmingly, that in his earlier work he "came in at too high a level and left the fundamental problems unsolved." "Too high a level" was the level of self-reflection—knowledge *of* one's states of consciousness. This leaves quite untouched the prior question of the nature of the mental states themselves—the pains, the tickles, the seeings of red, the smellings of roses. How do *these* spring from mere irritations of nervous tissue? Humphrey now sees the problem, correctly, as that of "explaining how states of consciousness arise in human [*sic*] brains": how do we get from brain cells to subjective sentient fields?

Humphrey's theory has two main parts: (1) a distinction between sensation and perception, with consciousness attaching directly only to the former; and (2) the suggestion that to have a sensation is for the brain to initiate a feedback loop from its core to its periphery. Both parts of the theory strike me as fundamentally flawed and crucially unclear.

Many theorists of perception have felt the need to distinguish between a component of sensory experience that acts as a sensation in or for the subject and a component that corresponds to the way the objective world appears to the subject. When we smell a rose, we have a sensation in our nose, it seems, as well as perceiving something to be so in the environment. Awareness of our own body thus seems somehow implicated in awareness of the external world: we perceive the world from a specific body and our experience seems to reflect this fact. Something happens *in* us when the outer world presents itself to our senses. The difficulty has been to formulate this intuition, or set of intuitions, in a way that does not misdescribe the character of sensory experience. When we see a scene, which aspects of the experience constitute the sensation we feel and which depict the outside world? What is strictly inside us, experientially, and what points outward? This kind of question has occupied philosophers for centuries and the pitfalls have been diagnosed. In particular, the need to preserve the essential intentionality of sensory experience has long been recognized.

Unfortunately, Humphrey shows little awareness of, or sophistication in, the conceptual and other issues that arise at this point, and often writes in ways that indicate a good deal of error and confusion. He fails to give any account of the representational character of sensory experience. It is totally unclear, in particular, whether he takes his category of sensation to be intrinsically nonrepresentational, or whether it is simply prejudgmental. Is he making a division within how things *look* to the subject, as he sometimes seems to be, or is he trying to identify a level of experience that has no world-directed intentionality written into it? Humphrey says repeatedly that sensations "represent what is happening to me," at my bodily surface. It is not clear how he is using "represent" here (itself a crucial issue), but it is surely false to suggest that in typical visual experience the way in which my retina is being physically stimulated is part of how things *seem* to me—I have no experience *of* my retina.

Nor is it acceptable to predicate color words of my sensations themselves, supposing that when I see something green there is literally something green inside me—a "green sensation." This is the old mistake of transferring to the experience what properly belongs to its intentional object. In fact, Humphrey unwittingly (I assume) treads the old path of the sense-datum theorists, with its debates about the status of secondary qualities. Maybe such theories are more defensible than they have seemed to recent philosophers of perception, but Humphrey is too naive about the philosophical issues involved to persuade us of that. The central question he needed to work harder on is this: is the sensation/perception distinction, as he wishes to draw it, a distinction *within* the way the world appears to the subject? That visual experiences have affective corollaries does not show, *pace* Humphrey, that there is a sensational component to them which can be hived off from the way they represent the world, since this might be extrinsic to their content.

Equally problematic is Humphrey's conception of what the perception side of his contrast is supposed to be. Sometimes it seems to consist in the judgments the perceiver makes on the basis of his experience, in which case it is not a component of experience at all, since it goes beyond how things appear. At other times it seems intended to capture anything about experience that represents the world outside the subject—say, its looking to one as if there is a red round thing there—in which case its distinctness from sensation becomes problematic. Matters are not helped by saying, as Humphrey does, that perception is not modality-specific, which is analytically false, and by an alarming tendency to conflate percepts with the objective facts they represent. Nor is it clear what he could mean when he argues that perception, as distinct from sensation, does not involve consciousness, since surely how the world appears to me enters into the determination of my state of consciousness.

The trouble is that Humphrey is playing with a number of distinctions and failing to pin down precisely which one he has in mind. Talk of two "parallel channels" is either unhelpfully metaphorical or downright mistaken if taken to imply that there is a dual representation (in the proper sense of the words) in every sensory experience. I don't, after all, see my retina every time I see something that isn't my retina.

The point of this distinction, for Humphrey, is to pave the way for his theory of consciousness: it is offered as a theory of the sensation component. I find this theory bizarre, unmotivated, and inadequate. The idea appears to be this: to have a sensation, say a pain or a visual experience, *is* for the brain to send a signal to the periphery of the body, so creating a physical disturbance there, and for this disturbance to be registered, via a feedback loop, in the initiating segment of the brain. The theory is that a sensation resembles, and descends from, such actions as the wiggle of an amoeba in response to an impinging stimulus: in other words, it's an activity that originates centrally and has effects at the body's surface. A visual sensation of red is thus (is nothing more than) the action of causing the retina to fire in response to incident light—as it were, wiggling the retina. Consciousness reduces, then, to the neural causation of peripheral bodily disturbances.

To be sure, Humphrey is compelled to modify the original (intuitive!) statement of his theory to handle the fact that we can have sensations without anything occurring in the body, as with phantom limbs: his amended claim is that the body finds a surrogate in a "cortical map," so that sensations become instructions to cause physical disturbances at the surface of the cortex—"cerebral sentiments," he calls them. Feeling something consists in making your cortex wiggle. But this does nothing to make the theory any more palatable—quite the contrary. To repeat, a conscious sensation *just is* the physical action of the brain as it causes changes in outlying portions of itself or in the body if there is one, where these changes are themselves kept track of by means of a feedback loop. The immediate presence of sensations to the conscious subject is held to consist in such "loopiness." Since brains can do these physical things, and since that is all a sensation is, we have an explanation for how brains generate sensations. Success!

This is a very disappointing solution to the original problem. First, the theory is really just a variant of familiar physicalist theories. Like behaviorism, it sees the essence of a mental state in the disposition to cause bodily changes, though in the sensory receptors, not the motor system. Like central-state materialism, it ends up identifying mental states with neural events in the brain. Like functionalism, it stresses the "software" descriptions of the underlying brain processes, thus allowing for different physical realizations of the reverberating feedback loops that constitute sensations. And it faces all the standard problems that beset these doctrines, without making any real advance on them.

Second, what about bodily changes initiated internally and subject to feedback that manifestly doesn't involve any consciousness—healing of the skin, muscle growth, digestion, blushing? Since these involve essentially the same physical processes yet don't generate consciousness, the feedback loop theory cannot provide sufficient conditions for our being in a conscious state. Indeed, it is hard to see why, according to Humphrey, a thermostatically controlled heating system doesn't have conscious sensations, since it meets his conditions for consciousness. Physical feedback loops come too cheaply to add up to mentality.

Third, the distinctive sense in which sensations are owned by the subject can hardly be captured by this theory, since all bodily states are similarly "owned." No special link with the introspecting self has been established.

Fourth, it is quite implausible to maintain that the phenomenal type of a sensation is explicable in terms of the bodily characteristics of the site of peripheral disturbance. That would imply that the type *seeing red* is constituted by the face that my retinal rods and cones are firing in a certain way—as if that were how things seem to me when I see something red! The physical properties of my receptors, for example, the inside of my nose, are not what individuate the phenomenal type of my sensations, for example, the smell of a rose. This kind of physicalist reductionism is no more plausible when the physical facts obtain at my surface than it is when they occur further in. And calling the bodily disturbances the "adverbial style" of the cerebral action does nothing to make the theory more attractive. We are still being told that the feeling of pain is just one kind of physical wiggling among others.

In fact, after a lot of preliminary stage-setting Humphrey spends a breathtakingly small amount of time explaining how his theory is meant to capture the characteristic properties of sensations, and his explanation is obscure and unpersuasive. What he seems to be offering, at bottom, is a kind of peripheralist identity theory: a sensation is identical with a bodily perturbation of a certain sort. I see no good reason for this variant on familiar central identity theories, save for a kind of half-suppressed behaviorist urge somehow to get the wiggle into the act.

Toward the end of the book, Humphrey quotes me on the difficulty of the mind-body problem and the inadequacy of our current modes of thought, and he issues this challenge: "If McGinn still wants to deny that it"—Humphrey's theory—"is the wine of consciousness, let him taste it and say what is missing." Well, I found the taste elusive at first, though finally it revealed itself as the usual old plonk. What was missing? Oh, not much—just the presence of any real grapes. Seriously: despite some interesting incidental reflections, and an admirable breadth of reference, Humphrey leaves the mind-body problem exactly where it was. His excurus into speculative mental history has turned up nothing to alter the basic geography of the issue.

A puzzling question I would like to have seen discussed is why consciousness is so prevalent in the biological world; beyond the simplest organisms all animals seem to have some. This could either be because it has great and unique biological utility or because it is written deep into the nature of matter and can't, so to speak, help emerging when particles coagulate in certain ways. The first alternative is hard to reconcile with the fact that it seems quite possible to imagine even complex organisms reproducing efficiently without their behavior being guided by sentience—so why aren't there any (complex) robot species on the planet? But if the second alternative is the case, then there is something amiss, after all, with trying to understand consciousness biologically, as if its emergence must have a direct biological rationale. It might, on the contrary, odd as this may sound, be simply a by-product of traits that do have such a rationale. One of the great puzzles of evolution is why sentience seems to be the preferred method for handling adaptivity to the environment. Why not process information without any inner feeling at all? Why, that is, does consciousness exist?

It is common to hear theorists insist that consciousness must be viewed as a natural phenomenon with a natural history, subject to the rules that govern other evolved characteristics. Fine. But the same biological perspective should encourage a more sceptical thought: namely, that the human power to understand the world is itself a natural biological phenomenon, subject to the usual constraints and limitations. There is no empirical or a priori reason to suppose that our capacity to understand nature extends to all the things that puzzle us; it would be amazing if it did. Consciousness may be one of the subjects that our biology has not equipped us to understand. This should be regarded at least as a live possibility by anyone who takes the biology of mind seriously. For all his vaunted naturalism, Nicholas Humphrey is, like so many others, unwilling to take his naturalism the whole way. The reason he can't produce a good theory may be that his brain won't let him.

11

Churchland: A Problem Ignored

Neurophilosophy: Toward a Unified Science
of the Mind/Brain
by Patricia Smith Churchland
MIT Press, 1986

Contemporary cognitive science—that recent and fertile confluence of philosophy, psychology, and computer science—is apt to represent the human mind (or its underlying mechanism) as a proposition-manipulating engine, a device for processing language-like symbols. Thus, philosophy of mind investigates the so-called propositional attitudes (belief, desire, intention, etc.), those central pillars of commonsense or "folk" psychology; scientific psychology tries to uncover the mechanisms and algorithms whereby the mind constructs its representations of the world, these processes being seen as symbolic computations; and the builders of computer models of mental accomplishments program their machines with appropriate languages in which the machine takes instruction. On this view, the mind is conceived as a kind of word-processor.

But if you examine the brain—its neural nuts and bolts, its electrochemical transactions, its biological architecture—you do not observe the operations of the propositional engine: nothing sentential appears to lurk in its fissures and nuclei. Higher brains (like ours) seem to resemble lower brains (like reptiles') in this respect; and these lower brains look plainly infralinguistic. One reaction to this invisibility of the informational is to suppose that we are looking from the wrong level: we have mistakenly allowed the eye of theory to be fixated on the brain's hardware; indeed, we shouldn't really be *looking* at all. What needs to be recognized is that the brain can be described

Reprinted with permission from the *Times Literary Supplement* (February 6, 1987).

at different levels of abstraction; and at the more abstract level talk of propositional machinery comes into theoretical focus. It is the existence of this more abstract level—the "software" level—that secures a certain autonomy for the sciences of mind with respect to neurobiology. This is, roughly, the Standard View.

But there is another, more radical view, namely Eliminative Materialism, which urges that invisibility in the hardware is a sign of outright nonexistence. We strain our eyes seeking for the brain's propositions only because we are shackled by obsolete prescientific conceptions of what the mind is. Folk psychology, a theory of the mind developed before people knew what science was all about, has created theoretical figments that we are tempted to hypostatize into scientifically real structures and processes. A long hard look at the biological brain should serve to disabuse us of our ancient folk-psychological superstitions, and open the way for a genuine science of what goes on in our heads. This is, roughly, the view held by Patricia Smith Churchland (and others of her persuasion). Their motto might be crudely put: if you can't find it in neuroscience, that's because it isn't there.

Neurophilosophy is a five-hundred-page dithyramb to the brain sciences. Churchland's mission is to convince philosophers and psychologists that detailed knowledge of the biological workings of the nervous system is the answer to their problems. Instead of theoretical autonomy, they should seek integration, reduction—or, failing that, elimination. Psychology, philosophical or scientific, should thus be prosecuted as a branch of neurobiology. She conducts her crusade with impressive zeal; tremendous energy has gone into the campaign, and there is something awesome about her conviction. But the excesses of evangelism obtrude disturbingly: mesmeric repetitiveness, hectoring the audience, rhetoric masquerading as argument, blindness (or blind-sightedness!) to the opposite point of view. Of this sales-resistant reader, at least, she has not made a convert to the faith. The sparkling new discipline of "neurophilosophy" does not live up to its advertising. It fails to vanquish the competition from more traditional approaches.

The book has three parts. Part 1, the lengthiest, offers a fairly potted survey of the history and current state of neurophysiology. We learn about the behavior of individual neurons, about the functional architecture of grosser structures, about the various techniques that have been developed to figure out what is going on deep inside the brain. Naturally, this is all fascinating stuff—especially, perhaps, the impressive progress that has been made in understanding the precise nature of the nerve impulse. As far as I can judge, Churchland does a competent job of presenting this material—though I suspect that many philosophical readers will find the details a bit too technical for their taste. One wonders, however, quite what the point of reproducing this material is, since it can be readily found in standard textbooks of neurophysiology. And there is no real attempt to locate the scientific facts in a philosophical context. It serves to demonstrate Churchland's credentials as a philosopher of neuroscience who has done her homework, but that is hardly a sufficient rationale. No significant gap in the literature seems to be filled by these 235 pages. The dominant impression they leave is how far *away* from the nature of the mind detailed knowledge of the brain's physiology leaves us. Knowing little about the brain, we are inclined to endow it with magical powers that suffice to explain consciousness, thought, freedom, and so on; but once we start to understand its nature as a physical-biological object, we realize that there is nothing supernatural in there, and then it becomes even *harder* to see how the brain could subserve the mind. Understanding the precise chemistry of neural transmission makes it seem even more baffling how a few pounds of soggy biological tissue could be the basis of a conscious mental life.

Part 2 broaches some relevant philosophy concerning theory reduction in general and reductionism about psychology in particular. Churchland's exposition of intertheoretic reduction is clear and workmanlike, though pretty standard. She gets more interesting when advocating her version of eliminative materialism. Suppose psychology (folk or scientific) failed to be reducible to neurobiology: what would that show about psychology? There are two main options: psychology is a respectable autonomous discipline with its own well-defined subject matter; or: the principles and taxonomy of psychology as we have it are bogus and deserve to be unceremoniously eliminated from science and ordinary thinking. The second view takes propositional psychology to be a falsifiable empirical theory whose prospects are not bright: it might well turn out, for example, that there are no such things as beliefs and desires, or indeed pains and emotions, since these commonsense psychological categories do not map neatly on to neurobiological categories.

I do not think that Churchland provides any good reason to suppose that this elimination is likely to happen, and the prospect is virtually inconceivable. You might as well say that physics is likely to show that there are no objects in space which causally interact with each other. When Descartes asserted that he could not be wrong in supposing himself to be a thinking being he was not being misled by his ignorance or neuroscience. Tell him all the neuroscience there is to know, and he will not be justified in concluding "Oh, so I'm not really thinking, after all." At any rate, it is this kind of intuitive conviction that Churchland needs to undermine—and no amount of tired rhetoric about the intellectual conservativeness of philosophers is going to turn the trick. Of course, ordinary folk may well harbor some pretty funny ideas about how their minds work, ideas that deserve prompt elimination; but it is another matter to claim that the general scheme of psychological understanding that we employ every day might, as a realistic possibility, turn out to be simply *false*.

What would we lose if we junked the resources of folk psychology? Well, without the ascription of mental states with propositional content, we would lose the idea of ourselves as rational (or irrational) beings: for the normative notions of correct and incorrect reasoning require that logical relations hold between mental states. In consequence, logic itself would be deprived of its raison d'être, since logic is the means by which people's propositional reasoning gets evaluated: if there is no such thing as propositional reasoning, logic loses its point and purpose. Nor is it clear that anything recognizable as art could survive the repudiation of the categories of folk psychology: for how, without these categories, could we characterize the artist's intention? Certainly the major (and minor) works of literature would not have existed had their authors been persuaded of the truth of eliminative materialism. How, too, are we to apportion blame and responsibility without the notions of motive and intention? And what would ordinary human relationships be like if we could only talk brain physiology? It sounds like a very dystopian prospect indeed. (This is not to say that scientific psychology must slavishly follow the contours of folk psychology; it is only to insist upon the value and utility of the latter as an autonomous mode of person understanding.)

Churchland is on much firmer ground in part 3, unfortunately much the shortest section of the book. Here she expounds a theory of sensorimotor coordination developed by Pellionisz and Llinás known as "tensor network theory." The basic idea is that perception and action might be coordinated in the brain by means of metrically deformed mapping relations between banks of neurons. This theory is philosophically interesting because it characterizes the underlying neural machinery in nonsentential terms. It is presented in some detail, but Churchland does little to put it into theoretical context and derive appropriate general conclusions. She does not see that it is compatible with propositional psychology, even when generalized to higher cognitive processes, as a glance at the relevant philosophical literature would have made clear (we just need the idea of propositions *indexing* underlying nonpropositional structures). Neither does she relate the tensor network theory to other theories in psychology of the same general shape—notably mental model theory and the analog theory of mental imagery. These are areas in which the synoptic vision of a philosopher might have been expected, but Churchland's vision is too tunneled on to the details of the neurophysiology to supply this kind of perspective.

A disturbingly antiphilosophical vein runs throughout the book; beginning with its very first sentence: "In the mid-seventies I discovered that my patience with most mainstream philosophy had run out." It would be widely agreed, I think, that the period in question was an exceptionally rich one philosophically: Davidson, Kripke, and Putnam, to choose just three philosophers, were doing important work around that time, much of it centering on the mind-body problem. Churchland, however, was impatient with it. It emerges later that she is impatient with philosophical method in general— she sees nothing coherent or valuable in the kind of conceptual investigation typically undertaken by philosophers, past and present. (The present reviewer is mockingly berated for believing that it is possible to do interesting philosophy of mind in this traditional way.) She thus consigns most of the best work in philosophy of mind this century (and earlier) to the rubbish heap. No remotely convincing justification is given for this hubristic dismissiveness, and one can only assume that she has succumbed to a severe case of scientism. Churchland is, of course, quite within her rights to find science more interesting than philosophy—in which case she should have become a scientist. But it seems to me deplorable to convert this personal preference into a wholesale condemnation of philosophy as a serious subject. There is really no need to downgrade philosophy in order to proclaim the importance of neuroscience. In fact, I think her attitude to philosophy in this book is simply absurd.

It might have been different if she had succeeded in showing how some standard philosophical problems could be solved by means of neuroscience; but nothing of the kind is shown in the course of this very long book. So far, then, "neurophilosophy" is the name of a nonexistent subject, at least if it is intended to offer a new approach to the old problems of philosophy. As it stands, it amounts rather to a proposal to *ignore* most of the problems that have occupied philosophers. Like the old discredited positivists, Churchland will have none but empirical questions; but unlike them, she has no colorable philosophical motivation for this parochial view. It is certainly no defense of her neuroscientism to cite Quine as having "shown" that there is no analytic-synthetic distinction. Nor does it cut any ice to go on as if traditional philosophers are constitutionally "antiscientific." It really shouldn't need saying that both philosophy and science are perfectly respectable enterprises, each in their own distinctive way: but apparently it does.

This book is clearly intended to appeal both to philosophers and to neuroscientists (as well as to psychologists), but there is a real question whether it is necessary at all. The great bulk of the material covered is readily available in standard works of neurophysiology and philosophy; putting it between the same pair of covers seems not to be a very great advantage. And Churchland's own contribution to the issues could have been condensed into a much shorter book. As it is, the book contrives to be both long and superficial. There are, to be sure, some worthwhile ideas in it, but they are swamped by irrelevant technical detail and by the fervid excesses of the proselytizer.

12

Marcel and Bisiach:
The Language of Awareness

Consciousness in Contemporary Science
edited by A. J. Marcel and E. Bisiach
Clarendon Press, 1992

To casual inspection, the history of the universe would appear to have been marked by three great upsurges. In the beginning, came matter in space—particles, planets, galaxies. Physics is the science of this primordial being: it seeks to say what the laws of matter are, and (if possible) how matter came to exist in the first place. After this initial upsurge, nothing essentially novel came on the scene for an unconscionably long time. Then living organisms arrived. Self-replicating macromolecules begat single-cell organisms, which led eventually to big, complex, warm animals like ourselves. Matter became intricately arranged into living forms. Biology is the science of this new arrival, and evolutionary biology the study of how it came about. The third major upsurge was consciousness. Now here was a genuine novelty, scarcely predictable from what preceded it. Consciousness would need a science all of its own, as special as it is, a science that would try to understand its inner workings, why some things have consciousness and some don't, how it emerged from what came before, how it develops in the individual, how it relates to behavior, and so on. Psychology sounds like a good name for such a science: the systematic study of perhaps the most remarkable of nature's products.

Yet the science that has gone by that name has been notably unconcerned with consciousness—its laws, functions, origins. Indeed, psychology has, despite an early flirtation with introspection, prided itself on repudiating con-

Reprinted with permission from the *Times Literary Supplement* (April 14–20, 1989).

sciousness, and come to be the science of physical behavior. Consciousness was supposed to be "private" and hence not a suitable subject for objective scientific study. It was as if the third upsurge had never happened. But consciousness is now making something of a comeback, at least as a topic of serious discussion, and *Consciousness in Contemporary Science* is an attempt, by sixteen authors—neuroscientists, psychologists, philosophers—to evaluate its status in the contemporary sciences of mind. Is consciousness unitary? How does it relate to the brain? What causal role does it play? What are its pathologies? How does it map on to the constructs of computational psychology? What conceptual illusions might it spawn?

The reason for this burgeoning interest is not so much a tardy reappraisal of earlier (philosophical) dogmas; it is, rather, the occurrence of a variety of pathological syndromes in which ordinary awareness is curiously abolished or disrupted. Consider "blindsight," a condition much cited in this book. Normally we are aware of what we see: our eye-based discriminations are accompanied by visual experiences of which we are conscious. But in cases of blindsight, caused by lesions to the striate cortex, there is a strange dissociation of visual consciousness from visual receptivity. Blind-sighted patients can identify stimuli presented to their visual field remarkably well, yet they protest that they cannot *see*—they claim to be merely guessing. They can "see" but it does not seem to them that they can.

It is not immediately clear how these findings should be interpreted. Is it that the blind-sighted have visual experiences but cannot judge that they do, so that it is their introspective capacity that has been impaired? Or is it rather that they simply have no visual experiences to make introspective judgments about? The latter interpretation seems more plausible, since their introspective capacity remains intact when directed on to input from other senses, and the damaged area of cortex is concerned with early visual processing; but contributors to this book can be found saying both things interchangeably, not realizing the difference between them. At any rate, we have here an abnormal case in which the absence of normal consciousness forces us to acknowledge its presence in ordinary cases of sight. It is as if a biologist had living things brought to her attention by observing the fact of death.

Then there is Anton's syndrome, in which patients are "blind" to their own blindness: they think they have normal visual experiences but they don't. And, of course, there are the well-known split-brain patients, whose left hemisphere does not know what the right hemisphere is up to. These are all cases in which bizarre dissociations in what we normally think of as seamless capacities seem to occur. To describe these conditions at all we have to adopt the language of awareness and its lack, and listen to the introspective reports of the patients suffering them.

While some contributors to this volume (Lawrence Weiskrantz, Michael Gazzaniga) feel that consciousness is forced upon them by the clinical data, others suspect that the concept is too ill defined to be helpful (Alan Allport, Patricia Churchland, Daniel Dennett perhaps, Kathleen Wilkes). These latter authors produce papers in which one detects a lurking agenda behind the inevitable caveats and retreats. They clearly distrust the idea of consciousness, fearing it will tempt us into bad science, but they cannot bring themselves simply to forswear it, as the old-style behaviorists did. Allport brings a somewhat chaotic positivism to bear on the problem of defining consciousness, smothering some of his more interesting points in bad old philosophy. Churchland issues dark warnings about clinging too fondly to folk psychology; she has a dream in which consciousness has gone the way of caloric fluid or vital spirits (i.e., there is no such thing). I don't know whether Dennett thinks his eliminativist nibbles at the taste of soup remove all the mysteries from consciousness, but it does not seem to me that we need to believe in "qualia" in his sense (as ineffable, private, intrinsic, self-proclaiming) in order to believe in the essential subjectivity of consciousness. Wilkes hints (her word) that our terms "mind" and "consciousness" lead us into harmful reifications, and that a look at other languages (Greek, Chinese, Croatian) should stop us worrying about the phenomena seemingly referred to. Here I cannot better her own words upon concluding this linguistic survey: it "proves nothing." If this is the best that can be said for eliminating consciousness from respectable society, then I think I will hang on to mine for the time being.

Among the other contributors, some embrace consciousness and see no special scientific problem in doing so (Marcel Kinsbourne, Philip Johnson-Laird), while others accept it as a difficult challenge to natural science (Anthony Marcel, Tim Shallice, Richard Gregory, Robert van Gulick). Kinsbourne thinks it is enough to say that consciousness is an "interactive" property of groups of neurons, no more mysterious in principle than macroproperties of matter. Johnson-Laird finds the secret of consciousness in the hierarchical parallel processing of computers. Sceptics will wonder whether their confidence is misplaced: is it really *that* easy to see how a physical system could be conscious? Van Gulick has a useful discussion of subjective experience and intentionality, effectively criticizing Searle, and making some interesting (though sketchy) suggestions of his own that link consciousness with the degree to which a system understands its own internal representations.

I may have seemed somewhat negative in my assessment of these contributions. It is true that a number of the papers are routine, ground-grazing, confused. They sometimes seem to have been composed to meet a conference deadline rather than because the author had anything original to say. But the book is worth reading as a survey of how science and consciousness now stand to each other. No consensus emerges. And it brings out the intractability of the problem of consciousness, how difficult it is to say something illuminating on it.

13

Nagel: The View from Nowhere

The View from Nowhere
by Thomas Nagel
Oxford University Press, 1986

In his introduction to this important book, Thomas Nagel writes: "There is a persistent temptation to turn philosophy into something less difficult and more shallow than it is" (p. 12). No one could accuse Nagel of shallowness; nor is his book easy reading. He tackles some of the hardest problems in philosophy with unblinking determination: the mind-body problem, the self, the possibility of objective knowledge, thought and reality, freedom of the will, the status of moral value, the happy life and the moral life, death and the significance of living. His treatment of these issues is consistently illuminating, elegant, and provocative; and he is properly modest in the face of the problems. It is hard to see how one could become one of those philosophers who are "sick of the subject and glad to be rid of its problems" (p. 11) when there are philosophy books like this to read. *The View from Nowhere* is alive with the true spirit of philosophy.

Nagel's book ranges widely, but its concerns are not unconnected. His unifying theme is an opposition or tension between two sorts of standpoint we can take on the world: a subjective standpoint, which reflects our particular and peculiar point of view on reality; and an objective standpoint, which detaches itself from this specific point of view and aspires to conceive the world *sub specie aeternitatis*. And his central thesis is that it is the simultaneous existence of these two inharmonious standpoints that generates many of the basic problems of philosophy: we are torn between these two ways of seeing

Reprinted with permission from *Mind* (April 1987).

the world and cannot satisfactorily integrate them into a coherent conception of things. Because of this split philosophers are prone to accord undue dominance either to the subjective or to the objective, thus producing a distorted picture of reality; the proper course is to acknowledge both stand-points and try to live with the intellectual discomfort. "Absurdity comes with the territory, and what we need is the will to put up with it" (p. 11). I think Nagel is remarkably successful in bringing this general structure to bear on a variety of seemingly disparate problems, and the benefits of reciprocal illu-mination are considerable. Who would have thought that the mind-body problem, scepticism and the meaning of life might all exhibit the same ab-stract form!

The topics treated fall naturally into three groups—mind, knowledge, value—and I shall discuss Nagel's views on these in turn, concentrating on the first group, where my disagreements are most substantial.

Mind

Chapter 2 is about the question what notion of objectivity is appropriate to states of conscious subjects, if any is. How can we conceive our own minds as just one example of the many possible forms of consciousness, not all of which will be "subjectively commensurable" with ours? Nagel rejects the idea that this objective conception of the subjective can be a kind of *physical* objectivity: all brands of physicalist reduction of mind are misguided because they cannot acknowledge the irreducible subjectivity of mind—they cannot capture what it is *like* to be a (certain kind of) conscious subject. Rather, we must seek a notion of "mental objectivity" that recognizes the subjectivity of mind but which does not view our own minds as privileged. To do this we need to form a conception *of* our own point of view which is not *from* that point of view—a conception that is in principle available to creatures with a different point of view from ours. Nagel's thesis is that we do in fact possess such a general conception—the conception of consciousness in general—but that it necessarily omits what is specific to different kinds of subjectivity. Accordingly, not all aspects of reality are representable objectively—even when the notion of objectivity is extended beyond the physical paradigm. There are some facts that can be grasped *only* by means of "subjective imagination."

Here we must pause to clarify how the terms "subjective" and "objective" are being used by Nagel. His usage is not, I think, altogether consistent; indeed, his employment of the notions is haunted by a systematic ambiguity throughout the book. His official formulation is this: "Objectivity is a method of understanding. It is beliefs and attitudes that are objective in the primary sense. Only derivatively do we call objective the truths that can be arrived at in this way" (p. 4). In other words, "objective" is a predicate (primarily) of conceptions, not of the facts or properties conceived: and a conception is said to be objective in proportion as it is detached from the specific point of view of the conceiver. Thus the distinction between subjective and objective is "really a matter of degree" and we may "think of reality as a set of concentric spheres, progressively revealed as we detach gradually from the contingencies of the self" (p. 5). Notice that, in spite of his official stipulation, Nagel is here already slipping into predicating objectivity of bits of reality, a practice he engages in all through the book. I would myself say that both uses are legitimate and that much potential confusion can be obviated by being explicit about the relations between these uses. A fact or property is subjective if it is part of (or essentially involves) a specific point of view; otherwise it is objective. A conception is subjective if it represents a fact *from* a specific point of view, exploiting that point of view as a medium of representation; otherwise it is objective. Combining this pair of distinctions yields four possibilities, each of which has instances: (1) a subjective conception of a subjective fact, for example, our imaginative acquaintance based conception of our own conscious states and others like them; (2) a subjective conception of an objective fact, for example, our perspectival perceptual representation of a primary quality such as shape; (3) an objective conception of a subjective fact, for example, our schematic conception of consciousness in general—which may include in its extension forms of consciousness not imaginatively accessible to us; (4) an objective conception of an objective fact, for example, the theories of physics. Note that, on this way of using the words, the subjectivity or objectivity of a fact does not dictate whether the fact is conceivable subjectively or objectively. Nagel's stipulation, by contrast, has the consequence that manner of conception transfers itself to truth conceived—a result at odds with his own views. We can also see that it is only the objectivity of conceptions that coherently admits of degree: a conception can be more or less detached from an initial subjective perspective, but it makes no sense (in this sense) to say that the distinction between subjective and objective *facts* is a matter of degree: facts either involve consciousness or they do not. We can conceive of a sensation of red or the squareness of an object more or less objectively, but there is no sense in the idea that the squareness itself is *more* objective than the sensation of red. The tempting mistake here is akin to a use/mention confusion: we shouldn't confuse the nature of a fact with the nature of the conception we have of it. The mistake is easy to make when we are discussing points of view *on* points of view, but it is a mistake nonetheless. (I am not saying that Nagel himself makes this mistake, just that he does not sufficiently warn us against it.)

We can now say that Nagel's question in chapter 2 is whether the subjectivity of (the fact of) consciousness allows us to detach from it to form a conception of consciousness that is not constrained by this subjectivity: must the subjectivity of consciousness invade our conception of it? His qualified positive answer consists of an existence argument and some negative considerations about the workings of this general concept: that is, we do in fact seem to operate with the concept, and it cannot be explained in terms of subjective imagination. But he says little positively about the content of this general concept: it seems to be simply the concept of an inconceivable perspective. A more full-blooded characterization would be: a perspective that can be grasped fully only by an imaginatively omniscient being. But this also seems too thin and schematic—as well as being insufficiently objective. A functionalist account (say) would supply what is positively needed; but Nagel has (rightly) rejected that. So it remains unclear whether we can really possess a general notion of consciousness that has any more content than the totally inspecific notion of existence discussed in chapter 6: the notion of an aspect of reality we are constitutionally unable to grasp. In sum, the idea of an "objective phenomenology" looks too much like a *contradictio in adjecto*.

Chapter 3 wrestles with the relation between irreducibly subjective mental states and the physical world in which those states are somehow located. Nagel undertakes to explore and defend double-aspect theories of the mind. It is a fascinating discussion, but it seems to me seriously flawed by a persistent failure to distinguish importantly distinct double-aspect theories: moving carelessly from one version of the theory to another, Nagel ends up making implausible and inconsistent claims about the nature of mind. Surprisingly, the conflations turn upon neglect of the type/token distinction. Perhaps I am wrong about this, but I have not been able to convince myself that I am.

Let me begin by distinguishing three theories one might wish to call double-aspect. DA1 is the thesis that each entity (substance, event, state) satisfying a mental property also satisfies at least one (nontrivial) physical property (Davidson's anomalous monism falls into this category). DA2 says that mental kinds are analogous to natural kinds such as gold or cats in that they possess, in addition to their superficial appearance properties, underlying physical essences that need to be discovered empirically (early type identity theories said something like this). DA3 is the obscure Spinozistic claim that both mental and physical properties are joint products of some hitherto unknown third kind of property of which they are both somehow "aspects"—in somewhat the way that the temperature and pressure of a gas are both "aspects" of the underlying motion of molecules (I cannot cite a contemporary adherent of this type of view). Each of these three theses crops up at some point in chapter 3, but they are never clearly distinguished. In particular, Nagel tends to pass from DA1 to DA2 as if nothing were at stake in the slide. He wishes to claim that mental concepts are "incomplete" in the way natural kind concepts are, that is, they leave open what the empirical essence of the kind is. The way is then open for him to identify selves with brains and mental states with brain states: for this might turn out to be what mental phenomena essentially *are*. Intuitions to the contrary can therefore be put down to a confusion of epistemic and metaphysical possibility, resulting from the neglected incompleteness of the concepts: they do not tell us everything about what they refer to.

Now it is crucial to distinguish two sorts of incompleteness claim that might be made on behalf of a double-aspect theory. The first says that mental concepts do not contain within them specifications of every essential property of entities satisfying them: this would be maintained by a two-property token identity theory after the fashion of DA1. That kind of conceptual incompleteness is uncontroversial and trivial: x's being a table does not include every other essential property it might have. The second says that mental concepts contain a blank space which might be filled by an empirical specification of *the very property* denoted by that concept. Clearly we cannot infer the second kind of incompleteness from the first; it is a much stronger claim. The second supports the natural kinds analogy; the first does not. It is not, in fact, at all clear which view Nagel wants ultimately to defend. Is he identifying each human self with that human's brain, or is he identifying the *property* of being a self with the *property* of having a brain of the same physical kind as the human? The former thesis is compatible with the variable physical realization of selfhood; the latter is not. In some places Nagel appears to commit himself to the stronger thesis (pp. 31, 39, 41, 47). But if he were to take this thesis seriously, he would undermine his own insistence on the irreducibility of mental phenomena; for natural kind concepts precisely *do* admit of reduction to concepts specifying the empirical essence of the kind. Pain would be C-fiber stimulation in the way heat is molecular motion. What it is like to be a bat might turn out to *be* a certain neural configuration. And so mental objectivity would be reducible to physical objectivity after all. The only way to block this result is to deny that mental kinds could be identical with physical kinds, which is what DA1 does but DA2 does not. DA2 allows for a duality of "aspects" only in the sense that the *conceptions* are distinct; but this is not enough to frustrate physical reduction.

Nagel's position is rendered yet more puzzling by his remarks on supervenience. He thinks it likely that most mental properties supervene on physical properties (sufficiency without necessity), but that there may be some mental properties, for example, the taste of chocolate, for which there are also necessary physical conditions. Read in the usual way, I think these remarks are, respectively, not consistent with the natural kinds picture and not consistent with Nagel's own antireductionism.

It might be thought that DA3 best represents his considered opinion: for it seems to allow us to steer between reductionism and a no-connexion thesis about mental and physical properties. But this is not in fact the theory that occupies Nagel's attention most of the time, and it has troubles of its own. First, it is obscure. Second, it does not sustain the strong conceptual incompleteness claim—as DA2 would. Third, the comparison with the temperature and pressure of a gas (p. 49) implies that mental and physical properties may turn out to be properties of the same fundamental kind, in which case the mental *would* be a special case of the physical and mental objectivity would not be *sui generis*. On balance I think it is DA1 that Nagel mainly wishes to maintain; but then he should drop the natural kinds analogy. He does not need it for his claim about persons and their brains, and it flies in the face of his own antireductionism.[1]

In chapter 4 Nagel invites the reader to be startled about who he is. How could it be that *I* am CM, that "*small* and *concrete* and *specific*" (p. 61) particular person? By what metaphysical miracle could the centerless world of individual persons come to contain *me*? The connexion between me and CM must strike me as deeply "accidental." I have to confess right away that I have never reeled at the thought that I am CM, so I bring no antecedent intuitive perplexity with me to Nagel's discussion. And even after studying it with as open a mind as I can muster I still do not feel the force of the problem—at least not as Nagel elucidates it. My own identity with CM still strikes me as a rather boring fact. I can, of course, imagine circumstances in which it would not be boring: I might have amnesia and live in a hospital where trick mirrors prevent me from recognizing which reflection is mine; it might then come as a considerable surprise that the person I have learned to call CM on the basis of his reflection is in fact me. But Nagel's claim is not that such an identity judgment *could* be startling; it is that it *is* (metaphysically) startling, even when all the facts are in. So we must not let the thought of such special circumstances creep into our assessment of the surprise value of such judgments. The problem is said to be analogous to the problem of how a particular time can be *now* (he says nothing about the judgment that Oxford is *here,* and I don't know whether he thinks this raises the same kind of question).

Casting around for a suitable perplexity to associate with "I am CM," one naturally turns to Cartesian intuitions: it is remarkable that I, this consciousness, should *be* a particular spatiotemporal physical organism. This at least gives us a sense in which it might seem that I am "accidentally" linked to a particular public person. A Cartesian will certainly profess incredulity at the suggestion that *he* can satisfy both mental and physical predicates. But this is not Nagel's point: he is not merely approaching his earlier concerns from a fresh direction. I can also agree that there is something vertiginous about the recognition that I am for others no more than they are for me: all this vivid pressing consciousness reduced in their eyes to a mere behaving physical organism, as if my consciousness *shrinks* when conceived from an objective standpoint. But this feeling seems to be a reflection of the asymmetry between first person and third person access to a mental life: I subjectively seem to myself to be the hub of the universe because of the shortness of the epistemic distance between me and myself. But again this is not Nagel's point. What he finds remarkable is the fact that my "objective self" apprehends the world through the subjective viewpoint of CM. That is to say, "I" refers to me under the mode of presentation "bearer of an objective conception," while "CM" refers to me under the mode of presentation "creature

---

[1] I am indebted here to discussion with Anita Avramides.

with this specific subjective point of view." What is held to be surprising then is the thought that I—one thing—can represent the world in these two ways. No doubt my capacity for both sorts of representation is remarkable and in need of philosophical account, but I can see no intuitive force in the idea that this thought is what "I am CM" naturally evokes. Since this diagnosis is not offered as an account of the *meaning* of "I am CM," it is hard to disagree with Nagel about whether he has interpreted the statement correctly: all I can say is that it seems to me overly contrived to suggest that the identity judgment is naturally or spontaneously associated with the kind of thought Nagel pins on it. The Cartesian thought seems to me much more naturally expressible in this way. Indeed Nagel's own earlier formulation of the problem—how a centerless world can contain "the point of view from which I observe and act on the world" (p. 56)—seems closer to the Cartesian thought than his own preferred diagnosis is. I therefore remain puzzled at Nagel's puzzlement. But perhaps I have lived with myself for too long to still be amazed at whom I am.

Nagel's use of the notion of an objective self calls for comment. He is apt to speak of it as *another* self, numerically distinct from the subjective self, but coexisting with it. The question then is how to bring harmony to the uneasy relations between these two competing selves. But in his more cautious moments he repudiates this suggestion: he prefers to speak of our objective *capacity,* though he still says that "the objective self functions independently enough to have a life of its own" (pp. 65–66). What is not clear is whether Nagel relies essentially upon the incautious formulation, at least rhetorically, in his treatment of problems: could he reformulate his theses without loss in terms of the sober literal interpretation of the phrase? I think he needs to say more about how exactly he conceives the ontological status of the objective self. He tends to waver between the dramatic idea of a conflict between selves and the more prosaic idea of a conflict between ways of thinking possessed by the same self. How much mileage does he get out of this wavering?

Knowledge

Nagel's epistemology is dictated by his metaphysics. And his metaphysics is uncompromisingly realist: We are contained in the world, it is not contained in us, and there is no guarantee that we can know and understand its objective nature. We are limited creatures thrown up by evolution, just one species among others, and the world is not about to cut itself down to our size. Our view of the world is fixed by our peculiar manner of interaction with it: and it is by no means certain that we can transcend the appearances to discover how the world is in itself. The gap between our beliefs and their grounds is wide and perilous. It may even be that there are aspects of reality of which we cannot, even in principle, form any conception: for reality is not constrained by our contingent conceptual powers. A properly robust sense of objectivity thus brings with it the threat of scepticism. Scepticism is, indeed, a sane and sensible reaction to our actual predicament in the world.

I find myself in considerable sympathy with these views. Nagel provides a powerful corrective to certain idealist trends in contemporary philosophy, Kantian, Wittgensteinian, Davidsonian. He makes some good criticisms of current attempts to foil the sceptic by invoking causal theories of meaning (in particular, Putnam): these theories suspiciously resemble earlier verificationist attempts to stop the sceptic in his tracks; they fail to demonstrate the unavailability to the envatted brain of the general concept of independent existence in space and time; such semantic theories are actually refuted *by* scepticism, rather than refuting it. These points are well taken, but Nagel does not attempt to show what is wrong with these semantic theories independently of their relevance to scepticism; and unless this is done proponents of such theories will regard Nagel's position as mere assertion (indeed there are a number of places in the book where this charge may be expected). But chapters 5 and 6 come like a breath of fresh air across the somewhat arid wastes of contemporary epistemology.

I do, however, have a couple of relatively minor misgivings about these two chapters. The first is that the sanity of scepticism is apt to seem less solid when we inquire what its logical consequences are for the truth of our ordinary epistemic claims. It seems fine to say that we can never get outside ourselves to certify that how things seem to us is how they really are, but acute discomfort sets in when we are told that none of us knows anything or has any justified beliefs—that it is simply *false* to say (e.g.) that I know that I am typing a review. Nagel does, it is true, say that the sceptical standpoint is not one that we can happily integrate with our ordinary confident beliefs: but he does not really confront the question whether realist-inspired scepticism *contradicts* our ordinary epistemic assertions; he tends to describe the conflict in psychological (not logical) terms. Recent discussions about the closure of knowledge under known logical implication are relevant to this question, but Nagel says nothing about such attempts to protect commonsense knowledge claims from the ravages of scepticism. His discussion proceeds at a rather lofty and general level; I would have welcomed a bit more analytic detail on the consequences of scepticism. Technicality is not always to be shunned.

Secondly, Nagel advocates a significantly rationalist epistemology: he thinks there is an indispensable and nontrivial a priori component in our knowledge of the external world. His reason for this is that the human mind is capable of generating from within itself hypotheses about how the world might be: experience can select among these but it cannot create them. (He compares his position here with Chomsky and Popper.) It is true that this conception of knowledge is contrary to certain traditional brands of empiricism, notably crude Baconian inductivism; but it does not follow that the conception is genuinely rationalist, that is, assigns a nontrivial role to a priori knowledge. Nagel (like most philosophers) says little about what he means by "a priori," but as a first shot we can say that a priori knowledge is knowledge of truths that is not justified by experience—as knowledge of mathematics and logic have traditionally been supposed to be. But this definition does not fit Nagel's "a priori component": for that provides only knowledge of *possibilities*—and knowledge of what *is* the case comes only when the possibilities are tested against experience. I do not think that either Chomsky or Popper are speaking of genuinely a priori knowledge either: they are not saying that we have knowledge of facts that cannot be (and need not be) justified by experience; they are not likening our knowledge of language or science to mathematical knowledge. Of course there is more than one strand in the "rationalist tradition," but it seems to me misleading of Nagel to speak in an unqualified way of a priori knowledge of the external world.

In chapter 6 Nagel shows that we have a conception of reality that permits us to formulate the thought that there may be features of reality that we could never conceive: the probable incompleteness of our conceptual scheme is thus allowed for from within our conceptual scheme. This sounds paradoxical, but it is not: we need to distinguish between *specific* conceptions of reality and the *general* notion of the real. We can have a general notion of truth that goes beyond the particular truths we can conceptualize. Nagel argues for this thesis by inviting us to think of a species of intellectual nine-year-olds: their conceptual repertoire will be truncated relative to ours, but surely they can form the idea that this is so. A nine-year-old Davidson who claimed that there could be no conceptual scheme not translatable into theirs would be mistaken. Similarly, *we* might have a conceptual scheme that is truncated relative to some superior species, and the real Davidson among us would be wrong to deny this. The underlying point here is that reality consists of independent facts that we may or may not have concepts for—we may just be constitutionally incapable of grasping certain truths about the world, as other species certainly are. This argument seems to me thoroughly convincing and, as Nagel says, a particularly powerful refutation of one kind of idealism (to be is to be conceivable). My only quibble concerns the scope of this realist claim: might *any* sector of reality transcend our conceptual powers? Nagel seems to have physical reality chiefly in mind (he makes an exception of ethics and aesthetics), but we can ask the question about other areas too: logic, mathematics, our own minds. Might there be truths in these areas that we cannot in principle grasp? If there are, the explanation of this transcendence is liable to differ from the case of physical reality. Is it sheer complexity that prevents conceptualization or might there be simple properties that our minds are not tuned to get themselves around? Certainly the idea of our *containment* in reality has no natural application in these other areas. What is it that *makes* a particular sector of reality possibly concept-transcendent?

In the course of this chapter Nagel introduces and makes use of a distinction between the "form" of a thought and its "content." He thinks that all our thoughts incorporate the human viewpoint in their form, but that it does not follow that their content also does—this relates rather to what in the world makes the thought true. In other words, thoughts necessarily have a subjective form but their truth-conditional content can yet be completely objective. This distinction is not entirely perspicuous, but I think I understand it well enough to disagree with it: indeed it seems to me an abnegation of one of Nagel's own main theses, which is importantly correct. For, if the subjective point of view inevitably colors our thoughts, so that they always represent facts *from* our point of view, then after all we cannot really be said to possess a view *from nowhere*. It is as if Nagel is incorporating the human perspective into our ostensibly most objective thoughts in rather the way our peculiar perceptual perspective enters into our perception of primary qualities: the "form" of our experience is admittedly subjective but *what* is perceived might yet be entirely objective. It is true enough that we need not think *about* the point of view *from* which we think, but so long as our point of view enters into the *way* in which we represent the world it will make that representation subjective. I would say that our objective thoughts, say in physics, contain conceptual constituents that are wholly innocent of subjective invasions: they represent the world from *no* point of view, and so the very *same* thoughts are available to creatures who do not share our point of view. It is, of course, tautologically true that any thought had by a human being must be accessible to human beings; but it does not follow that the thought incorporates the human perspective, either in form or content, for the same concepts are available to other perspectives too. In the relevant sense, the objective self *has* no point of view, so its characteristic mode of thinking is untainted by any point of view. (This is not to say that Nagel is wrong to scotch the non sequitur from form to content: it certainly does not follow from the subjectivity of our way of representing something that that thing itself is subjective, or else we could never perceive what is objectively there.)

Value

The second half of *The View from Nowhere* explores the tension between objective and subjective standpoints in relation to intentional action, motivation, and ethics. Parallels with the earlier discussions are duly noted. Thus the subjective perspective of the autonomous agent is brought face to face with an objective account of the causal antecedents of action: free will is the main casualty in this collision. From the objective point of view it is not even clear what freedom would *be;* yet we seem unable to shed the conviction of freedom in our engaged doings. We seek to enlarge our freedom by taking a more objective view of the determinants of our actions, but at the limit this search undermines itself and freedom seems to evaporate. Nagel's presentation of incompatibilism is vivid and compelling; attempts (like Strawson's) to save free will simply fail to address themselves to the real problem. But the whole issue is so difficult and perplexing that one cannot but agree with

Nagel's concluding remark: "nothing approaching the truth has yet been said on this subject" (p. 137).

His defense of normative realism is masterly: he persuasively argues that there are reasons for action that we can discover by taking up an objective standpoint, and these reasons exist whether or not we recognize that they do. He efficiently disposes of some popular antirealist arguments (Mackie's "argument from queerness," nihilism about value, relativism). He puts up a strong case for the modest thesis that pleasure and pain provide objective reasons for action—reasons that lay claim to engage with anybody's will. He is less convincing on what distinguishes preferences with objective significance from preferences that only the agent himself has reason to satisfy: this is said to turn on whether the preference is for an experiential state or not— "the more subjective the object of desire, the more impersonal the value of its satisfaction" (p. 170). This seems wrong: surely my preference for listening to rock music over classical music has no impersonal force. A more promising place to look is the notion of need: my basic unchosen human needs are what provide reasons applicable to agents other than myself. These needs will be typically *associated* with experiences of pleasure and pain, but those experiences are not themselves the sole repository of objective value. Of course this suggestion would need working out, but it seems to me to be roughly on the right track. There is a very good discussion in chapter 9 of the dilemmas that arise through the clash between deontological moral principles and consequentialist considerations; Nagel shows how this clash reflects (again) the tension between subjective and objective viewpoints (the objective self can make nothing of an agent's deontological scruples).

Chapter 10 investigates the relationship between having a good life and living a moral life. Nagel rejects views that try to define the one in terms of the other (Aristotle, Plato), as well as the Nietzschian contention that the good life overrides the moral life. He favors instead the view that the moral life rationally overrides the good life: morality may give us reasons to act that rationally outweigh the reasons we have to pursue our own good—this is indeed part of the standard (reluctant) admission that morality may require great self sacrifice. Moral reasons come from the acknowledgment, by the objective part of our nature, that others have interests that provide us with reasons to act—and these interests may well, if we are unlucky, conflict with our own. Nagel is surely right in taking this to be part of received morality, but it is a question whether his opponents are not recommending a revisionist morality: morality needs to be humanly livable, so where it is not it should be pruned accordingly. (I do not support that revisionist view myself; I am only trying to give the opposition a run for its money.) I think Nagel expresses an important insight when he says that the demands of impersonal morality issue from our objective capacity, so that we do violence to our own nature as objective beings if we turn away from such morality: impersonal morality may conflict with the agent's well-being, but it is not straightforwardly against human nature. We might indeed say that the suppression of the objective self's impersonal morality is itself a form of "self sacrifice." So the imperious claims of morality need not be looked upon as *completely* unnatural.

The book ends, appropriately enough, with a chapter on "Birth, Death, and the Meaning of Life." In this chapter Nagel dwells upon the awful contingency of his birth, the insignificance of his life, and the outright evil of his death. Again, it is the objective self that is responsible for producing these disturbing feelings. Anyone inclined to be unperturbed by such reflections should read this chapter (or perhaps should not). While not at all wishing to dissent from Nagel's bleak conclusions, I think there is *a* respect in which our objective insignificance can be quite soothing: it can make us more reconciled to our many misfortunes, personal as well as universal. It is consoling to reflect that from a cosmic standpoint none of it really *matters* all that much, even our own death. It is something of a relief to recall that all those too human problems don't objectively *count* for much. Imagine being a child again when all your worries and disappointments took on the dimensions of the universe—better to be able to detach yourself from your projects and passions once in a while. Too much meaning in life can be a burden; insignificance can lighten the heart. We need not worry that our desires and ambitions will crumble under the objective gaze: they are resilient enough to take care of themselves. Objectivity makes us aware of the absurdity of our mortal plight, but it also enables us to find some consoling irony in this absurdity.

14

Chalmers: Wise Incomprehension

The Conscious Mind
by David Chalmers
Oxford University Press, 1996

It is very hard to devise a theory of consciousness that is not open to decisive objection. This is not because consciousness is so amorphously ill defined that anything goes and we find it impossible to choose among a plethora of options. Rather, no matter what theory we come up with, it always seems to run into some shattering difficulty. The problem of consciousness is like a chess game in which a series of forced moves always ends in checkmate, more or less humiliating. Sometimes it seems that the best we can hope for is some teetering ad hoc contrivance that just manages to evade outright refutation—for the moment at least. Philosophy is like that, we know; but with consciousness the constraints are especially tight.

David Chalmers's book is an attempt to develop a theory that escapes knockdown refutation, while tolerating some counterintuitive and uncomfortable features. The book is very well argued, thorough, sophisticated, honest, stimulating—and almost plausible. It is certainly one of the best discussions of consciousness in existence, both as an advanced text and as an introduction to the issues. One feels that Chalmers has done about as good a job as could be done on this most intractable of problems. That said, I do not think the position he defends ultimately works, and for reasons that are not surprising. Still, there is much to be gained by following his argument: checkmate, yet again, but an impressive game nonetheless.

The book has two central theses, one negative, the other positive. The negative thesis is that materialism is false, because the mental is not logically

Reprinted with permission from the *Times Higher Education Supplement* (April 5, 1996).

CHALMERS: WISE INCOMPREHENSION

supervenient on the physical. The mental is not explained and necessitated by the physical in the way that the observable macroproperties of water are explained and necessitated by the molecular structure of water. Since facts about consciousness are not entailed by physical facts, the former are something over and above the latter. This is argued to follow from the conceivability of zombies—entities physically just like us but without any consciousness: since these are logically possible, the physical facts alone cannot conceptually guarantee the presence of a conscious life. We cannot then come to know anything about conscious experience itself just from knowing all the physical truths of the universe; nor, *a fortiori*, is it possible to analyze experience in physical or functional terms. Experience is irreducible. It follows that dualism of some form must be true.

The positive thesis now is that this dualism consists in fundamental laws that connect physical and mental properties by mere natural (not logical) necessity. We cannot reductively explain experience in physical or functional terms, but we can suppose there to be a contingent empirical lawlike connexion between them. This is nomological dualism instead of the rejected reductive monism. The physical does indeed "give rise" to the phenomenal, but it does so only with the force of natural necessity. Experience is thus a basic feature of the universe, like space and time, tacked on (as it were) to the swarms of particles that constitute matter.

In addition to these two main theses Chalmers speculates that the notion of *information* might provide some sort of link between the mental and the physical. Since the concept of information he employs is correlative with the notion of causation (the Shannon-Weaver concept of selection among possibilities), it turns out that experience is ubiquitous in the world—which leads Chalmers to endorse a version of panpsychism. Thermometers can now boast consciousness of some primitive form, a result Chalmers declares himself willing to live with. He also ingeniously defends a version of functionalism that makes experiences lawfully correlated with (but not reducible to) computational-functional properties. The argument here turns on the implausibility of dissociating qualia from the subject's first-person access to them, as would have to be so if experience could float free of a subject's cognitive processing.

There are two large problems with the theory as presented. The first, which Chalmers fully acknowledges, is that epiphenomenalism about experiences is entailed. Since my zombie and I share our physical and functional constitution, nothing in our behavior differs, so that the doings of *both* of us can be explained without ascribing conscious states to *either* of us—yet I have them and he does not. In particular, we make the same judgments—including, for example, "I am conscious and currently having a red experience"—despite the vast difference in respect of conscious experience. But now it follows that my utterance of this is not explained by what makes the judgment true, since my zombie's utterance cannot be so explained—it being false in his case. My experience thus turns out to be epiphenomenal with respect to my self-ascriptions of experience. Chalmers himself spells out this consequence and tries his best to draw its sting; but he is clear that it would be better if it could be avoided, and he does not succeed in removing the attendant air of paradox. What needs to be noted is that it is the denial of logical supervenience that leads directly to epiphenomenalism; so we need to be very sure that this denial is compulsory.

The second problem, which he nowhere confronts, is that just as the alleged conceptual contingency of the link between the physical and the mental leads to the logical possibility of zombies, so also does it lead to the logical possibility of disembodied consciousness. For if the link is merely that of natural necessity, then there are possible worlds in which the laws are abrogated—which means that the correlated properties could be instantiated independently of each other. There are pure spirit worlds as well as zombie worlds! I do not know whether this consequence would alarm Chalmers, but I suspect it would—and rightly so. How would such disembodied experiences be connected to the rest of nature? What might their causal powers depend on? How could they have any dynamic role in anyone's psychology? Where would they *come* from? The trouble is that once the psychophysical link is loosened to mere natural necessity the ontology of mind comes out looking pretty radically Cartesian.

Both problems have a common source: the denial of logical supervenience. It is therefore extremely important that this denial be shown undeniable. Chalmers is aware of this and argues that putative notions of a posteriori supervenience, in which there is no *conceptual* entailment from one level to the other, will not provide a viable alternative. Only logical supervenience can block the conceivability argument to the possibility of zombies. I find him quite convincing on this, but he underestimates how pressing it is to find some way to defend strong metaphysical supervenience, in view of the problems that arise from denying it. The crucial question here is whether all forms of logical supervenience must be epistemically transparent to us. Must our present concepts allow us to appreciate the nature of the supervenience relations that constitute the psychophysical link? Might we not instead be confronted by a case of *opaque* logical supervenience? If that were so, then there would exist concepts of both the physical and the experiential, and of whatever relations might connect them, such that there is an a priori explanatory connexion between those concepts—*even though they are not concepts we do or even could grasp.* The conceptual dependencies would go outside of the circle of concepts we bring to bear in thinking about mind and body. Indeed, these concepts cannot be within our grasp or else it *would* be plainly inconceivable to us that zombies are logically possible. In other words, zombies *seem* possible to us only and precisely because we do not grasp the concepts that render them *im*possible. There is logical supervenience after all, but it is hidden to our epistemic faculties.

This is surely a coherent position, and it provides an alternative to the other relations Chalmers mentions. In fact, he does briefly discuss something like this at one point, correctly attributing it to me. But he does not see how serious are the consequences of rejecting it, since it seems to be the only viable way to avoid the twin problems of epiphenomenalism and disembodiment, while accepting that we cannot reduce experience to physical properties. It is not dogmatic materialism that prompts insistence on strong supervenience but the need to escape the two problems cited. Indeed, the thesis of opaque logical supervenience is not materialist at all, if that means that the terms of current or foreseeable physics are adequate to explain consciousness. The view is actually quite compatible with theories that regard the physical as itself just the appearance of some deeper currently unconceived reality—or with idealism for that matter. Of course, the view assumes that we do not *know* the concepts that are necessary for a satisfying explanation of consciousness; what it does is use this fact to explain why it is that we can be misled into denying logical supervenience, with all the problems that stem from this.

It helps here not to be too wedded to the old framework of "materialism" versus "dualism." Both notions assume that materialism is a useful well-defined doctrine, but it is not, since the notion of the "material" is entirely theory-relative. We don't want to limit our theoretical concepts to those of current physics, but if we make the notion more inclusive it comes to include anything that might be relevant in explaining what happens in the world. There are really just a *lot* of properties that might be identified and used in explanations of consciousness. Perhaps because he sticks to the old materialism-dualism dichotomy, Chalmers finds it hard to imagine how there could be concepts that transcend those now used in physics or commonsense psychology, and hence finds the idea of opaque logical necessitation difficult to accept. The first order of business here is not to declare materialism false, but to question its very significance.

The speculations on information and panpsychism are admitted to be a bit on the wild side, but the problems go beyond mere incredibility. Not only do we see no evidence in nature of the experiential properties allegedly associated with every causal process; it is also not the case that physics finds any need to postulate such properties in explaining the behavior of matter. If all matter has experiential properties, should not this be relevant to the correct science of matter? Yet there seems no gap in the physics of the inanimate that calls for the ascription of mental properties to things. These alleged properties make no difference to the way a rock falls or water flows or any other purely physical interaction. The only motivation for invoking them is in order to provide an explanatory account of consciousness; they are idle otherwise. Subtract them from that thermometer and you will not observe any change in its behavior.

Chalmers's defense of a weak form of functionalism uses some intriguing thought experiments, but the conclusion that there is a lawlike relation between functional properties and consciousness is too weak to be of much interest. We might equally claim that there is also a lawlike relation between experiences and underlying neural states: if you keep these constant you will always get, as a matter of law, the same experiences. No *asymmetry* is established between the functional and the neural if lawlike dependence is all that is asserted; so it is wrong to suppose that any interesting form of functionalism has been established. All we have is a three-way lawlike relation between the mental, the neural, and the functional.

The only way to avoid being checkmated by consciousness is to assume you do not understand it. Chalmers has done his level best to understand consciousness, but the result, despite its many merits, shows the wisdom of incomprehension.

15

McGinn: Out of Body, Out of Mind

Take our own nature as conscious beings—something of unique fascination to us all. We want to know, among other things, how our consciousness levers itself out of the body. We want, that is, to solve the mind-body problem, the deep metaphysical question about how mind and matter meet. But what if there is something about us that makes it impossible for us to solve this ancient conundrum? What if our cognitive structure lacks the resources to provide the requisite theory? That would be distressing news for the knowledge-manufacturing industry. And the bringer of the news might expect the opprobrium that traditionally greets the unwelcome messenger: Don't *say* that.

I became a proponent of mystery one dark night in Oxford, seven years ago. At about two in the morning—and I don't know, maybe the moon was full—I was seized with the terrible conviction that our cognitive apparatus simply does not fit the mind-body problem. The reason the problem is a problem is not that consciousness is intrinsically outré (ontologically anomalous, as we analytic philosophers like to say); rather, the human intellect has been biologically set up to deal with other sorts of questions, and this one happens not to lie within its given modus operandi. We seem pretty good at answering questions about material objects in space, and also at handling the terms of ordinary psychology, but nature has not prepared us to answer the

Reprinted with permission from *Lingua Franca: The Review of Academic Life* (November–December 1994).

question about how mind and body come together. To a Martian, with a different innate cognitive structure, the problem might look easy, while elementary mechanics might prove terminally baffling. It is all a question of whether the appropriate intellectual equipment happens to have been installed in one's head. Problems only seem profound when we lack the mental gear with which to crack them. The profundity of the mind-body problem is thus neither a mark of objective miracle nor a misconception in the formulation of the problem. It is just the perimeter of our conceptual anatomy making itself felt.

But one can have some odd thoughts in the dead of night and maybe I was succumbing to small-hours delirium. I rose and wrote down some notes, the better to conduct a sober morning perusal. And lo! the thought still clung to me the next day. I had an acceptable explanation of the theoretical intractability of consciousness. Our modes of concept formation, which operate from a base in perception and introspection, cannot bridge the chasm that separates the mind from the brain: They are tied to the mental and physical terms *of* the relation, not to the relation itself. This solves the metaphysical problem in a way, because now we are under no pressure to think that the world contains something heavy with intrinsic impossibility: from the fact that *we* cannot make sense of something it does not follow that *it* makes no sense. We know that consciousness exists and that it is robustly natural, though we cannot in principle produce the theory that would make its nature manifest. There is thus nothing mysterious about the existence of the mystery.

I began expounding this position in conversations and seminars, often causing a marked widening of the eyes. At that time I was Wilde Reader in Mental Philosophy at Oxford, and some waywardness was assumed to come with the title. (Brian Farrell, who had held the post for thirty years before me, reported that his newly acquired mother-in-law had said to him, "So you're the Mental Reader in Wilde Philosophy, are you?") I boldly announced to anyone who would listen that I had finally dismantled the mind-body problem. Sir Peter Strawson, Waynflete Professor of Metaphysical Philosophy (a position of considerable seriousness), once retorted, good-naturedly, "But I thought *I'd* done that."

A year after my sleepless night, I managed to write a paper on the topic called "Can We Solve the Mind-Body Problem?" which I submitted to the *Journal of Philosophy,* one of the leading American journals in the field. Hitherto, they had accepted every paper I had ever sent them, but this one was rejected without explanation. Eventually, it found its way into the British journal *Mind* in 1989. I now sometimes feel as if it were the only paper I had ever written, so identified have I become with its content. And it is obviously perceived as some sort of provocation. "Oh, so *you're* the guy who thinks it's all a mystery," people begin, eyes aflame. "Well, just listen to *my* solution."

I then wrote some other papers expanding on the position, where were to come out as a collection, *The Problem of Consciousness* (Oxford), in 1991. Soon afterward, Owen Flanagan of Duke University dubbed Thomas Nagel and me the "New Mysterians," an allusion to a defunct 1960s rock band called Question Mark and the Mysterians. In a famous 1974 paper, "What Is It Like to Be a Bat?," Nagel argued that consciousness constitutes a serious obstacle in the way of materialism—though he has never in fact embraced the insolubility thesis that I defend. Noam Chomsky should also have been brought under this ironic honorific, since he has for years held the view that the human cognitive system divides the class of intelligible questions into the mere problems and the insuperable mysteries; indeed the term "mystery" in its present use is a legacy from him. I have derived much low-fat nourishment from Chomsky's writings on this subject, and discussions with him have been important to my own development of the basic viewpoint. The modular conception of mind, with linguistic competence as one module among others, is integral to my picture of cognitive limitation.

The label "mysterian" is potentially misleading, however: none of us regards his conviction of the limits of human understanding as in any way mystical or romantic. On the contrary, the view is motivated by a ruthlessly naturalistic perspective on the human intellect. As Chomsky often observes, the human mind is just a collection of specific finite organs, as biologically natural as the organs of the body. There are therefore limits to our knowledge in the way that there are limits to our motor abilities.

The reviews of my book were, as one politely says, mixed. They tended toward the edgy and distancing. The two extremes were represented by philosophy professors Jerry Fodor, my colleague at Rutgers, and Daniel Dennett, author of *Consciousness Explained* (Little, Brown, 1991). Fodor sympathized with my position, though he dissented from some applications I make of it. Dennett began his review by declaring that he was embarrassed to be in the same profession as me, and went on to suggest that I belong to a sinister cadre of "New Jersey Nihilists" intent on destroying cognitive science as we know it. ("New Jersey" because I moved from Oxford to Rutgers in 1990—though this move had nothing to do with my views about the dark roots of consciousness.) My fellow Garden State nihilists were said to include Chomsky, Fodor, and Nagel—all fearfully dangerous chaps. The label lacked factual accuracy: Chomsky was and still is at MIT, Nagel at NYU; Fodor formulated his notion of "epistemic boundedness" while at MIT; and I had my idea at Oxford. Moreover, there is nothing nihilistic about the position, any more than it is nihilistic to suggest that human beings cannot learn every possible language by means of their innate human language module. Sometimes pessimism is just the rational upshot of realism, not an urge to tear down the good and the beautiful. My response to all this ad hominem labeling was to suspect the operation of what might be called Tufts's syndrome (Dennett is a professor at Tufts)—a condition characterized by the patient's hysterical hostility to anyone who questions his grandiose ambitions. But here I ruefully begin to play a game I deplore.

In general, the reactions I have received, other than those I have outlined above, have fallen into three main categories. One grudgingly admits the logical possibility of my thesis's being correct but insists that there is absolutely no reason to take it seriously: the solution may be just around the corner; we should get on with our researches undaunted by the fear that our intelligence might be the wrong shape for the mind-body problem. Another sort of reaction is brutally pragmatic: we should proceed as if the deep problems are soluble, despite all the evidence to the contrary, so that we can continue to receive funding for our work and keep up our motivation. Put less cynically: since the value of a theory of consciousness would be very high, and since there is at least a nonzero probability of the problem's solubility, it is rational to keep aiming for a solution in the hope that fate will smile upon us.

A third response is to associate my view with religious tenets, either favorably or unfavorably. Thus I have had people congratulate me on finding a place for God in our soulless contemporary worldview—my position being thought to imply that the supernatural soul is alive and well and living in New Brunswick. Then there are the secular scientific types who think they have found the chink in the otherwise hard glaze of my official atheism. Next, they insinuate, I will be extolling panpsychism, ESP, or the spirit world.

Perhaps the most unexpected response came from a woman attending a conference I participated in with mathematician and philosopher Roger Penrose and Dennett at Dartmouth in April. The conference dealt with consciousness, computers, quantum physics, and similar abstract topics, though it was intended for the general public. I was expounding my usual position, putting special emphasis on the point that while consciousness is a nonspatial phenomenon, human thought is fundamentally governed by spatial modes of representing the world, so that our ways of thinking tend to force consciousness onto a Procrustean bed of broadly Euclidean design. The woman, who seemed oddly agitated, objected, saying that while it might well be true that the male mind could not solve the problems raised by these areas, the *female* mind would be much better at handling them. I explained that my position was that the problem goes much deeper than that, applying to the human cognitive system as such. After all, I noted, it is not as if when asked about the mind-body problem or the puzzles of quantum theory women come right out with the correct solution. She retorted that I was not entitled to make this claim, since there were no female philosophers or physicists at the conference to ask.

The least common reaction is the one that seems to me the most obvious: that my diagnosis of this particular philosophical problem is simply too facile, too convenient. But, I must reply, most of the great dead philosophers have been as pessimistic as I am about solving the core philosophical problems. What is new about my position is not the unsolvability thesis as such but the particular explanation I give of it. I suspect the reason for the opposition is, in part, that my cognitive pessimism collides with the kind of indelible optimism characteristic of modern (especially American) culture. Instead of can-do and leave-it-to-me, I am preaching don't-try and it's-never-going-to-work. I deny, in effect, the perfectibility of man, epistemologically speaking.

I recently published a book, *Problems in Philosophy: The Limits of Inquiry* (Oxford, 1993) that sets out these general views in a systematic and explicitly metaphilosophical way. In addition to consciousness, I discuss free will, the self, meaning, mathematics, knowledge—extending my treatment of consciousness to these other topics. Cognitive closure, I argue, turns out to be rather pervasive. I also suggest that while human reason is not equipped to solve the problems in question, there may be other epistemic systems that can do better. Thus the genetic code arguably contains precisely the information about our mental makeup that we cannot acquire by the exercise of our rational faculties, since the genes have to encode the information necessary to organisms with consciousness, free will, and so on. I can hear the howls of protest now: "It's bad enough to downgrade human reason by drawing boundaries around it, but now you are suggesting that DNA molecules are better philosophers than we are!" Well, yes, that is my suggestion, put crudely. Human reason is an adventitious biological organ whose job description plainly does not include solving every problem about the natural world—while the genes have the biological task of engineering organisms from the ground up, so they had better have access to the information needed to perform this feat.

I once gave a talk on this to some biologists and they construed my argument as a reason to back the Human Genome Project. I pointed out, however, that it was a consequence of my view that, whatever valuable philosophical information the genes might contain, it was not going to be translatable into human language. Our conceptual scheme does not, according to my argument, coincide with the informational resources of the genes. This is not to say that we are "stupider" than the genes, since plainly we can do many things with our minds that they cannot do. The upshot of these reflections is rather that the concept of intelligence needs to be understood much more subtly than we are anthropocentrically inclined to think.

Earlier this year, *Scientific American* ran an article on whether science can explain consciousness. There is a rather eerie photograph of me, seated on a gothic rocking chair with a curling dead twig seeming to grow out of my skull. Some say I resemble the film actor Anthony Hopkins in the role of Hannibal Lecter. I certainly look severe. I would have preferred one of the shots taken of my cat and me pretending to play chess together, the point being that chess is to the cat mind what consciousness is to the human mind—out of cognitive reach. The caption beneath the picture describes me as a "Hard-Core Mysterian," which is I suppose pretty much what I look like. If I'd been asked, I'd have preferred to be called a commonsense noumenalist, following Kant's use of the term "noumenal" to denote that region of reality that is incognizable by us. But by now I realize that once in the public realm one's identity is apt to become detached from one's own conception of it.

From now on, a hard-core mysterian is what I am condemned to be—a guru of ignorance, a high priest of mental lack.

By chance, a man from Con Edison came to read my gas meter with that very issue of *Scientific American* stuffed into his back pocket. I indicated the picture of me, to his intense amazement. I awaited hushed inquiries. He confided that he was particularly interested in the article on wasps that lay their eggs in the bodies of live grubs and that he hadn't gotten around to the consciousness article yet. I had to agree that wasp child-rearing was indeed an interesting subject. The next time he came he made no mention of the article in which I had figured. Clearly, grubs and wasps were a far more fascinating subject than consciousness.

What difference has being a mysterian made to my life? From an internal point of view, it has released me from the uncomfortable sensation that philosophical problems have always stimulated in me—the feeling that reality is inherently preposterous, ill formed, bizarre. Now I believe that the eeriness of consciousness and allied enigmas is just a projection of my limited intellect interacting with the phenomena—it is not a feature of the phenomena themselves. I also feel less intellectually embarrassed in the face of problems than I used to, as if I really *ought* to be able to do better. It is not that I have been given the right tools but lack the necessary skills; rather, nature has given me a toolbox with other jobs in mind. A happy side benefit is that I feel no temptation to deny the existence of things that are terminally puzzling. I can now, for example, see my way clear to believing in free will again after twenty-five years of denying its very possibility—on the ground that neither the random nor the determined could accommodate it. Free will is, indeed, I still think, a phenomenon about which we can form no intelligible theory, but given the idea of cognitive closure it does not follow that it is unreal. We can be free without being able to understand the conditions of the possibility of freedom.

On the other hand, it is disappointing to arrive at the conclusion that the problems that have always most interested me are not humanly solvable. I would, truth to tell, dearly love to see these problems grandly resolved in some new large-scale theory of the cosmos—as Newton, Einstein, and Darwin resolved their daunting problems. I don't really *want* to stop trying to solve the mind-body problem, futile as the effort now appears to me to be. As Wittgenstein remarked, grappling with philosophical conundrums is something that we human beings cannot easily shake off, even when our metaphilosophy assures us of their unanswerability. As a consolation, though, I have a reason now to work more on ethics, which looks to be an area in which the human intellect can get some real purchase. Ethics is an area of mere difficulty rather than blank mystery.

My mysterian identity does have its down side. I work in a university and assert that the central aim of universities will remain thwarted. This is not a very popular line to take. It discourages the students. It casts something of a pall over the proceedings. People no doubt think I am a traitor to the noble cause of knowledge. But let me observe that knowledge of our limits is, after all, one sort of knowledge, and quite an interesting sort. Psychologists study perceptual and memory limits: why can we not study the limits of theoretical reason? And whoever said that the human mind, at this transient evolutionary moment, has been so constructed as to be able to deliver the answer to any question about that vast intricate world we live in? It is amazing that we know as much as we do, but we should be wary of epistemic greed. There is a lot to be said for species modesty.

16

Lycan et al.: Imagining an Orgasm

Mind and Cognition: A Reader
edited by William Lycan
Blackwell, 1990

Acts of Meaning
by Jerome Bruner
Harvard, 1990

Modelling the Mind
edited by K. A. Mohyeldin Said
Oxford, 1990

The more philosophically interesting a science, the less secure or transparent are apt to be its theoretical foundations, given that philosophy thrives on perplexity. It is some time since chemistry produced much of a reaction in philosophers, but biology can still get their juices flowing, though not so freely as in the days of the Bergsonian *élan vital*. Quantum physics is a contemporary focus of philosophical attention—despite the suspicion of some that it is only a dispensable antirealism that generates the putative puzzles. Mathematics induces periodic bouts of fascination, even of deep distrust—as with Brouwer and Wittgenstein—but its rigor and finality tend to keep the perplexities at bay. In the case of psychology, however, philosophical interest reaches its highest pitch, and never more so than at present: perhaps to the chagrin of practicing psychologists, philosophers are now *very* interested in what they are doing—or at any rate in what they ought to be doing.

The reason for this intense scrutiny can be summed up in two words: "meaning" and "consciousness." These crop up with increasing frequency in psychological writings, after a long period during which they were anathematized. And the topics they refer to have never ceased to occupy philoso-

Reprinted with permission from the *London Review of Books* (May 9, 1991).

phers; indeed, the theory of meaning might justly be regarded as the central concern of twentieth-century philosophy. Together, the two concepts are definitive of what we ordinarily mean by "mind." It is largely because psychology is turning again to these constitutive marks of mentality that philosophers have once more become intrigued by that science. They found little to grip them while psychology perversely defined itself as the "science of behavior," entirely eliminating the notions of meaning and consciousness from its purview. Put differently, now that scientific psychology is acknowledging its continuity with commonsense or folk psychology, in which philosophers have maintained a steady interest, psychological theories contain concepts that provoke difficult philosophical questions. There is no shame for the scientists in this: it was misguided to defenestrate the mind just because the concepts that characterize it are philosophically rich and demanding. On the contrary, it is good to see one of the more philistine legacies of antiphilosophical positivism finally melting from the scene.

I do not mean to imply that the notions of meaning and consciousness are in good odor with all philosophers of psychology: they are certainly not. But the philosophical issues that surround these notions are now part of what a reflective psychologist needs to be sensitive to: they can no longer be left to those reactionary old philosophers. For these issues determine the shape and content of empirical theories. A central question here is whether theories that make serious use of these notions can be properly "scientific"—whether, that is, their employment calls for a distinctive methodology. Specifically, can the study of meaning and consciousness conform to the theoretical paradigm set by the natural physical sciences? The physical sciences deal with quite different sorts of phenomenon, at least on the face of it: does this mean that a psychology so conceived cannot take the form assumed by physical theories—with their laws, causes, mechanisms? What happens to the structure of psychological theories, and the empirical procedures that lead to them, when you make psychology go consciously semantical? How does a psychology of belief and desire compare to a physics of gravity and electric charge?

There are basically three schools of thought on this issue, with much variation within them. One school, which we may call the nomothetic realists, holds that (ideal) psychology consists of an explanatory set of content-involving causal laws: psychology is just one more special science, but one in which intentional properties are the domain of interest, as factual and nomic as geology or biology. General statements like "If an agent desires that p and believes that making it the case that q is a good way to bring it about that p, then that agent will, *ceteris paribus*, bring it about that q" are thus comparable in status to causal laws like "Free-falling bodies accelerate to earth at a rate of thirty-two feet per second squared."

This is the school of which Fodor is the most forthright and formidable member: on his view, psychological attributions are made true by real internal sententially structured states of the subject that stand in certain kinds of reference-creating nomic relations to environmental contingencies—in a word, by a meaning-endowed language of thought. According to nomothetic realism, there is no good reason why invoking meaning should disqualify psychology from taking its place among the other natural sciences. Fodor is less robustly sanguine about consciousness, however: he tends not to mention it at all.

In opposition to the Fodorean school, stand eliminativists and instrumentalists of varying degrees of boldness. The Churchlands, following Feyerabend and Quine, assert that folk psychology is a discredited prototheory, and that the language of neuroscience states the only psychological facts worthy of the name: there simply are no beliefs and desires, no meanings, no states of consciousness—period. Somewhat less drastically, Stich has suggested that psychosemantics in the style of Fodor should give way to unadulterated psychosyntax: cognitive science should restrict its theoretical concepts to purely formal or structural features of the internal code, regarding semantic interpretation as so much pointless mythmaking. One reason for this recommendation is the difficulty of seeing how referential properties of internal symbols could exert a causal hold over the subject's behavior, once it is granted that such properties are not supervenient upon the total internal physical state of the subject: if meanings are not "in the head," then they are not where the causes of bodily movements are located. An ostensibly weaker position undertakes to define a type of meaning that does not diverge from the causal taxonomy determined by the inner syntax, so that folk psychology comes out as approximately fifty percent true. In any case, there is to be no room for the ordinary notion of meaning in theories of cognition.

Dennett, for his part, rejects the psychosyntactic story about intentional states, with or without a semantic component, preferring to construe our ascriptions of belief and desire in an instrumentalist spirit: folk psychology is merely a "stance" we adopt toward the behavior of people, animals, and computers—a useful scheme that enables us to predict what they will do. It isn't an attempt to depict an inner landscape of the mind. His most recent thesis, indeed, is that human intentionality is just as derivative as the intentionality we attribute to our artifacts: the nearest thing to original intentionality in the world is exemplified by the blind processes of natural selection. The aboutness of our conscious beliefs is thus merely "as-if": we can retain such talk as a convenient heuristic, but we should not credit it with more factual solidity than this.

The third school might be called "interpretationalism": talk of meaning and content is literally true, and truly literal, but it is not talk that lends itself to canonical lawlike formulation. The concepts of belief and desire are agreed to be causal concepts, and the denoted states taken to be as real as reality gets, but they are concepts that belong to a kind of understanding that differs from that typical of the natural sciences: their business is *Verstehen*, not the expression of nomic regularities. One mark of this specialness is their essential involvement with normative notions—consistency, consequence, good reason—from which it follows that there can be no reduction of folk psychology to anything purged of the normative. This type of view is championed by Davidson and those influenced by him, as well as (latterly) by Putnam. If psychology is to immerse itself in the intentional, then it must expect to sacrifice the kind of scientific rigor for which its exponents have hankered. It must join the intellectual B-stream of history, anthropology, literary criticism, corner gossip. Each of these schools, which I have so crudely summarized, has its representatives in the volumes under review. *Mind and Cognition,* in particular, offers a broad sample of philosophical opinion on these matters, though it seems biased toward the more "hard-nosed" end of the spectrum.

What should become clear to theorists of cognition once the issue of meaning is explicitly raised is that the computer model of mind is a good deal less straightforward than it might have seemed. I suspect that the enthusiasm of cognitive scientists for the computational conception of human cognition was nourished by a certain unclarity about what precisely a computer program is. For, as Bruner observes in *Acts of Meaning,* the cognitive revolution in psychology was welcomed precisely because it was not properly understood: it was made to seem like less of a departure than it really was. With the idea of a computer program as their inspiration and paradigm, psychologists felt that they could speak of human information-processing without fear of departing from standards of scientific purity. But the picture becomes substantially less reassuring when the idea of a program is scrutinized more carefully. As Searle never tires of reminding us, a program is a list of purely syntactic or formal instructions; in itself it contains no semantic interpretation for the symbols manipulated. We cannot therefore expect that program rules will explain to us what meaning is, thus rendering semantics scientifically reputable. Indeed, it seems highly plausible that such meaning as computer codes have is conferred by their operatives, and is therefore presupposed rather than explained. Once we inquire what could determine the semantics of a machine code independently of human interpretation, all the usual perplexities about meaning begin to surface. The idea that a program is both well understood in virtue of its purely formal character and at the same time accurately simulates human thinking is thus illusory: it will simulate thought only if it carries genuine intentionality (*pace* Dennett)—but then the program cannot be defined purely formally. So the computer model doesn't answer the deep problems about meaning raised by the cognitive turn in psychology: it simply presupposes an answer to them, or else passes them by. In other words, you can't expect artificial intelligence programming competence to let you off doing the messy philosophical work—not if you are serious about a semantics-based psychology.

I have said little so far about consciousness. That is because even philosophers find this one a bit of a hot potato. Whereas it is possible to say a lot of quite interesting things about meaning, it is hard to say more than a little about consciousness (beyond the merely rhetorical)—and most of this is a touch *too* interesting. On the one hand, there are those who insist, startlingly enough, that, appearances notwithstanding, states of consciousness reduce without residue to neural states or physical causal roles of such states. On the other hand, there are those who stoutly declare it as self-evident that no amount of physical information about the brain could ever imply the possession of a state of consciousness, so that conscious experience falls radically outside the domain of physical science. This dispute has recently centred on the question of what one's own experiences teach one about consciousness that could not be taught otherwise: *Mind and Cognition* contains a useful section on this. Nagel and Jackson hold that there are real features of experience that only direct acquaintance with it can reveal: these features cannot then be comprised in physical information about the experiencer, which can be taught discursively. Nemirow and Lewis, on the other hand, contend that undergoing an experience confers only an ability to imagine experiences; it does not reveal special nonphysical properties of experience that are accessible only by acquaintance. The question dividing these disputants is whether what is referred to by one side as an irreducible subjective state can be exhaustively explained by the other in terms of an ability to imagine. As a student of mine remarked, the latter thinkers hold, in effect, that the feeling of an orgasm is equivalent to imagining an orgasm—an equation that she felt (perceptively) not to be very plausible.

As to the place of consciousness in theoretical psychology, it is almost a reflex among psychologists to cry "Epiphenomenalism!" and reach for Occam's razor. However, it is far from clear that conscious events suffer causal inertness in any sense beyond that true of events described in any of the special sciences—biology, geology, even chemistry. From the explanatory universality of basic physics we cannot infer that other modes of explanation fail to capture causally significant patterns in nature: the hierarchical arrangement of the sciences should not be confused with epiphenomenalism about all but the bottom layer. What is wanted here is not a priori dismissal but a serious investigation into the properties and processes of consciousness: its developmental history, both phylo- and ontogenetic; its contribution to our modes of cognitive processing; the nature of its pathologies (e.g., blindsight). Psychologists should shed their dated philosophical hang-ups about consciousness, as in fact they are now beginning to do, and apply themselves to carrying out some empirical work on what their forebears regarded as taboo. If nothing empirically worthwhile turns up, *that* will be the time to abjure interest in the topic and leave it to the philosophers to puzzle over.

A question seldom raised in these discussions is whether meaning and consciousness are susceptible of deep investigation by human knowers. (Admittedly, I discuss it myself at some length in *The Problem of Consciousness*.) A properly general naturalism should leave open the possibility that human cognition is not designed in such a way that we can gain any real scientific insight into the underlying workings of our own minds (or those of other animals). Certainly, it is painfully plain that we have not achieved in this area anything like the theoretical depth we have attained in understanding the physical world: there appears to be a systematic elusiveness about the ultimate science of mental phenomena. Despite our fairly advanced understanding of brain function, for example, we seem no nearer than Descartes was to explaining how conscious states result from neural excitations. As an ancillary investigation to the science of meaning and consciousness, then, we should also try to develop a higher-order science of our capacity to understand these phenomena—a science of our ability to arrive at psychological knowledge. It may be the case, not that meaning and consciousness are in themselves suspect or mythical since our science cannot plumb their depths, but rather that our science, as a natural product of human cognitive capacities, has the wrong kind of structure to take in all that the world objectively contains. Transcendent nomothetic realism may in the end be the truth of the matter. The philosophical interest of mental notions might thus be an artifact of the human inaccessibility of the ultimately correct mental science. Psychology might be philosophically boring after all, objectively speaking, if only we could come to know its deep principles. But given the limiting parameters of human cognition, it is possible that the science of mind is condemned to perpetual philosophical interest.

17

Fodor: Mentaĺ Representations

Representations: Philosophical Essays on the
Foundations of Cognitive Science
by Jerry A. Fodor
Harvester, 1981

In *Mental Acts,* published in 1957, P. T. Geach proposed that judgment be understood in terms of "mental utterances" in an "interior language." Judging, he supposed, consists in the mind's exercise of concepts, and the content of a judgment comprises a complex of Ideas which represent things in the world; his suggestion was that these Ideas be identified with words—to judge that the sky is blue is to say in one's heart "the sky is blue." This theory, or something very like it, has recently been advocated by Jerry Fodor (among others) under the title "the language of thought," though Geach's early statement of the theory is not mentioned. In this new collection of essays, mostly reprints of earlier publications, Fodor's chief concern is to expound and defend what he calls the Representational Theory of the Mind (RTM). RTM, as Fodor expounds it, is the thesis that to have thoughts is to be related to internal formulae in a (probably innate and universal) language, these formulae having both syntactic and semantic properties; mental processes such as reasoning consist in computational operations performed upon these formulae.

Fodor holds that RTM is (a) a substantive and controversial thesis and (b) an empirical thesis, one whose acceptability must finally turn upon how successfully it serves the theoretical needs of the cognitive psychologist. But Fodor's way of presenting the issues is misleading. Surely everyone (except behaviorists and the confused) would agree that thinking involves the structured deployment of concepts; and that concepts are (or correspond to)

Reprinted with permission from the *Times Literary Supplement* (January 29, 1982).

mental elements that somehow represent the world. What is substantive and controversial is not RTM as such, but the linguistic turn Fodor gives to it. Fodor's presentation obscures this because he writes as if the choice were between accepting the language of thought and rejecting altogether the idea that thought involves the mental exercise of concepts. Geach's original exposition properly separated the platitudinous from the contentious: he first introduced the idea of mental representation, leaving it open what the representations were to be, and only later proposed that words play the role of representing Ideas. The real issue, then, is not whether RTM is true, but what sort of item a mental representation or concept is.

It is partly this conflation of issues that explains Fodor's insistence that RTM is an empirical thesis. For whereas it is arguable that the internal language theory is answerable to the theoretical requirements of empirical psychology, it is scarcely to be imagined that psychological experiments should induce us to abandon the philosophical thesis that thinking consists in the exercise of concepts. Fodor is well aware that he is reviving a philosophical account of thought at least as old as the works of Descartes and Locke, but he likes to suggest that nowadays the philosophers can and should hand over their problems to the scientists and await their verdict. But really it is not that RTM is philosophically respectable only so long as psychologists find it experimentally fruitful; rather, psychologists are obliged to conceive the mind in this way precisely because RTM is (or is not) acceptable on pretheoretic or philosophical grounds. Contrary to what Fodor suggests, philosophy of mind is not in the process of being engulfed by "cognitive science."

The thesis that thinking is the internal manipulation of sentences invites the question how these sentences acquire semantic significance: in virtue of what do they have a meaning for the thinker? Fodor treats this crucial question with notable caution, but his view seems to be that the internal sentences enjoy significance in virtue of two sorts of property: syntactical or "formal" properties, which determine the role of a thought content in the thinker's mental life; and genuinely semantic properties—reference, satisfaction, truth—relating the internal words to the world. Anyone familiar with Frege's writings will wonder what has happened to the level of *sense,* that is, the association of cognitively significant concepts with words considered as syntactic objects. What Fodor seems to want to suggest is that mere syntax can discharge the duties of sense, that the "shape" of internal symbols can function as their cognitive meaning.

But once this suggestion is made explicit the idea looks hopeless—mere uninterpreted syntax has no representational significance; we need some apparatus that assigns concepts to the internal words or else they will be literally senseless. The relational semantic properties will not do the job since, as Fodor recognizes, they cannot account for the different ways in which the same object may be mentally represented (the "opacity" of thought contents). Nor is the idea that syntactic properties might do duty for sense just a detachable aberration: for once the need of sense is acknowledged the question becomes acute as to whether there remains any useful work for internal sentences to perform. If we require nonsyntactic mental representations anyway, then why not make do with these and let the internal words go? Of course we are then left with the real question—what a concept is. But the language of thought, so far from answering that question, conceals the need to ask it, while silently helping itself to resources whose characterization is the point at issue. Perhaps Fodor's proneness to suppose that syntax can add up to sense comes from the feeling that words in a mental medium, unlike spoken words, are somehow intrinsically interpreted—this along with undue concentration on the workings of computers.

RTM and the language of thought are not the only topics discussed in *Representations;* there is independently interesting material on functionalism, on realism about the mental, on reduction, artificial intelligence semantics, and the doctrine of innate ideas. Most of this seemed to me salutary and often stimulating—the mental is held to be real, irreducible to the physical, and more perplexing than some people suppose—but there are a number of shaky points, mainly concerning the relation between mental and physical, and the issues of innateness.

Fodor wishes to argue, reasonably enough, that the explanatory role of thought content is not preserved under neurophysiological reduction. His ostensible reason for this is that the "standard notion" of reduction permits the loss of structure in mental content. The argument is obscure, and the claim is so hedged that it often looks empty; at any rate, the alleged consequence of reduction seems easily circumvented simply by requiring that the predicates in the reducing neurophysiological theory preserve the complexity of the predicates in the reduced psychological theory—a requirement one would think it natural to impose from the start. There is also what must be some sort of slip on Fodor's part about the distinction between identifying mental particulars with brain events (token identity) and identifying mental properties with brain properties (type identity). Fodor asserts, incorrectly, that the former identification relates only to all *actual* mental particulars, while the latter identifies all *possible* mental particulars with physical events. This is a mistake, since the latter identification does not entail that for any possible instance of a given mental property the corresponding physical event is of the *same* physical type: every possible colored object is identifiable with some object having a mass, but it does not follow that the property of being red is identifiable with the property of having a certain mass.

About the innateness of concepts Fodor makes a surprising claim: he suggests that, understood correctly, both empiricists and nativists agree that primitive concepts are unlearned and so innate; they disagree fundamentally only over *which* concepts are primitive, the empiricist finding conceptual complexity where the nativist descries simplicity. This latter point is interesting and probably right, but Fodor is surely in error in his claim that this is the only disagreement—in particular, in his claim that empiricists accept the innateness of primitive concepts. He arrives at this unorthodox position by too crude a use of the idea that for both empiricists and nativist experience is needed to "trigger" the acquisition of concepts. For the nativist, experience functions merely to activate concepts that are already latently present in the intellect; but for the empiricist, concepts are attained by abstraction from what is sensorily given and are not present in the intellect before such abstraction gets to work. Experience is, it is true, necessary under both theories, but its "triggering" role is conceived quite differently by them.

Fodor is encouraged to overlook this obvious point by a tendency to conflate the idea of innately determined constraints on which qualities are perceptible to an organism with the idea of innately given concepts: that a certain concept is accessible to an organism only because of its innate sensory capacities does not imply that the concept *itself* is innately present; and an empiricist who accepts innate constraints of the first kind will still think that abstraction on experience is required before any concepts are possessed by the organism. Once this point of difference between empiricists and nativist is clearly acknowledged, Fodor's novel reconstruction of the dispute collapses. He does, however, have other worthwhile things to say about the acquisition of concepts—particularly about the old doctrine of "mental chemistry."

Fodor's prose style, though heavily larded with jargon, is very informal and facetious. After the initial shock, the jocose manner becomes just about bearable; but it is not a style to be imitated.

18

Fodor: Using Common Sense

Psychosemantics: The Problem of Meaning in the Philosophy of Mind
by Jerry A. Fodor
MIT Press, 1987

What is the scientific status of commonsense psychology? Should it be taken as a sound basis from which to build a psychological science—needing to be deepened and extended, certainly, but right in essentials? Or should it be discarded wholesale as so much outworn superstition, fit only to be replaced by some quite new kind of theoretical structure? The latter attitude prevailed during much of the infancy and adolescence of scientific psychology, but the former attitude seems to be gaining ground in the (relatively) mature period we know as cognitive science.

Jerry Fodor is a firm conservationist: he thinks that modern cognitive psychology vindicates the constructs of ordinary belief-desire explanation—in particular, he thinks that the idea of mental representation is common to both and is a fine thing in itself. His aim in this book is to protect folk psychology, as a solid basis for mental science, from a range of objections that have been brought against it in recent years, mainly by philosophers. He does so with verve, clarity, and wit, generally getting the better of his revisionary opponents. The book is vintage Fodor: clever, stimulating, challenging, infuriating. It will undoubtedly become the target of much critical discussion as the philosophy of psychology moves toward its adulthood.

According to Fodor, folk psychology works wonderfully in ordinary life and is practically indispensable. Its predictive power is no accident, he claims, because it is a *deep* theory, in the way that physics is deep. The depth comes from two features of the theory: the fact that it postulates unobservables, and its preference for causal intricacy over proliferation of theoretical primitives. This is a neat point against old-style positivistic behaviorists, making unobservability a virtue rather than a liability; their mistake, ironically, was to fail to take the model of physics seriously enough. But Fodor neglects to mention an equally salient feature of folk psychology: the fact that it postulates introspectables—for we also have direct first-person access to our beliefs and desires. By Fodor's criterion of depth, this feature should make us say that folk psychology is *superficial*. Here is where it differs from physics. What would he say about this difference?

The scientific theory that vindicates belief-desire psychology, Fodor assures us, is the computational conception of mental processes. This kind of psychology treats the mind as a symbol-manipulating system, the mental symbols having both causal and semantic properties. Just as we commonly suppose a rational harmony between what a belief logically implies and what it is disposed to cause, so the idea of a language of thought integrates syntactic shape and semantic content—thus explaining how a rational mechanism might be constructed. This may be, as Fodor says, "a perfectly terrific idea," but it is not—contrary to his repeated assertions—the only idea in the field. Psychologists (such as Philip Johnson-Laird) who frame their theories in terms of mental models will be surprised to find their approach declared to be nonexistent. In general, Fodor is far too ready to move from the need for structured mental representations to a specifically sentential conception of the form of these representations. In arguing for the language of thought, indeed, he focuses on an example of a mental representation, namely a tree-structure representing an understood sentence, that is in fact more a model of a sentence than a verbal description of one—supposing this to support his specifically linguistic theory of mental representation.

With folk psychology shown to be, on the fact of it, in good theoretical standing, Fodor goes on to rebut three potential threats to its security: externalism, holism, naturalism. Externalism claims that the content of a belief can be pulled apart from its causal powers, so that any science geared to capturing causal generalizations will have no use for the ordinary notion of content. Fodor accepts this argument, stating it with considerable force, but evades its alleged conclusion by confecting a notion of content ("narrow content") that cannot be divorced from causal powers. Supervenience on the physical is thus respected, but at the price of ineffability in the kind of content that so supervenes.

I think Fodor is right to discern this kind of content, but he underestimates the magnitude of the concession he makes by banning wide content from psychology. For, by his own showing, narrow content cannot be (exclusively) specified in the terms of folk psychology: so a psychology based on narrow content will be neither expressible nor a version of ordinary folk psychology; it will not have available the form "*x* believes that *p*." The lesson is to look more critically at the original demand to make psychology the study of the causal powers of mental states.

Holism takes the content of a belief to be fixed by the totality of beliefs with which the given one has "epistemic liaisons." It thus blocks generalizing over believers, since believers will always differ in their total belief sets. Fodor convincingly demolishes a number of arguments for this extreme holistic thesis, and opts for a local denotational theory of content. He also rejects theories that regard content as the fusion of internal and external factors, though far less convincingly. First, he mistakenly assumes that "two-factor" theories take each factor to determine a unique proposition: but the whole point of such theories is that this is not so. Second, his own earlier notion of narrow content supplies precisely what the two-factor theorist needs to rebut Fodor's criticism. Third, Fodor's reluctance to allow any place for functional role in the fixation of content sits ill with his previous claim that content is conferred by a harmony between inferential propensities and logical consequence.

Naturalism would be a threat if we could not explain mental reference in naturalistic terms. Fodor tries to develop a causal covariation theory of reference, thus explaining where meaning fits in the natural order. This is an ingenious discussion, but problems bristle—in particular, the problem of explaining the possession of content in the absence of appropriate environmental entities. What would he say about the brain in a vat? It looks as if he has to say, implausibly, that the causally isolated terms in its language of thought either have no content or some very bizarre sort of content concerning nerve-endings or some such. I think Fodor should reconsider the prospects for a teleological theory, which he dismisses too quickly. Pure causal theories face formidable problems, especially with respect to the phenomenological content of perceptual experience—a type of content he conspicuously fails to discuss.

Fodor may not have the last word on all issues, as he would be the first to admit. But his forthrightness and intellectual daring are the best way to push our understanding forward. *Psychosemantics* is a notable contribution to the old question of how the mind represents the world.

19

Davidson: Cooling It

Donald Davidson
by Simon Evnine
Polity, 1992

Donald Davidson's Philosophy of Language:
An Introduction
by Bjorn Ramberg
Blackwell, 1989

Donald Davidson is perhaps the most distinguished philosopher in history never to have written a book. Indeed, he did not get round to writing articles until he was into his forties (he is now seventy-six). Yet those articles—short, intense, allusive, hard—have changed the shape of contemporary analytical philosophy. They were in mid spate when I was a graduate student at Oxford in the early seventies, and they acted as a kind of philosophical IQ test for the young philosophers of my generation. I well remember poring with tormented excitement over "Truth and Meaning" and "Mental Events," two of the most influential (and contested) articles of recent times. These cryptic texts gave the impression of well-honed conjuring tricks, in which the deepest of problems were given tantalizingly rigorous and ingenious solutions. In those days you were either a "Davidsonian" or you weren't; you certainly had to find out where you stood. But it wasn't easy, because each Davidson article presupposed the others, and they assumed you were good at logic. It became clear that Davidson had a system, but it needed to be pieced together by the reader, as best he or she could. Puzzlement about a particular Davidson piece would be met with a knowing look from the initiated and the query "But have you read 'In Defence of Convention T'?" The very plainness of his name (often transmuted to David Donaldson) lent an aura of mystique to the plosive economy of the Davidson corpus. And the man himself, with his startling blue eyes and precisely articulated mode of speech, his unhurried

Reprinted with permission from the *London Review of Books* (August 19, 1993).

confidence, his immersion in his own vision, his neatness, certainly encouraged the feeling that he had it all figured out, and all you had to do was figure him out. It did no harm, too, to discover that Davidson had been an enemy aircraft spotter in the U.S. navy in World War II, that he was a trained pilot, that he went gliding for a hobby, that he has climbed mountains, that there are very few places in the world he hasn't visited. Davidson wasn't just profound: he was cool (and there aren't many philosophers you can say that about). Davidson had *nerve*.

The principal appeal of the Davidsonian system lies in its attempt to combine two conceptions of human beings that have traditionally been taken to be rivals. One conception, advocated by the positivists, though not unique to them, draws inspiration from the physical sciences and formal logic: it seeks to reduce mental discourse to physical discourse, and it offers to replace ordinary language with the kind of formalized language devised by Frege and his successors. Ultimately, there is nothing more to us than an arrangement of physical facts expressed in the notation of the predicate calculus. This conception effectively displaces our commonsense picture of mind and language in favor of a kind of pared-down physical naturalism in which we are represented as continuous with the rest of nature. The other conception, associated with the later Wittgenstein, but by no means unique to him, insists on the autonomy and legitimacy of our ordinary ways of thinking about human psychology and human language: these are not to be replaced by some austere physical theory or gleaming logical apparatus—for they are perfectly in order as they stand. We are, in fact, what we commonsensically take ourselves to be: rational agents with free choice. Man is not just an irregular clump of vibrating particles, nor need he be coached in the language of the logician: he has beliefs and desires and intentions, and his natural mode of expression is not to be improved on. He eludes physical science, at least in his mental and linguistic part: he is separate from the rest of nature and needs to be studied by methods peculiar to himself.

These two conceptions seem to represent radically incompatible ways of thinking of ourselves, and no middle ground appears to be available. But it is not as if either conception can be comfortably adopted to the exclusion of the other. The first view suffers from the problem that no such reduction or translation has ever been carried out, so that limiting ourselves to physical description will inevitably involve abandoning the idea that we have minds at all. Also, there seems to be a lot about natural language that cannot be reconstructed in terms of the usual logical systems, so that we would not be able to say as much if we spoke only Formalese. The price of seeing ourselves in these restricted ways is that what we see is no longer ourselves, but only some desiccated residue. On the other hand, if we remove the mind from the scientific domain completely, as the second view suggests, regarding ourselves as beyond the reach of causation, law, and material composition, we run into equally severe problems. Do we not have brains that subserve our minds? Is not our behavior somehow governed by natural law? Are we not in some clear sense ultimately made of matter? And is not formal logic an object of great beauty and power, giving undeniable insight into the structure of thought, whose services we should solicit and exploit? Hence the classic dilemma: how can we both be and not be an object of natural science?

Davidson's key idea is that the dilemma is unreal; we can enjoy the benefits of both conceptions without incurring the disadvantages each appears to entail. What we must do is compromise, not pushing either conception beyond its legitimate sphere. Yes, but the question has always been how exactly that is to be achieved. The beauty of Davidson's philosophy of mind is that this massive question is held to turn on a simple—but neglected—logical point. Once this point is made plain we can be all we want to be. No ideological posturing will be necessary; no spurning of the obvious; no deep unifying revisionary metaphysics will have to be generated. All we need to recognize is (a) that there are events and (b) that events, like material objects, admit of a type-token distinction (about which more in a minute). We don't even need a theory specific to the mental: once we get clear about our talk of events in general we will already have the necessary resources with which to explain how the mind can be both rational and natural, irreducible and physical, causal and lawless. To put it differently, once we properly grasp the distinction between events and their descriptions we will be in a position to be both materialists and mentalists.

It works like this. First, it is obvious that we talk of events as well as objects, as when we say that the bridge collapsed because of the explosion, or that Smith went to the shops because it occurred to her that she needed some milk. That is, we routinely include mental and physical events in our ontology. Secondly, and only slightly less obviously, we allow that there can be different instances of the same general type of event, as when two bridges collapse on different days, or when the same milky thought occurs to Jones. These instances are the event tokens and the universals they exemplify are the event types. You have to count types differently from tokens, since many tokens can correspond to the same type and a given token can exemplify many types. In other words, distinct particular dated events can fall under the same general description, and one and the same particular event can fall under many descriptions. Accordingly, mental events, too, admit of a type-token distinction, requiring as to distinguish particular events from the descriptions that apply to them.

And now Davidson's master stroke is just this: every mental-event token is identical with some physical-event token in the brain, but mental-event types are not identical with physical-event types, nor are they reducible to them. Ontologically, then, every mental particular is a physical thing (falls under a physical description), but it is not possible to reduce mental concepts or properties to physical concepts or properties. According to this position, which Davidson christened "anomalous monism," every mental event falls under a physical law, but there are no laws of psychology; indeed, psychology is not really a science at all. The reason is that mental descriptions

apply to things that also satisfy physical descriptions, but no systematic relation between mental and physical discourse is entailed by this identity of
events. Thus we can be, as it were, natural under one description and rational under another; lawlike when described one way but lawless when described another way. We consist of a single series of events, but this series
admits of quite distinct and irreducible modes of description. (Technical
note: the type-token distinction as here invoked is really a special case of the
use-mention distinction—we *use* descriptions to *mention* events.)

On the one hand, then, we can say that mental events are physical, that
reasons cause actions, and that everything is subject to strict law; while, on
the other hand, we can insist that mental concepts are irreducible, that action
explanation is essentially normative, and that there are no psychophysical or
psychological laws. We do not need, on this Davidsonian view, to *explain* the
relation between mental and physical properties of a person: we ascribe these
properties under appropriate criterial conditions, following distinct sorts of
principle, and that is all that needs to be said. In order to solve the mind-body
problem, then, we do not need to represent mental properties as physical
properties in disguise, nor do we need to effect a conceptual revolution that
will bridge the gap, or even to acknowledge that there are facts about the
mind-body relation that we cannot grasp. We need merely to observe that
one and the same event can be described in these two ways. We may also, if
we like, hold that mental descriptions are supervenient on physical descriptions, so that physical twins must also be mental twins: but this is an optional
extra, in no way entailed by the thesis of anomalous monism. There are
indeed two very different sides to our nature, but from an ontological point
of view we are undivided beings.

Simon Evnine's introductory book does a creditable job of bringing all this
usefully together, enabling the student to grasp how the various parts of
Davidson's philosophy cohere. He has a sure grip on the metaphysical and
logical bases of Davidson's distinctive approach, particularly as regards causation, laws, and ontology, and he puts the essential points in such a way that
only the most determined could miss them. His book should take a lot of the
pain out of learning and teaching Davidson. He is also well aware, on the
critical side, of the tensions that lurk within his subject's hybrid picture of
human mentality. The heart of the trouble, as he notes, lies in maintaining
both a causal and a normative account of the nature of propositional content.
Davidson invokes causation at three critical junctures: to relate reasons (*qua*
reasons) to actions; to confer content on beliefs, by identifying the object of a
belief with its environmental cause; and to account for cases of irrationality,
where the notion of a mental cause that is not a reason is brought into play.
These three causal theses correspond to three threats to the other component of Davidson's overall conception. First, if reasons (*qua* reasons) are
causally relevant to action, then there must after all be psychological laws of
some sort, just as there are laws in other special sciences: and this means that
there is no inherent conflict between normativeness and lawfulness. Second,

if belief content is fixed by environmental impingements, then it is hard to see how it could also be holistically determined by principles of rationality that essentially advert to the agent's other beliefs and desires—any more than the identity of the impinging objects is so determined. Third, if we are allowed, in cases of irrationality, to make ascriptions of content that violate conditions of rational justification, so that lack of rationality does not undermine the possession of content, then it becomes unclear why we cannot push this separation further, until the point at which the agent is preponderantly irrational. The trouble with causation, as the cement of the mind, is that it has the wrong properties to sustain Davidson's hermeneutic-holistic-normative picture of mentality. Once causation is allowed to flow through the mind's channels it threatens to flush out the kind of anomalism Davidson wishes to combine with it. If this threat cannot be convincingly repelled, then we shall be forced into one or other of two kinds of extreme position: either a position like Jerry Fodor's in which causality reigns and rationality be hanged, or a position like Daniel Dennett's in which rationality is prized but the idea of inner causes is fed to the dogs. Certainly, Davidson needs to say more about why he is not forced in either direction. To be sure, it would be nice to be able to combine both viewpoints; but mere conjunctive affirmation is not enough to bring this off.

Davidson's philosophy of language is intimately connected with his philosophy of mind, but it raises questions of its own. Evnine also does a good job with this more technical aspect of his subject, which is more than I can say for Bjorn Ramberg's ill-expressed attempt to convert his reader to the Davidsonian faith. This could not be used as an introductory text, despite its title, because of its failure to explain technicalities and its general sloppiness; nor does it contain material of sufficient originality to be of interest to those already acquainted with the literature of Davidson. It is exactly the kind of book he doesn't need: an exercise in undisciplined banner waving. What would have been more helpful is a clear tracing out of the several strands that link Davidson's work on semantics with his epistemology, and ultimately with his view of how the mind contrives to confront reality. For here we can discern an instructive evolution, in which an initially technical problem leads to a questioning of the entire empiricist tradition.

I remarked earlier that Davidson seeks to dissolve the traditional opposition between reverence for formal systems in developing semantic theories and respect for the structures actually present in natural languages. By pairing vernacular sentences with suitable formal counterparts, and providing a theory of the latter, Davidson proposes indirectly to give a theory of the former. Hence his claim that Tarskian truth theories—in which the predicate "true-in-L" is rigorously defined for a formal language on the basis of a finite set of axioms—provide the basis for a theory of meaning for natural languages such as English. Davidson is able to suggest this thanks to his considerable success in ingeniously translating logically recalcitrant idioms of natural language, such as adverbs and indirect discourse, into formulas of a standard logical language. Logical form is what we need if we are to provide a theory for natural language at all, rather than being a rival to it.

Details aside, however, there is the question whether this entire approach can capture the full meaning of sentences, given that it operates with the apparently much weaker notion expressed by "is true if and only if." Davidson's response to this persistent problem has been to enrich the set of notions used to capture meaning to include those that would feature in an account of how we would empirically verify that a given truth theory successfully interprets the speech of a particular community; specifically, to employ such psychological notions as belief and desire. The question has become: what are the right assumptions to make about the mind of a speaker who holds a sentence true in certain environmental conditions? And here Davidson applies a principle that has figured increasingly in his philosophy—the so-called principle of charity.

In order to arrive at an attribution of belief to the speaker we are to assume that his beliefs are true, so that we can use the surrounding facts to determine a content for his belief. If he holds "It's raining" true when it is in fact raining, then we should take it that he believes that it's raining and so interpret his sentence to mean that it's raining, instead of assuming, uncharitably, that he has made a mistake and thinks it's not raining when it is. This sounds like sensible enough practical advice to the would-be interpreter, but it raises the question of how we can be so confident that people regularly believe what is true. Isn't it at least conceivable that a community could speak an interpretable language and yet be massively deluded about the extralinguistic facts? Couldn't I be a speaker of English and yet be a brain in a vat, as Cartesian sceptics have long assumed to be possible? Davidson's shocking answer is that actually I could not: he thinks that it is a necessary conceptual truth about belief that one's beliefs are mainly true. Beliefs must not only be rationally consistent with each other in order to be possessed at all: they must also veridically represent how the world is. But this yields a startling result: scepticism must be incoherent, since it tries to envisage situations in which people have beliefs but get everything wrong. Davidson justifies this result by insisting that the content of belief is fixed by its actual cause, and not by any epistemic intermediary such as experience. He is thus led to reject the empiricist dichotomy of scheme and content, of concepts and the given. That is, in sum: in order to make up for the logical extensionality of "is true if and only if" Davidson is led first to interpretation, then to charity, thence to a rejection of scepticism, and finally to an abandonment of the third dogma of empiricism. Where the empiricists took meaning to be possible only if it stems from sensory experience, Davidson takes the theory of meaning to be possible only if experience plays *no* role in fixing meaning. Meaning, for him, results from a direct collision, or collusion, between belief and fact.

This is stirring stuff, but it is far from obvious that it is correct. What powers the whole argument is the initial claim that interpretation can only get going if we make a charitable assumption about belief, since mere holding-true is mute as to what is believed. But isn't there something Davidson is forgetting? Agreed, mere assent to sentences will never by itself decide between different hypotheses about what is believed, so that something else must take up the slack if we are to interpret at all. But we are not compelled to leap to a fixed policy of charity, since we can always appeal to the speaker's *nonlinguistic* behavior to narrow the options down. Suppose our speaker assents to "it's raining" in broad sunshine: we might be inclined to suppose that he can't really believe it's raining—so we charitably assign to him the belief that it's sunny, reinterpreting his words accordingly. Of course his assent is not all we have to go on: we might observe him scampering under a tree, swearing, dabbing at his face with a hanky—giving all the signs of a man who is convinced it's pouring down. Well, that would be evidence that he actually believes it's raining, in plain contravention of the facts. And we might then go on to assemble further evidence that he is suffering from delusory perceptions, perhaps caused by malnourishment or whatever. None of this would be conclusive—he *might* be trying to deceive us into thinking he believes it's raining when he knows it isn't—but then no empirical evidence for anything is ever conclusive.

The point is that we are not, as interpreters, stuck merely with inscrutable assent, so that we have to go by the charitable assumption or not go at all: there is other behavior to appeal to. I take this to be a Wittgensteinian point: mere ostension is always multiply interpretable, and the only way to give it specific content is to bring in an extensive range of behavior and "forms of life." Furthermore, since it is certainly coherent to keep a subject's behavior fixed while varying his environment, we have here a basis for interpreting his speech that does not presuppose that his beliefs fit the facts. Beliefs are not just caused by things outside us: they are also that on which we act, so that how someone acts gives purchase in deciding what he believes. The upshot is that Davidson's antisceptical argument does not go through: there can be true and warranted attributions of predominantly false beliefs. The good news, so far as Davidson's overall scheme is concerned, is that it becomes possible to accept his semantics without embracing his epistemology.

Davidson's work combines rigor with imagination, caution with boldness. He shows what analytic philosophy can be like at its best. In tackling head on some of the most profound and perplexing questions he has opened up new areas of inquiry, and it is impossible not to learn from thinking through his ideas—even when one disagrees with them. There is a well-known genre of philosophical joke—"X's proof that p"—that parodies a given philosopher's characteristic style of argument. Davidson's proof that p goes: "Consider the bold conjecture that p. Therefore p." (That, for a disciple of Davidson, goes: "Davidson has considered the bold conjecture that p. Therefore p.") Of course, this is as unfair as it is meant to be (it is actually a good deal milder than other examples of the genre): but it does signal one very commendable feature of Davidson's work—its courage. Davidson wants to answer the big questions, and he is not afraid to muster whatever degree of boldness is requisite to the task. What is amazing is that he has done this while remaining as scrupulously analytical as even the most inhibited of thinkers. Read "In Defence of Convention T."

20

Davidson: Weak Wills

Essays on Davidson: Actions and Events
edited by Bruce Vermazen and
Merrill Hintikka
Oxford, 1985

Donald Davidson has this year been George Eastman Visiting Professor at Oxford: only the second philosopher to hold the august position (the first being W. V. Quine, a teacher of Davidson's at Harvard and his greatest philosophical influence). This honor reflects his present stature in the academic world. Last year he was the subject of a massive conference held in New Jersey, organized by the indefatigable Ernie Lepore. It was probably the largest philosophical conference ever held, and it attracted nearly all of the world's leading philosophers. Most of the papers delivered were addressed (often critically) to some aspect of Davidson's work. For a philosophical event, it was undoubtedly a great occasion, if a somewhat overwhelming one (especially for Davidson, who attended as many of the papers as was humanly possible). Probably no other philosopher now working has been discussed as much during the last decade.

It was not always so. Davidson was something of a late-developer, or at least a late publisher. His publishing career did not seriously get off the ground until the early sixties, when he was into his forties. It was in the seventies that his writings really took hold, passing from cult status into virtual orthodoxy (in certain circles). There has yet to be a significant reaction. He has still not published a single book setting forth his ideas systematically, preferring to publish short pithy articles, intricately interrelated, which have eventually been bound together into collections. Davidson is not

Reprinted with permission from the *London Review of Books* (September 5, 1985).

an easy writer. He makes free use of technical ideas and results, which he assumes the reader to have mastered, and his predilection for economical and aphoristic formulations sometimes shades into elusiveness. But there is a firm respect for our ordinary thinking, and his feet never lose contact with the ground. Hard persistent thinking is always much in evidence—Davidson always pushes the subject just that little bit further (the bit that makes all the difference). A Davidson paper invariably gets somewhere.

Davidson has worked principally in philosophy of language and philosophy of mind, occasionally spilling over into metaphysics and (latterly) epistemology. *Essays on Davidson,* a collection of papers by "students, colleagues, collaborators and adversaries" of Davidson's, deals mainly with the work relating to philosophy of mind, though there are three essays (by Chisholm, Strawson, and Thalberg) addressed to the metaphysics of events and causation. Davidson's treatment of intention is discussed in five papers (by Bratman, Grice and Baker, Peacocke, Pears, and Vermazen), three of which also discuss the allied topic of weakness of the will. The third main section of the book is about Davidson's views in the philosophy of psychology, in particular his theory of the mind-body relation (here the discussants are Lewis, Smart, and Suppes). There is one rather strange three-page piece by Dan Bennett on pride. Davidson gets to reply to each paper at the end of the volume, and a new paper by him called "Adverbs of Action" has been included. Before commenting on these various contributions it is as well to remind oneself of Davidson's principal doctrines.

Practical reasoning (the kind addressed to the question "What shall I do?") consists in a transition from premises expressing beliefs and desires to a conclusion expressing an intention to act. This type of reasoning is not deductive in character, since the addition of new premises can invalidate the inference: what it is reasonable to do in the light of one set of beliefs and desires may not be reasonable when further reasons for actions are adduced. So we cannot represent the conclusion of a piece of practical reasoning, premissed on a particular pair of belief and desire, with an unqualified "Doing *a* is desirable." Instead, Davidson suggests, we should compare practical reasoning with inductive or probabilistic reasoning, in which the addition of new evidence can also serve to discourage us from drawing the initially reasonable conclusion. What we should then say is that the agent's reasons give *prima facie support* to a certain practical conclusion. Thus the form of a practical inference is something like this: "Reason *r* gives prima facie support to doing *a*"; in symbols "pf(doing *a, r*)," which resembles the "prob(*H, e*)" (where *H* is a hypothesis and *e* some evidence) of probabilistic reasoning. However, this cannot be the end of the story, for an agent must act, and prima facie judgments of desirability don't get him there—an agent can make far too many of these at any given time. A new type of judgment is therefore needed: this is what Davidson calls an unconditional or "all-out" judgment of desirability, and it has the adventurous form "Doing *a* would be best." This unconditional judgment Davidson identifies with intention. Accordingly, the agent is seen as engaging in three stages of practical reasoning: first, he makes a number of prima facie judgments, each relativized to a particular desire; second, he judges on the basis of this that, all things (desires) considered, he should do *a*, thus making a generalized conditional judgment; third, he makes the all-out judgment "*a* would be (is) best." When the agent reaches the third stage he is intending to do *a*, and if he does not temporize he is actually doing *a*.

This apparatus is used by Davidson to give an account of the reasoning of the weak-willed agent—the *akratic*, as he has quaintly come to be called. To act akratically is, pretheoretically, to act against one's better judgment. Thus the akratic judges that he should do *a* rather than *b* (his preference is for *a*), yet he does *b*, and does it intentionally. How, Davidson asks, is this possible? If the intention to do *b* is, or involves, the judgment that doing *b* is best, then how can the will be weak—won't it always follow the counsels of practical reason? The solution to this apparent paradox, Davidson suggests, lies in the distinction between conditional and unconditional judgments of value: the akratic judges that all things considered he should do *a* rather than *b* (a generalized prima facie judgment), but he does not detach the corresponding all-out judgment—indeed, he judges all-out that *b* is better than *a*. His error resembles that of the scientist who judges that all his evidence supports a certain conclusion but then irrationally believes its opposite. The akratic lets his all-out judgments get uncoupled from his prima facie judgments: this is irrational all right, but it is perfectly possible—it does not require the agent knowingly to believe a contradiction. The key idea here is that the akratic agent's intention fails to be shaped by his practical reasoning in the same sort of way that the theoretical reasoner's beliefs about the world may fail to be determined by his evidence. The nondeductive gap in both cases is the point at which the weak of mind trip up. What happens every day has thus been shown possible.

This account of practical reasoning and its deformation is criticized by several contributors. The results do not make light reading; one might be forgiven for nominating the topic of weakness of will for the prize for the driest treatment of a juicy-sounding topic in analytical philosophy. Much heavy technical weather is made of Davidson's writings on intention and prima facie judgments. Davidson cuts through this thicket in his replies, which contain many accusations of misunderstanding. These protests seem to me largely justified: one has the impression that Davidson's critics have become swamped in technical detail and allowed the wood to be occluded by the trees. Incidentally some worthwhile points are made, but the core of Davidson's theory emerges unscathed, as he is not slow to point out. This is not to say that the theory is unfaultable: indeed, I think it contains some highly questionable elements. The central implausibility is the ascription to the akratic of the all-out judgment that his weak act is best. For the weak-willed agent acts *against* his better judgment, not in conformity with it: he precisely does *not* judge that what he is doing is the best thing to do. Davidson's distinction between two sorts of value judgment does not help overcome this point, since his theory still represents the akratic as having his will shaped by his best judgment—the kind of judgment that in ordinary cases triggers *non*akratic action. Surely it is more plausible, if we are to use Davidson's apparatus, to suppose that the akratic judges *both* that all things considered he should do *a* rather than *b* and that he should do *a tout court*—yet he weakly does *b* rather than *a*. On this way of representing the agent's state of mind, the intention to do *b* cannot be identified with (nor can it entail) the all-out judgment that *b* should be done, so Davidson's theory of intention goes by the board: but this, too, strikes me as a welcome result, since that theory assimilates the will too closely to the cognitive faculty. Intending belongs with trying, and surely it is unplausible to think of trying as a kind of *judgment*. Weakness of *will* is a failure of the ratiocinative faculties to shape the executive faculties; it is not, as Davidson's theory describes it, a foul-up *within* the ratiocinative faculties. So there is no paradox to resolve about how the agent can form conflicting *judgments* about what he should do.

Weakness of will is in a certain respect analogous with perceptual illusion. It is possible for a perceiver to see the world otherwise than he believes and knows it to be, as when a straight stick looks bent in water. The operation of the perceptual system is here not being controlled by what the perceiver's beliefs tell him. How is this possible? It can seem that there is a puzzle here if one insists that experiencing is a species of judging: for it will then seem that the illuded perceiver must be making contradictory judgments about how the world is—he must believe both that the stick is straight and that it is bent. The solution to this alleged puzzle is clearly *not* to distinguish two categories of judgment differing in their logical form—such that the illuded perceiver judges that all things considered the stick is straight but also judges all-out that it is bent. Rather, we must recognize that the perceptual system can operate autonomously with respect to the belief system. Seeing is thus not a kind of judging—and nor is willing. In both cases the solution is to acknowledge what has come to be called the modularity of mind. At any rate, this sort of approach seems to me to make the right assumptions.

The middle section of *Essays on Davidson* deals with events, causation, and states of affairs. Much of this is routine (which is not to say without value), but an issue of some significance crops up in the exchange between Strawson and Davidson. This concerns whether causation and causal explanation are relations "in nature." Both Strawson and Davidson wish to distinguish between the relation of causation holding between events in the world and the relation of causal explanation which "holds between facts or truths." Strawson scolds certain unidentified authors for employing the confused locution "under a description" when speaking of causation and explanation. Since Davidson has used this locution himself, he naturally wonders whether he is one of those Strawson has it in mind to censure. He points out in his reply that it is directly contrary to his view of causation to speak this way of what events do causally to other events, but that he has spoken in this way of

explanation, and, moreover, has warned of the misunderstandings the locution can invite. Properly construed, talk of explanation "under a description"
is simply a handy way of acknowledging the intensionality of explanation
claims, and is thus entirely innocent of the confusion Strawson stigmatizes.

On this point Davidson seems to me completely in the clear. But there is
another potential confusion lurking, and I am not sure that it is avoided by
either Strawson or Davidson. Strawson describes causal explanation as "an
intellectual or rational or intentional relation," and Davidson comes close to
calling it "language-dependent." The suggestion in both authors is that while
causation is objectively out there in the world there is something essentially
mind- or language-dependent about that which is reported when we explain
one event in terms of another. If this were so, then natural laws would be
similarly people-dependent, since these are what provide our (best) explanations of what goes on. But this cannot be right: nature was governed by laws
before we came on the scene to say so. And events have explanations whether
we are here to give them or not. Laws and explanations (considered as
sentences) pick out *properties* of events and substances that are lawfully and
explanatorily related: these properties are just as independent of mind and
language as the entities that instantiate them (or if they are not, this has
nothing in particular to do with the nature of laws and explanation). It does
not follow from the fact that a certain type of sentence is semantically inten-
sional that what it reports is mind- or language-dependent. Perhaps neither
Strawson nor Davidson thinks it does, but then I cannot see what other basis
their claim might have.

The third section of the book discusses Davidson's doctrine of "anomalous
monism"—the thesis that all mental events are physical but there are no
psychophysical laws. The importance of this doctrine is that it offers the
hope of reconciling the ontological materiality of the mind with its conceptual irreducibility to the physical. It does this by identifying mental events
with physical events while insisting that the mental properties of those events
are not physical properties. The papers in this section raise some natural
queries about Davidson's arguments—in particular, his reasons for removing
psychology from the realm of the strictly lawful. Thus Suppes claims that
physics is less strictly lawlike (deterministic) than Davidson suggests and that
psychology is more so. Again, it seems to me that Davidson's fundamental
contentions survive, though his earlier formulations need to be qualified
somewhat. Nothing particularly new emerges from the three papers in this
section. I think again, however, that Davidson's critics have here missed the
chance to urge deeper objections: I will mention just two.

First, Davidson's reasons for contesting the reducibility of mental notions
focus on the logical and semantic features consequent upon the possession of
propositional content. This has the look of a sound thought when the reducing vocabulary consists exclusively of terms from physics and chemistry. But
what about the vocabulary used by cognitive scientists to describe the informational and computational properties of the brain? This vocabulary has the

resources to speak of propositional content—so might not the mental vocabulary be reducible to *it*? And if it is, as many cognitive scientists believe,
then how will matters look when we inquire how the physical and computational properties of the brain are related? Perhaps this intermediate way of
describing the brain will bring mind and matter closer together than now
seems to us possible. There is, at any rate, an issue here for Davidson to
address.

Secondly, what are we to make of those irreducible mental properties of
the brain—what is their "ontological status"? They are said to be fixed by
physical properties of the brain, but how *can* they be, given their categorical
difference from physical properties? What kind of dependence is this? What
is its explanation? How in the course of evolution did merely material things
come to have irreducible mental properties? These are natural questions, but
we search in vain for an answer to them in Davidson's writings (this is why
many materialistic philosophers feel that anomalous monism does not say
enough). I suspect that Davidson does not get himself worked up about these
questions because of a more or less tacit instrumentalism about mental ascriptions: to have mental properties is to be interpretable by the ascription of
mental predicates—having a mind is as much dependent upon the interpreter as the interpretee. Suppose one were such an instrumentalist, then
one would not be excessively concerned about how the physical properties of
a subject fix his mental properties, since these latter properties are possessed,
as it were, only by courtesy—they are projected onto the subject by the
interpreter. I think this kind of instrumentalism does alleviate the worry
about irreducible mental properties—but at an obvious cost. The question to
worry about is: can one rest content with anomalous monism if one believes
that mental properties are objectively determined?

In a charming postscript to the volume Davidson says that he used to think
that replying to critics was easy and so didn't bother to do it, but that replying
to his critics in this volume has changed his attitude: critics sometimes have
good points, hard as it may be to admit it. Davidson here shows a degree of
honesty and modesty seldom found among philosophers, but I have to say
that on this occasion his critics have not given him a particularly hard time.
For all they have said, the Davidsonian edifice still stands.

21

Davidson: When Is an Action Intentional?

Essays on Actions and Events
by Donald Davidson
Clarendon Press, 1980

This volume usefully assembles Davidson's hitherto scattered writings on events, action, and the mind-body problem. Their juxtaposition brings out the system in Davidson's thought: one has the sense of a tightly knit garment held ingeniously together by a few carefully interwoven strands—the points of vulnerability may be few but the consequences of snapping are more calamitous.

The master threads of this system are the twin notions of event and cause. These notions, especially that of event, are scrutinized and tested with relentless persistence. The spirit of the enterprise is undogmatic and theoretical: events are to be recognized, not so much because of their commonsense or metaphysical credentials, but on account of their utility in devising attractive and rigorous theories—of logical form, intentional action, the nature of mental events. Davidson's influence is owed as much to his *attitude* toward philosophical problems as to the specific doctrines for which he is justly celebrated.

The proposal to acknowledge an ontology of events can seem banal, for surely things change—and changes are events. What is not banal, though once perceived is compellingly obvious, is the idea that events are *basic particulars*: they are not to be conceived as logical constructions from substances, times, and properties, but are genuine objects of discourse susceptible of multiple characterization. This conception of events enables Davidson to

Reprinted with permission from the *Times Higher Educational Supplement* (September 5, 1981).

treat adverbial sentences reporting change as conjunctive predications of such particulars; and it motivates the detection of opacity where others have supposed extra entities. Thus unintentional actions always have intentional aspects, and explanation is always "under a description." It also makes possible the claim that mental events can be described physically even though there is no reducing mental descriptions to physical ones. The nontriviality of the event ontology is shown in the frequency with which one needs to press the question "Do you mean *token* or event *type?*" And surely this conception of events is not to be denied. This is not to say that all of Davidson's applications of the conception are plain sailing: there are adverbs that resist the Davidsonian treatment; there are certain actions, namely, omissions, that are hard to see as events; and it is less than obvious that a single event *can* have both mental and physical characterizations, especially if one thinks (as Davidson tends not to) of conscious sensations. But it must be said that Davidson's framework is what permits a sharp statement of these questions. An ontological issue he does not discuss is whether we should welcome *properties* as we have been advised to welcome events; the answer to this will affect, among other things, our assessment of the purport for physicalism of the irreducibility of mental descriptions.

In his 1963 paper "Actions, Reasons, and Causes" (reprinted as the first essay in this collection) Davidson defended a "causal theory" of intentional action: a bit of behavior counts as an intentional action if and only if it is caused by the agent's desires and beliefs, and it is explained by citing those causally operative desires and beliefs. The stark economy of this theory is not preserved in Davidson's later papers, as he comes to appreciate its inadequacy as originally stated. First, we have to cope with the notorious problem of "lunatic causal chains," cases in which a reason causes a piece of behavior that we would not call intentional. Davidson himself despairs of solving the problem, but unless it can be accommodated within a broadly causal framework (which I concur with Davidson in doubting) we really have no right to speak of a causal *theory:* perhaps some conceptually quite novel ingredient is needed to fill the gap, or perhaps the notion of intentional action is just irreducible. This admission of Davidson's leaves us with the rather more modest thesis that it is merely a *necessary* condition of acting intentionally that the action be caused by a reason.

Secondly, Davidson comes round to enriching his earlier minimal account with the notion of intending, which he wishes to construe as an all-out judgment of desirability. This suggestion keeps down the enrichment, but for that reason seems to miss something essential: for surely it is possible for me to judge that doing *a* is best all things considered, yet at the same time refrain from intending to do *a?* Here we may need to reckon with the will, one of those mysterious faculties against which Davidson has always set his face. Intending threatens to spoil the simplicity of Davidson's theory in another way too. Davidson at one point concedes to Castañeda that intending always involves a certain reflexivity: Oedipus intended that *he himself* should seek the slayer of Laius—replacing "he himself" with "Oedipus" does not preserve truth conditions. That intention necessarily involves this kind of attitude toward oneself suggests that self-awareness is integral to the concept of agency—as integral as causation. But Davidson does not pursue the consequences of Castañeda's observation—perhaps we shall also have to make room for the self in our final account of intentional action.

Thirdly, there is the question in virtue of what reasons cause actions; in particular, how does the propositional content of an attitude play a causal role in producing behavior? To answer this question—which seems essential if we are to know what *sort* of causal nexus we are dealing with—we will need a theory of what constitutes propositional content, and of how the truth conditions of an attitude are connected to its explanatory force. It would be churlish to chide Davidson with failing to answer these questions, but those working in his wake must come to grips with the problems he leaves open.

Reading these essays it is not difficult to understand the mesmeric effect Davidson's writings are apt to produce. The combination of logical rigor with belles lettres, of grand theory with attention to detail, of seriousness with lightness of touch, of clarity with arch allusiveness—these make for an intoxicating mixture. But when the intoxication wears off Davidson's work stands forth as a major contribution to analytical philosophy.

22

Putnam: Ideal Justifications

Realism and Reason: Philosophical Papers,
volume 3
by Hilary Putnam
Cambridge University Press, 1985

Since the publication in 1975 of Hilary Putnam's second volume of collected papers, he has been changing his views; he has, indeed, been undergoing something of a conversion. As he confesses in the introduction to the present volume, there was a time when he was an unqualified realist, hostile to verificationism in any form; when he believed that reference to things in the world was unproblematic and semantically primary; and when he took truth to consist in a relation of correspondence between thought and a mind-independent world. But now Putnam has come to believe that all this is wrong, or at least highly misleading: the papers collected in this third volume set out to explain why.

There is much to commend in these efforts: his discussion is, as always, lively and stimulating; he takes on the big issues with uninhibited freshness; he ingeniously connects what may have seemed like separate questions. There are, however, some regrettable lapses in both conception and presentation: formulations of key positions are obscure and elusive, relying upon a liberal use of inverted commas to suggest that more is being meant by the quoted phrase than it literally says; there is a tendency to resort to shrill sloganizing when rigorous argument is what is wanted, possibly as a result of hasty composition; and there are moments of pretentiousness and self-congratulation. The topics treated range widely, from technical issues in quantum physics to meditations upon the place of analytical philosophy in

Reprinted with permission from the *Times Literary Supplement* (November 25, 1983).

"contemporary culture"—though the issue of realism is the central and re-current theme.

Putnam's primary target is someone called "the metaphysical realist." This species of philosopher is credited with quite a variety of convictions: he believes in a mind-independent world; he holds a correspondence theory of truth; he thinks there is a unique reference scheme for our language; he supposes there to be a single true theory of the world; he takes truth to outrun even idealized justification; he rejects the idea that we have "direct access" to objects; he cannot tolerate objective vagueness; he prefers ideal languages. Now it may be that there have been (and are) philosophers who have adhered to all these doctrines (Russell is perhaps an example), but it is not to be supposed that there is any *logical* connection between them—someone could consistently espouse a subset of them without being commit-ted to the whole lot. In particular, I see no reason why someone who believes in a mind-independent world and a nonepistemic notion of truth—surely the core beliefs of "the metaphysical realist"—should find himself saddled with the other doctrines listed. Putnam typically proceeds by attacking some of these doctrines and taking himself to have thereby undermined the others, thus insinuating guilt by association; whereas what is needed is a careful articulation of distinctions and of the advantages and liabilities of each com-ponent of the composite position he opposes. And where Putnam does at-tempt to show a real theoretical connection, as, for example, between a correspondence theory of truth and rejection of vague properties, his argu-ments are quite unconvincing: for the believer in correspondence and vague-ness can simply hold that the correspondence relation is itself vague (non-determinate).

But how good are Putnam's arguments against the several doctrines that make up his target? About the idea of a mind-independent world he says some curious things: his chief complaint seems to be that if we locate material objects wholly outside of the mind we *eo ipso* render them inaccessible to the mind. Putnam thinks that the mind has access only to its own representa-tions, so that if objects are distinct from mental representations the mind cannot reach out and embrace the objects; and if so, there is nothing the mind can do, so to speak, to select a determinate range of objects as the reference of its cognitive acts.

To this line of thought one is inclined to make a short and unsympathetic reply: namely, that an object does not need to be (literally) *in* the mind in order for it to be capable of coming *before* the mind. Do we not simply *see* objects, objects that would exist whether we saw them or not, even though (of course) such objects are not constituents of our minds? The puzzle is to understand why Putnam seemingly commits this non sequitur. I suspect he would say that in perception the mind has access to objects only as repre-sented in a certain way, so the short reply has not made sense of the idea of thought about mind-independent objects. But this would be to make the same mistake Berkeley made when arguing that to be is to be perceived. It does not follow from the fact that whenever we conceive of an object the object is conceived that we cannot conceive of what it would be for an object to exist *unconceived*, since our conceiving of the object need not be part of the content of what we conceive—as when we think of objects as they were before anyone had thought about them. Similarly, what we see need not be mind-dependent just because our seeing it is.

Putnam is clearer about his reasons for doubting the uniqueness of reference (though he tends to conflate this question with the question of whether *truth* is to be explained in terms of correspondence). His doubts have two sources: the difficulty of finding any suitable relation that could constitute determinate reference; and a technical result in formal logic (the Löwenheim-Skolem theorem) which appears to show that reference can float free of more global properties of a theory (a similar claim has been made by Donald Davidson and John Wallace). One natural reply to these doubts appeals to the relation of causation as what glues words to things in the world. Putnam dismisses this reply: his objection to it is that either it is the claim that our use of the word "causation" fixes the interpretation of "refers," in which case it simply raises the same question about *that* word; or it is the claim that it is in the nature of causation itself that it determines reference, in which case it is a pernicious form of "medieval essentialism."

Now, plainly, the first version of the causal reply is a nonstarter, for the reason Putnam gives, but his quick dismissal of the second version seems unpersuasive. For consider *any* question about the uniqueness and determinacy of a relation—spatial or familial relations, say—and try applying Putnam's arguments. Certainly our use of words for these relations will not settle their identity if the words have indeterminate reference; but why should it be thought objectionable "medieval essentialism" to take these relations as primitive features of the world, or to reduce them to other such relations? Putnam's dilemmatic argument thus appears to prove too much: it threatens to make *all* relations indeterminate. I would suggest that it is at least the beginning of a reply to Putnam to see linguistic reference as constrained by more basic natural relations in which one stands to one's environment—acting upon it, being acted upon by it, having one's goals fulfilled by objects in it, and so on. Perhaps Putnam's difficulties stem from assuming an over-"intellectualist" conception of reference; the problem starts to look less real when we remember the representational states of animals and infants.

The view with which Putnam would supplant metaphysical realism he labels "internal realism." Internal realism regards truth as not transcending idealized justification (hence "internal") while insisting that there is more to truth than believed truth (hence "realism"). Thus the normativeness of truth is preserved, along with its transcendence of what is presently assertible, while the metaphysical realist's conception of truth as quite independent of our capacities for justification is repudiated ("external antirealism" would I think be an equally apt name for this view).

Internal realism is unfortunately somewhat undercharacterized by Putnam, and it invites questions he does little or nothing to answer. The crucial question concerns the nature of the idealization: does he intend the idealization to be over our actual capacities for verification, or does he mean to abstract away from these to the condition of some kind of ideal knower? The indications are that he means the former, in which case there is a threat of an unacceptable relativism in the resulting notion of truth, since what is (is not) justifiable by the exercise of our actual capacities may not (may) be justifiable by the exercise of capacities possessed by other knowing beings—in other words, truth becomes relative to a species. According to internal realism, man is the measure of all things, but Martians and monkeys have their own measures, and the measures might give different results. But if Putnam wishes to avoid such relativism in the notion of truth, by prescinding from our actual capacities for knowledge, he will run the risk of rendering his position vacuous: if God is the shape the idealization takes, then it is not clear that this is not metaphysical realism by another name. It seems to me that this is a dilemma any equation of truth with justification must confront, and Putnam says nothing to show how internal realism escapes being impaled on it.

Putnam makes some surprising claims about the relation between metaphysical realism and the concept of necessity (notably in "Why There Isn't a Ready-made World"). He tells us that a consistent metaphysical realist cannot reject essential properties because such a realist needs to hold that there is an essential or intrinsic relation between thought and its objects. Putnam's reason for saying this is, apparently, that the metaphysical realist requires something ("metaphysical glue") to tie words and concepts to things outside the mind. I see no force whatever in this contention: what the metaphysical realist requires (as Putnam here describes him) is just uniqueness, not necessity—something that singles a reference relation out in the actual world. That our thoughts could have different objects in other possible worlds does not show that they fail to have unique reference in the actual world.

This puzzling claim is followed up with the suggestion that the most prominent contemporary form of metaphysical realism, namely, materialism, is incompatible with an objectivist conception of necessity—indeed that it is incompatible with the notion of objective causal explanation. This incompatibility is supposed to follow from the (alleged) fact that these concepts are not strictly definable in the vocabulary of physics—terms for mass, charge, and so on. But that is surely an unreasonable demand to impose upon the materialist: it would prevent him employing arithmetical concepts, or temporal concepts, or indeed the concepts of ordinary logic. What the materialist characteristically holds is that there are no irreducibly mental (including semantic) facts; he is under no obligation to provide a physicalist definition of *every* concept to which he appeals. Thus a materialist will typically claim that all events have physical causes and that everything has a physical explanation; he does not need to make the further claim that causation and explanation themselves have strict physical definitions.

Not all of this book is concerned with realism; it also treats of reason. And here too Putnam has changed his views: he used to hold (with Quine) that no propositions are rationally unrevisable—anything we now believe we can envisage rationally giving up as theory develops. Now Putnam is prepared to allow that there are absolutely unrevisable beliefs, notably the minimal principle of noncontradiction, "not every proposition is both true and false." To give up this principle would simply be to cease to reason, so there is no sense in the idea of rationally abandoning the principle. This certainly seems to me like a step in the right direction, though it must be said that Putnam offers rather little in the way of a detailed articulation of why reason should enjoy such absolute presuppositions. (This type of unrevisability thesis has also been put forward and developed by the Danish philosopher Peter Zinkernagel, but Putnam evidently does not know of his work.)

Putnam's new views are manifestly still in their formative phase, it is to be hoped that future work will clarify and sharpen his position, but I suspect that once the process of critical reflection has been pushed further, we shall witness yet another change of view.

23

Chomsky: Rules and Representations

Rules and Representations
by Noam Chomsky
Columbia University Press, 1980

Chomsky's new book restates, and somewhat amplifies, the contentions about language for which he is renowned. Its six chapters record (with modifications) sundry lectures given by Chomsky over the last five years. Perhaps inevitably, given their provenance, the chapters are exceedingly repetitious, and it is doubtful whether a lesser figure could have got away with this degree of underediting. Nevertheless, there is much interesting material here, and repetition has a way of sinking in. Besides, Chomsky might offer the excuse that some people never learn. My own opinion is that on some issues Chomsky clearly has the better of his critics, but there are others on which there are deeper and subtler worries behind objections whose typical formulation allows Chomsky's untroubled dismissals. Matters are philosophically and methodologically less clear-cut than he acknowledges. I shall divide my remarks into two parts, the first logically prior to the second, trying to spell out the deeper worries alluded to.

Psychological Reality

Chomsky repeatedly insists that linguistic theories, in particular generative grammars, be accorded the same realist significance as is standardly ascribed to theories of natural science; he opposes what he calls "the bifurcation thesis" as between cognitive psychology and (say) physics. Thus he urges that

Reprinted with permission from the *Journal of Philosophy* (April 1983).

a description of a grammar for a natural language *is* a theory of the cognitive structures in the possession of which linguistic competence consists: its rules are held to be represented somewhere in the speaker, so that a candidate grammar is true or false according as it does or does not correspond to those internally represented rules and principles. Chomsky challenges those who deny this to explain why it is that psychology should be methodologically different from natural science—to explain why studying linguistic competence on the basis of performance data is not analogous to studying thermonuclear reactions within the sun on the basis of data relating to its surface. In both cases our aim, he thinks, is to contrive true theories of the properties of unobservables, guided by rather limited empirical evidence. Let me distinguish three Chomskian theses here, of ascending strength, and then try to articulate the source of what seem to me reasonable qualms about the claim to psychological reality. The theses are (1) that a grammar characterizes an internal structure of representations and computational principles; (2) that this structure belongs to the *mind* of the speaker; and (3) that the structure is the object of propositional attitudes on the part of the speaker, specifically that he *knows* the propositions of grammar, particular and universal.

Thesis 1 is the least controversial and should, I think, be accepted. As Chomsky emphasizes, the case of grammar seems comparable with that of vision: recent empirical work has postulated a complex system of "feature detectors" implicated in the processing of visual information, to which it would be unreasonable to deny psychological reality of some sort; and the abstract structures of grammar seem equally good candidates as mechanisms involved in processing linguistic material, in hearing or speech. However, I think he underestimates the difficulty of immediately interpreting a grammar as a piece of psycholinguistics. He says that there can be no genuine distinction between the "goodness" of a grammatical theory and its correctness as an account of the actual principles of linguistic competence—as a theory of what goes on in the speaker. But surely, as I think Chomsky would agree, it is *possible* to approach the task of constructing a generative grammar with different aims in mind, and with respect to those aims the theory may be good, yet neither intended nor construable as psychological theorizing. Compare devising a logical system or proof procedure for some area of logic, say, first-order quantification theory. One may aim at a system that is sound and complete with respect to first-order validity (generate all and only the valid formulas) yet refrain from any suggestion that the system characterizes the mechanisms or principles whereby people reason; one's criteria of success may not (though they may) bear on psychological reality. Or again, one may devise a set-theoretic account of arithmetic and be indifferent with respect to its psychological reality. Similarly, it seems that a linguist could set himself the goal of devising a grammar capable of generating all and only the grammatical strings of some language and not commit himself on the matter of psychology. But then, if you *can* achieve the aims in question without venturing into psycholinguistics, it appears that the criteria of success for the enterprise do not *themselves* verify the psychological imputation; extraneous evidence will need to be invoked. Perhaps grammar differs from logic and arithmetic in some crucial respect here, but Chomsky needs to tell us what it is. What seems to me true is that grammar can legitimately be taken as a psychological theory of competence, but it requires empirical underpinning from considerations external to simply characterizing (however illuminatingly) grammaticality for the language in question. (In this respect we have a disanalogy with the case of vision.)

Thesis 2 raises some difficult issues, to which Chomsky does not seem sufficiently sensitive. It is plainly not entailed by (1), or else far too much would be mental—computers, retinas, and digestive systems, for example. What is wanted is some criterion for when a system of representation and computation is genuinely part of the mind. Chomsky rejects (as he must) the idea that the criterion is accessibility to consciousness, but he does not really offer any alternative suggestion. His tacit criterion, I suspect, is not that of *accessibility* to consciousness but rather systematic *interaction* with conscious knowledge, that is, being part of a mechanism whose operations explain what goes on consciously. However, this criterion is far from clear and precise: for, again, there is the danger that too much will count as mental—digestive mechanisms and retinal processing again seem to meet the criterion. One feels, perhaps, that grammatical rules, even those of universal grammar, are somehow closer to what is authentically mental—are more intimately bound up with it—but the issue clearly demands Chomsky's consideration. What may move Chomsky to be so cavalier on the issue is the conviction that such questions are of little relevance to the project of constructing models in cognitive psychology. That may well be so, but a philosophical (or indeed commonsense) account of the boundaries of the mind needs to respect distinctions insignificant to the cognitive psychologist. So I do not think that Chomsky has yet demonstrated his right to the claim that generative grammars have properly *mental* reality.

Thesis 3 is, *a fortiori*, disputable. Hoping to evade philosophers' doubts about attributing knowledge of grammatical rules, Chomsky introduces the word "cognize," which he glosses as "tacit" or "implicit" knowledge. He could make it easier for himself by claiming that linguistic knowledge is knowledge-how, a capacity conferred by (inter alia) an internally represented grammar; but no, he wishes to assert that there is *propositional* knowledge of (all) the grammatical rules that characterize a language. He tries to render this less outrageous by observing that, in his usage, a missile guided by a program embodying an astronomical theory cognizes various facts about its flight path. But this only makes it illicit to gloss "cognize" as "tacit *knowledge*." Either "cognize" means "know," in which case it is no improvement on the original strong claim; or it does not mean "know," in which case it cannot be glossed as "tacit knowledge" (unless "tacit" is intended as a privative adjective!). I cannot see that Chomsky's persistence in describing the internal representations as knowledge, in his attenuated sense, really adds anything to the bare thesis that grammar is internally represented. If he stuck to the ordinary full-blooded concept of knowledge, he would have the obligation to explain how the characteristic features of *belief* apply in respect of grammar. And would he be prepared to say that the abstract principles involved in vision were objects of the perceiver's beliefs? The correct description of the matter seems to me to be just this: a speaker knows a language—in particular, he knows that certain strings are grammatical—in virtue of possessing an internal representation of its grammar, the principles of which are not themselves known and are only dubiously part of the content of his mind. This formulation does not seem to sacrifice anything essential to Chomsky's conception of psycholinguistics; his stronger claims seem to me gratuitous and implausible.

Chomsky makes a number of other questionable claims about psychological reality. He is anxious to distinguish firmly between the capacity to use language and the "structured vehicle" that underlies this capacity; competence consists only in the latter, and so does not imply ability. Here I think he has been misled by his opponents. There are indeed those who wish to characterize mastery of a language as a bare capacity, devoid of structured basis in the speaker. I would agree with Chomsky that this is wrong, but the proper response is not to deny that competence is a capacity or ability or disposition; what should be rejected is the view of mental capacities that such people presuppose. To attribute a linguistic capacity *is* to impute an underlying categorical basis—a "structured vehicle"; just as to attribute a physical disposition, say fragility, is to commit oneself to the presence of an underlying categorical basis. Chomsky alleges an opposition between these two perspectives on competence (as distinct from a certain view of what the perspectives involve) because he fails (oddly) to appreciate that all dispositions have their enabling conditions. Thus he has us consider a motor aphasic whose speech centers are intact: such a one would, he says, have competence but not the ability to engage in linguistic behavior. You might as well argue that being a solvent does not consist in a capacity or disposition to dissolve things, on the ground that solvents cannot dissolve things when frozen, that is, will not manifest the disposition when the enabling conditions, normally taken as read, do not obtain. Chomsky's position is better put as the thesis that linguistic competence is an ability whose categorical basis ("structured vehicle") is an internally represented grammar.

The issue of Quinean indeterminacy is touched upon *en passant*. Chomsky is impatient with the thesis, insisting that it amounts to nothing more than a special case of empirical underdetermination of theory, with no antirealist significance independent of the bifurcation thesis, already rebutted. One might sympathize with Chomsky's view that the considerations advanced in support of indeterminacy do not imply the no-fact-of-the-matter claim, without agreeing that those considerations indicate mere empirical underdetermination, analogous to what we find in (say) solar physics. For it is arguable that the inability of behavioral dispositions to fix mental facts reflects something important and peculiar about the relation between mental and physical facts, something not assimilable to the relation between homogeneous sets of facts such as we find in the astrophysical example. Cases of inverted qualia seem to show that mental facts are radically independent of functional-behavioral facts; and Quinean permutations of propositional attitudes and meanings might be similarly viewed. At least it is not obvious that such failure of determination is a matter of mere evidential exiguity. Chomsky also misses the point of those (e.g., Dummett) who require meaning to be publicly mani-festable: he asks, rhetorically, why meaning should meet this condition and mental images (say) not. The answer would be that meaning, in contrast to some other aspects of our psychological life, cannot consist in what is hidden from view, or else it could not be a communicable object of knowledge. This requirement on meaning may be unacceptable, but the issue is not settled simply by a general endorsement of psychological unobservables.

Chomsky's analogy with solar physics invites scrutiny on another score. As he at one point acknowledges (p. 197), the theoretical entities and properties invoked in that case and in the case of grammar are rather different in character: in the linguistic case, we are imputing *abstract* conditions and structures to the speaker, not themselves physical but presumably instanti-ated somewhere in the brain; in the astrophysical case, we are dealing in actual physical entities and processes. Now this asymmetry may have greater significance than Chomsky recognizes, since it appears to require us to inter-pret the explanatory force of the theoretical terms in the respective theories somewhat differently: in the astrophysical case, we have causally operative unobservables conforming to causal laws; but in the linguistic case the rules of grammar do not seem to enjoy that status—such abstract conditions will not enter causal explanations in any straightforward way. This is not (yet) to say that grammatical representations are any less real than physical unob-servables, but it does make it intelligible why someone should hold that grammars are more descriptive than explanatory. I am not at all sure what should be said of the theoretical and explanatory status of abstract rules of grammar, but it does seem that there is a real question here about that in virtue of which grammars enter into the explanation of behavior: along with different levels of description we might have to recognize different types of theoretical explanation. This issue connects with Chomsky's view of the rela-tion between internal grammar and the brain, about which he seems not entirely clear. In response to the asymmetry just mentioned, he has recourse to the in-principle availability of the neurophysiological facts underlying grammatical competence. This would help remove the asymmetry if gram-mar were *reducible* to neurophysiology, for then the difference from the astrophysical case would come down to a merely empirical-ethical infea-sibility. But Chomsky elsewhere indicates that he does not believe in such reducibility, as in his reference to variable physical realization of internal grammar (p. 226). So it is *not* just a matter of practical infeasibility, but of the very nature of the facts in question. As the functionalist literature has made

plain, the level of description occupied by grammar corresponds to an irreducible species of fact. Symmetry with the physical case cannot then be
restored by gesturing in the direction of future neurophysiology. Once
again, the issue of psychological reality is subtler than Chomsky allows—
which is not to say that he is wrong on the central point.

Ontogenesis of Language

Innateness is the other major theme of *Rules and Representations*. Chomsky's
chief argument for the thesis that universal grammar is encoded in the
genetic program of human beings is from "the poverty of the stimulus":
grammatical rules are so highly detailed and specific as to be unextractable
by standard mechanisms of learning from the linguistic data to which the
child is exposed. In order to bridge the gulf between stimulus and mature
competence we therefore need to postulate a rich system of articulate linguistic principles built into the child's genes; this system grows and matures with
the triggering (and partially shaping) effect of linguistic experience. The
development of the language faculty is thus comparable with the development of physical organs of the body: like them, language (more strictly,
grammar) grows according to restrictive innate principles, and is not literally
learned at all. This conception of the ontogenesis of the language faculty has
the consequence that the mind (in its cognitive part) is modular in structure,
comprising separate and variously organized subsystems interacting in the
production of observable behavior. The initial state of our cognitive apparatus is neither simple and unstructured nor uniform and indefinitely plas-
tic. Accordingly, what makes us able to know as much as we do also and
thereby imposes limits on the potential scope of our knowledge and understanding.

All this is very interesting, and by no means obviously false: it is, as
Chomsky insists, an empirical question whether our cognitive apparatus is
thus modular and genetically preset. Moreover, he is surely right to assert
that classical learning theory is powerless to account for the cognitive systems
we attain. However, I think that he presents us with a specious dilemma: for
there is a third account of language acquisition, different from both classical
learning theory and Chomskian innateness, which seems to me to have notable merits. In the remainder of this review I shall try to outline this neglected
alternative, comparing it with Chomsky's own position.

Suppose we were out to explain how a scientist attains the cognitive state
of knowing a theory that massively transcends what has been given in his
experience of the phenomena with which the theory is concerned—say a
theory of the interior of the atom. Plainly, the acquired cognitive system
could not be explained as the outcome of the operation of classical learning
mechanisms; the poverty of the stimulus ensures that. But now should we
take the Chomskian line and account for the gap between theory and evi-

dence by supposing that the propositions of atomic theory are innately present in the scientist's genes? It is not, presumably, logically impossible that this should be the case (though hardly likely from an evolutionary point of view), but the assumption is surely extravagant and unnecessary; and Chomsky seems at one point to agree.[1] The natural suggestion here is that the final cognitive state is the result of intellectual *creativity*, the production of hypotheses seemingly *ex nihilo*. That is, the scientist has a faculty of creativity that enables him to generate hypotheses "from his own resources," but this is not a matter of the hypotheses being latently present, awaiting the merely triggering effect of experience. Chomsky speculates (p. 250) that there may be some innate principles at work in our "science-forming capacities," but to the extent that there is transcendence of stimulus that is not to be thus explained, to that extent we need to invoke a creative faculty. And once ingress is given to such a method of knowledge acquisition, the question presses as to whether the same method is more generally exploited. In particular, might not language acquisition be correctly explained in terms of such creative hypothesis generation? What is strikingly absent from Chomsky's discussion of these matters is any recognition that there is such an alternative to the two types of theory he canvasses. Somewhat on the model (but see below) of the creative scientist, we might conceive of the child as possessed of the capacity creatively to generate grammatical hypotheses about the language spoken around him, testing these in his own speech and by observing the speech of others. The child is said to have acquired mature linguistic competence when his grammatical hypotheses have reached maximum predictive and explanatory power. The rules of grammar, on this suggestion, would be no more innate than the propositions of quantum physics. Let me now mention some of the advantages, possible vulnerabilities, and consequences of this sort of approach.

It should first be observed that the issue between the innateness and creativity proposals concerns an empirical question of fact, though there are certainly questions of principle and initial plausibility that can be raised. The question of fact is this: is the language faculty creative in character, like (at least some aspects of) the science-forming faculty; or is it passive in the sense that its final state contains nothing that was not either initially present or given in experience? How to adjudicate empirically between the two proposals is a further question, but one can imagine the kind of evidence that might be brought to bear. If we could observe a child of our own species brought up in the linguistic community of another species (say Martians), that would afford differentiating evidence: if the language of Martians, with a different species-specific universal grammar, were as easy for the human

---

[1] He remarks that "scientific knowledge does not grow in the mind of someone placed in an appropriate environment" (p. 140), adding that the study of human knowledge should allow for "abductive" theory construction as well as innate predetermination and environmental shaping.

child to learn as a human language (other things equal), that would suggest that there is no restrictive innate schematism of the sort envisaged by Chomsky. Less fancifully and more positively, if the child were observed to make grammatical mistakes, at the level of universal grammar, which were not accountable to performance deficiencies, this would be some evidence for the suggestion that he was trying out interim grammars for confirmation and modifying them accordingly; excluding performance factors, such mistakes would not be predicted by the innateness proposal. None of this would be conclusive, but it does at least indicate the kinds of consideration that might help decide between the proposals.

One point that seems to me already to favor the creativity proposal concerns the connection between knowledge and justification. Chomsky considers the following objection to his view of linguistic knowledge: if competence had the ontogenesis he suggests, then it would have no justification or grounds and so could not properly qualify as knowledge. His reply to this objection is to deny that knowledge requires grounds; it is better conceived simply in terms of "mental structures." But the creativity proposal can accommodate our talk of knowledge and learning here without such revisionism: linguistic knowledge will rest upon an internal theory (a grammar) of the speech to which the child has been exposed and will receive its justification from its success in coping with the linguistic data. I conjecture that we think of children as learning language and knowing what is grammatical because we inchoately recognize that they are engaged upon the enterprise of constructing a theory of the linguistic data provided by adults.

The creativity proposal, as I have hitherto formulated it, faces an obvious objection: if that is the way grammar is acquired, then children should know grammar in just the way a scientist knows the laws of quantum physics; but, by my own showing, they do not—constructing an explicit grammar is not child's play. This is a serious objection, but I do not think it is unanswerable: what we need is a notion of subdoxastic hypothesis formation. The child does not, it is true, undertake conscious and deliberate theory construction; yet he may be so constituted as to generate hypotheses at an unconscious, indeed subdoxastic, level. Here we might appeal to an analogy with what some psychologists say about vision. They say that the visual system generates hypotheses about the presented array which determine how things are seen (what they are seen as); this is done on the basis of scanty visual cues, and the process is wholly unconscious.[2] How this capacity to interpret visual arrays in terms of hypotheses comes about in the course of ontogenesis is not generally accessible to the individual's consciousness; it is, in the relevant sense, an exercise of subdoxastic creativity. Somewhat so, we might postulate a similar capacity relating to what is heard: sentences may be heard as grammatical or ungrammatical according as they conform to the grammar that has been

[2] See, e.g., R. L. Gregory, *The Intelligent Eye* (New York: McGraw-Hill, 1970).

generated. At any rate, it does not seem to me obviously absurd to postulate such unconscious creativity. Nor could Chomsky very well lodge this type of objection to the creativity proposal, given his own liberality with unconscious cognitive processes.

There is a second, deeper, objection of principle, which I suspect is influencing Chomsky. It may well be felt that there is something profoundly problematic and mysterious about creativity; this feeling expresses itself in the idea, common to rationalists and empiricists alike, that in cognitive development nothing comes from nothing. It may be this idea that prompts Chomsky to pass over the kind of account under consideration. I am inclined to agree that creativity is something of a mystery, into whose workings we have no real insight, but I do not think this is a good reason to reject the proposal. First, it seems that we have to accept such creative emergence of cognitive systems in other areas—notably in the sciences and arts. Second, Chomsky is in no position to accuse the proposal of mystery-mongering, because he himself is keen to point to areas in which there are similar mysteries, for example, the phenomenon of free choice. Indeed, he employs the idea of creativity, admitted to be a mystery, in characterizing linguistic *performance;* so he cannot reject it as a matter of principle with respect to the ontogenesis of linguistic *competence.* It is curious that he does not seriously think to apply the notion of cognitive creativity to the acquisition of knowledge, linguistic and other.[3]

Chomsky derives the following consequences from the innateness hypothesis: that our cognitive apparatus is modular; that it has inherent limits; that cognitive systems "grow" rather than result from learning. The creativity

[3] Chomsky has reminded me (in correspondence) that he does consider and reject such a hypothesis-generation account in earlier publications, e.g., *Reflections on Language* (New York: Pantheon, 1975). The ground of his rejection is the significant qualitative difference between language acquisition and the developments of (say) physics with respect to speed of acquisition, general intelligence, and application required, and uniformity of final state. These differences must be admitted, but it is unclear (to me) how much weight should be attached to them. I am inclined to suspect that human beings are capable of different *kinds* of "creativity," and that we may be predisposed to generate hypotheses at a subdoxastic level during certain "sensitive periods" of ontogenesis. This has been claimed of the visual system; but it also appears that we need to invoke such a capacity to explain the acquisition of *particular* grammar, for the following reason. The rules of language-specific grammar are not (I believe) held by Chomsky to be innate, but, equally, they are not extractable from the stimulus by classical mechanisms of learning: they are complex to state explicitly and not easily assimilated at a conscious level later in life (try learning Finnish). So some third method of grammar acquisition has to be attributed to the child to account for its eventual competence in particular grammar; and hypothesis generation seems to be the natural suggestion. If so, we are anyway compelled to recognize a species of "creativity" implicated in language acquisition that differs importantly from that involved in the construction of scientific theories; and then the question is whether *universal* grammar might not be similarly acquired. At any rate, I do not think we should rush dogmatically to dismiss the creativity proposal just because language acquisition does not exactly duplicate the development of physics.

proposal has contrasting implications. Since it does not impute a rich structure of genetically fixed principles, it does not immediately imply any initial modularity. Perhaps there are discrete creative faculties, but this is not required by the proposal and seems gratuitous in the light of it. By the same token, the kinds of limits to knowledge and understanding contemplated by Chomsky will not be imposed: innate principles seem inherently restrictive, but a creative faculty is quite the opposite. This is not, of course, to say that there are no limits on human knowledge, but it suggests that such limits as there are will consist in *general* factors—finite storage or information-processing capacity, say—rather than exclude certain sorts of subject matter, for example, Martian grammar. Lastly, the metaphor (or literalism) of endogenously controlled growth will seem inappropriate; for there would be no preset genetic program fixing the specific shape and content that the language faculty will assume.

I have dwelt at some length on this alternative to Chomsky's own innateness hypothesis because it seems to me to offer the strongest challenge to his doctrines, a challenge he regrettably does not take up in the book under review. To what extent the alternative can be sustained, in principle or empirically, I do not know; but it should, at least, be given a chance.

Chomsky's use of italics invites censure from a logical point of view. He is prone to employ such locutions as "the meaning *John exploited Bill*" and "the meaning *die*" (p. 150); and it is unclear how he intends the italicized portions. There seem two possible interpretations. He might really be using italics to form designations of "meanings," so that the cited locutions have the logical form of a functor applied to a singular term denoting a meaning. Or he might be using italics simply as equivalent to quotation, so that the locutions are effectively translational in purport. In fact he seems to use italics ambiguously between such meaning specifications and ordinary quotation; and he appears also to treat these locutions and the form "the meaning of '. . .' " interchangeably (as at p. 151). If he intends the quotational reading throughout, then the meaning theory he is presupposing has the form of a translation manual. If on the other hand he intends italicization to form the name of a meaning, as I suspect he does, at least sometimes, then we need to be clearer about how this device is to be understood and about the form of the background theory of meaning. These questions, much discussed in recent philosophical work (e.g., by Davidson) on the proper form of a meaning theory, are essential for an adequate understanding of how meaning specifications are to be presented; but they do not seem to have made any impression on Chomsky—at least if his use of italics is symptomatic.

24

Quine: Theories and Things

Theories and Things
by W. V. Quine
Belknap Press of Harvard University
1981

Quine's latest collection of essays is somewhat of a miscellany: it ranges from the strictly logical, through the narrowly philosophical, to the accessibly popular. The slighter essays make for enjoyable reading, displaying Quine's flawless prose to good effect, while the weightier essays helpfully clarify and extend his already familiar doctrines. In this review I shall comment critically upon some of these doctrines as thus clarified and extended, in the hope that the issues, and Quine's stand on them, will come into sharper focus.

The opening essay, "Things and Their Place in Theories," begins, strikingly enough, with this sentence: "Our talk of external things, our very notion of things, is just a conceptual apparatus that helps us to foresee and control the triggering of our sensory receptors in the light of previous triggering of our sensory receptors" (p. 1). This conception of the point and payoff of referring to objects, in both ordinary talk and theoretical science, is recognizably <u>pragmatist in spirit</u>: saying what there is is wielding an instrument whose function it is to predict and control certain events ("sensory triggerings") in the speaker. Such a conception would not, of course, be shared by all philosophers of science. Those who conceive the task of science as telling how the world is objectively constituted, independently of how it strikes human beings, would be offended by the anthropocentric orientation of Quine's formulation: scientific theories may indeed be *based* upon sensory stimulations, but it would (for these philosophers) be a distortion of the

Reprinted with permission from the *Journal of Philosophy* (April 1983).

intended objectivity of science to regard it as *aiming* at "developing systematic connections between our sensory stimulations" (p. 2). The instrumentalism present in Quine's conception of the purpose of speaking of objects is
strengthened by a further Quinean thesis: this is the thesis that there exist
"proxy functions" that enable us so to reinterpret the ontology of a theory as
to leave verbal behavior and empirical content undisturbed. The lesson
proxy functions teach us, according to Quine, is that reference is inscrutable,
ontology relative, and that the "structure" of a theory is all that ultimately
matters. So not only is science a mere contrivance for linking sensory stimulations, but there are indefinitely many alternative contrivances which do the
linking job equally well. Which objects we speak of thus appears to become in
the end a matter of arbitrary decision, not to be settled by considerations of
simplicity or other canons of scientific method. One's ontology accordingly
comes to seem an inconsequential and wavering affair, in contrast to the
stability and fixedness of the sensory stimulations it is the business of ontology to organize.

But now we are brought up short, for Quine goes on to insist upon his
"unswerving belief in external things—people, nerve endings, sticks, stones,"
declaring himself in favor of "robust realism" (p. 21). Evidently, Quine
wishes to combine instrumentalism with realism: arriving at a theory of the
world is choosing from among a plurality of equally serviceable devices for
coping with the data, but once a device has been chosen, however arbitrarily,
there is no shirking the existential commitments of the chosen device. As he
remarks of ontological commitment to abstract entities, "to view classes,
numbers, and the rest in this instrumental way is not to deny having reified
them; it is only to explain why" (p. 15). Now on the face of it there is an
obvious tension between these two views, since the instrumentalist thesis
would seem to nullify the seriousness of our talk of objects—and Quine is by
no means insensitive to this apparent tension. In reply to the question how
these two strands in his philosophy are to be reconciled, he tells us that it is
"naturalism" that renders them consonant, "the recognition that it is within
science itself, and not in some prior philosophy, that reality is to be identified
and described" (p. 21). Grasping how it is that naturalism reconciles instrumentalism and realism is thus the key to understanding Quine's philosophy.
As I see it, the idea is that we must accept *some* theory—there being no
theory-neutral conception of the world—and we can comfortably acquiesce
in the theory we were brought up to accept, the theory we were accustomed
to before the proxy functions undermined our naive confidence in ontological uniqueness. The role of naturalism in permitting ontological complacency in the face of ontological scepticism reminds one of Hume's treatment
of our belief in "external bodies." For it was Hume's naturalism that (allegedly) defused the implications of his sceptical arguments concerning the
external world: instead of our received beliefs being devastated by scepticism, we naturally and inevitably cling to them; and this is as it should be. But
if the comparison of Quine's naturalism with Hume's is illuminating, it is also

disquieting; for just as Hume's naturalism fails to provide any *rational* release from his scepticism, so Quine's naturalism leaves us wondering how our habitual ontology and "robust realism" can rationally withstand the impact of the scepticism generated by his pluralistic instrumentalism. Inasmuch as Quine is attacking a naive attitude we have toward our talk of external things, he is undermining the confidence we commonly repose in such talk: sceptical reflections at the philosophical level thus make themselves felt at the ground level of ordinary belief, whether common sense or scientific. Pending a good answer to the question how naturalism and the "immanence of truth" manage to *justify* our habitual ontology and exclude the deviant ontologies delivered by proxy functions, I cannot see how Quine's realism is ultimately to be squared with his relativistic instrumentalism. (Perhaps there are philosophical perspectives of a Kantian cast that allow such a conjunction of views, but I doubt that Quine would be happy to rest his philosophy on such Kantianism.)

In "Two Dogmas" what lay at the periphery of the fabric of sentences comprising science was described as "experience"—experience was the tribunal faced by scientific theory. Subsequently, experience gave way to neural input at the sensory receptors: "surface irritations" became the point at which theory made empirical contact with the world. As Quine is careful to explain, he does not *equate* experience with receptor triggerings; rather he offers the triggerings as a naturalistic *surrogate* for experience. Thus sensory triggerings are to do the job assigned by the old empiricists to experience—the tribunal is now the scientist's nerve endings (p. 40). The job of experience was, of course, to provide evidence on which the scientist may reasonably base his beliefs; and Quine makes the same claim on behalf of his physiological surrogate: "By sensory evidence I mean stimulation of sensory receptors" (p. 24). This account of empirical evidence prompts a number of questions, to which I cannot see that Quine has given satisfactory answers.

Perceptual experience, as construed by the old empiricists, had two properties suiting it to the role of evidence: first, its availability to cognition suited it to serve as that on which a scientist might base his beliefs—experience was "given" to the scientist; second, a normative principle, needed for rational inference, was plausibly satisfied by experience, that is, "If you perceive/(or seem to perceive) that *p,* then you ought (*ceteris paribus*) to believe that *p.*" In effect, these are constraints upon anything that can serve as evidence, at least for anyone who calls himself an empiricist; and experience has the virtue of meeting them. But does Quine's surrogate notion meet them? It seems sufficiently obvious that sensory triggerings do not meet the first constraint; for, as Quine himself remarks (p. 40), the scientist typically knows nothing of the physiological processes at his surface that (partially) cause his beliefs. But if such processes are not ordinarily available to cognition, how can they function as evidence upon which beliefs may be based? Quine's surrogate seems to lack the essential property that, in the eyes of the old empiricists, qualified experience as a suitable evidential base. This seems an obvious enough point, but I cannot discover in Quine any response to it. But now suppose the scientist did know of the irritations of his nerve endings: would that knowledge then afford a basis on which to form beliefs about the external world of bodies? Can the scientist say, "Given that my nerve endings are firing thus and so, I ought to believe the world to be such and such"? This seems doubtful, for surface irritations do not have the representational content enjoyed by experience: in perceptual experience the world is represented as being a certain way, but nerve triggerings do not do this in any way that would allow one to derive a belief about the causative state of affairs. In his desire to expel mentalism from empiricism Quine has, in effect, jettisoned the notion of observation from his official story, leaving in its stead surface stimulations and observation sentences defined in terms of such stimulations: but these aseptic materials do not really supply a workable notion of empirical evidence.

The inadequacy of Quine's notion of evidence can be brought out by pressing the following question: why should the physiological processes to which assent to sentences is conditioned be located at the periphery of the nervous system and not further in, say in the afferent nerves or the cortex? Since nerve endings are not (typically) known about by the subject, it cannot be that more central physiological processes would fail to serve as facts suitable as bases for inference: neither sort of process meets the constraint of availability to cognition. But if no relevantly principled distinction between surface irritations and cortical agitations can be demonstrated, then Quine's theory of evidence looks no better off than a theory that invokes central physiological processes as the tribunal faced by theoretical beliefs.

Quine sometimes couples his hostility to experience with his preference for naturalized epistemology, that is, the supplanting of normative "first philosophy" with descriptive genetic epistemology; but it is worth noting that the two doctrines are independent. We can certainly construe epistemology as a chapter of cognitive psychology while retaining the mentalistic notion of experience: instead of divining how the fragmentary neural input is transformed into a full theory of nature, we study how the subject constructs his theory on the basis of what is given in his experience. So we cannot justify insistence on surface irritations as a corollary of the rightness of such a naturalized epistemology.

The point I have been urging about the inadequacy of Quine's conception of evidence has obvious repercussions for his account of meaning. Conformably with his empiricist convictions, Quine takes meaning to be empirical meaning—a matter of the relation of sentences to the evidence that warrants assent to them. But if sensory triggerings do not constitute genuine evidence, then the expressions on which semantic concepts are defined in terms of such triggerings will not come out as endowed with empirical meaning. Observe the contrast with the traditional empiricist's account of meaning: sentences have meaning in virtue of their experiential implications, and they are synonymous just in case they are prompted by the same experiences.

QUINE: THEORIES AND THINGS

Quine's proposal, on the other hand, is that synonymy be understood in terms of a propensity to elicit assent under like surface irritations. The problem here is best seen if we ask, as above, why cortical agitations are not invoked instead: why not say that two sentences are synonymous if they are assented to under the same conditions of cortical agitation? The two definitions seem equally good (or bad) as conditions of cognitive equivalence of sentences, and neither can really claim to be more closely linked with anything recognizable as evidence for assent. In both cases, it is true, assent behavior is causally responsive to the physiological events concerned, central or peripheral; but such responsiveness is plainly not sufficient to license talk of evidence.

The question of the relation between Duhemian holism and Quinean rejection of the analytic/synthetic distinction is addressed in "Five Milestones of Empiricism." Here Quine softens his earlier formulations to what he calls "moderate or relative holism," holding it to be somewhat of an exaggeration to speak as if every observation put total science on trial: "What is important is that we cease to demand or expect of a scientific sentence that it have its own separable empirical meaning" (p. 71). He makes it quite clear that it is acceptance of such holism that leads to the abandonment of the analytic synthetic distinction, rather than the other way about; but there seems to be a gap in the argument. For we can surely agree with the Duhemian thesis that it is only bundles of sentences that get tested by observation and at the same time insist that *some* sentences are immune from empirical test altogether. Quine says that holism "blurs the contrast" between analytic and synthetic sentences; but it is not at all clear that it does—unless we just *assert,* without argument, that Duhemian holism extends to *every* sentence of a theory. Nor should we conclude that the in-principle revisability of every sentence of a theory undermines the distinction between analytic and synthetic sentences, or between a priori and a posteriori truths, since not all cases of revision need have their source in the recalcitrance of experience. I am not clear that Quine does intend Duhemian holism as a strict argument for blurring these alleged distinctions (he says only that the blurring "follows closely on this holism"), but others have supposed as much: anyway, it is a non sequitur as it stands.

Another Quinean thesis that seems wanting in argument at a crucial point is the indeterminacy of translation. In *Word and Object* it was argued that two incompatible schemes of translation might be compatible with all the behavioral dispositions of the speakers under translation. The conclusion drawn was that there is no fact of the matter as to which scheme is correct. This reasoning is open to the objection that there may be internal physical conditions of the speakers that make one scheme true rather than the other: their brains might be in appropriate differentiating states. Then the fact of the matter needed to block indeterminacy would lie in the interior of the speaker's body and not in his dispositions to behavior. Presumably in response to this kind of objection, Quine has taken to formulating his thesis in a way that excludes the claimed possibility: "when I say there is no fact of the matter, as regards, say, the two rival manuals of translation, what I mean is that both manuals are compatible with all the same distributions of states and relations over elementary particles. In a word, they are physically equivalent" (p. 23). This formulation certainly rules out the response to the *Word and Object* formulation just mooted, but it leaves us wondering what the *argument* is for the indeterminacy thesis as so formulated: we need to know *why* the compatibility of two manuals with a given set of behavioral dispositions implies the stronger thesis concerning physical equivalence. Compare the following case: it is argued that there is no (physical) face of the matter about which color experiences someone has, on the ground that two incompatible schemes of color-experience ascription may be compatible with all the same behavioral dispositions (inverted spectra). Clearly such an argument would fail to reach its conclusion, since differentiating internal physical states might be compatible with the same behavioral dispositions. In the same way, Quine's argument for indeterminacy needs shoring up with further (hitherto unspecified) considerations.

There is a helpful essay, "On the Individuation of Attributes," which clarifies Quine's attitude toward classes and attributes in respect of their identity conditions. The individuation of classes is clear once the individuation of their members is, but not otherwise; attributes, however, want in clear identity conditions no matter how well individuated their extensions are. Quine considers and rejects necessary coextensiveness of predicates as a criterion of identity for the expressed attributes, on the ground that modality is too infirm a thing to bear such explanatory weight. He might have objected also on grounds of insufficiency: the determinable attributes expressed by "*x* has a size" and "*x* has a shape" are presumably distinct yet necessarily coextensive, and the same is true of the determinate attributes expressed by "*x* has three sides" and "*x* has three angles." A suggestion Quine does not consider, which makes no (explicit) use of modality and looks fairly promising, is this: two predicates express the same attribute iff they are intersubstitutable in all causal-explanatory contexts (in a sufficiently rich language) *salva veritate;* or, without the appeal to languages, iff the attributes are causally equivalent. I mention this suggestion because Quine at one point (p. 107) remarks upon the possible need of attributes in the theory of causation, immediately adding that the need could be filled only if the individuation question were satisfactorily answered.

At a number of places in *Theories and Things* Quine expresses his distaste for modality and its logic: thus "[a]nalyticity, essence, and modality are not my meat" (p. 116). But it is hard to make out what his reason is. It is not that modal locutions are irreparably tainted with nonextensionality, for in "Intensions Revisited"[1] Quine shows how modality can be delivered from this

---

[1] I have reviewed this article elsewhere (*Philosophia*, July 1982; submitted 1978) and will not repeat here what I said there.

logical impurity. Aside from repeated complaints of "unclarity," which merely invite retorts about one man's clarity, the only substantial point I could find was the suggestion that "the very notion of necessity makes sense to me only relative to context" (p. 121). This suggestion is not, of course, uncontroversial and Quine gives no suasive argument for its truth; but even if it were true, why exactly is it a reason to "write off" modal logic? Is it a good reason to "write off" indexical logic, *à la* Kaplan, that its expressions are relative to context for their interpretation? A modal logician who agreed with Quine about the context-relativity of ascriptions of necessity might, for all Quine has said, interpret his formulas as relative to some parameter, and proceed as before. Here one feels that Quine is casting around for something solid to back up his distaste; but he needs to do more if he wishes to dislodge the modal logician from her calling. (It isn't that I think there are no respectable worries about modality; it is just that *Quine* does not present us with anything looking like a real argument.)

On ontological commitment to abstract entities Quine writes: "The numbers and functions contribute just as genuinely to physical theory as do hypothetical particles" (p. 50). Presumably some reconsideration of this claim will be called for in the light of Hartry Field's *Science without Numbers*.[2]

Quine pursues his philosophical vision with an uncompromising consistency of purpose that makes his doctrines impossible to ignore. You either go with him or define your position in reaction to his. And this is one mark of a great philosopher.

---

[2] Oxford: Blackwell, 1980. Field's claim is that sentences about physical-theoretical entities contribute to physical theory in a radically different way from sentences ostensibly about mathematical entities. It would be interesting to know Quine's reaction to Field's defence of a nominalist interpretation of applied mathematics.

25

Strawson and Warnock: Reputation

The Secret Connection: Causation, Realism,
and David Hume
by Galen Strawson
Oxford, 1989

J. L. Austin
by G. J. Warnock
Routledge, 1989

Philosophical reputations come and go—they surge and gutter—according largely to the prevailing intellectual climate, and are only tenuously tied to the actual merits of the views put forward by the reputand in question. To have a reputation is to have something perishable and fleeting, an imposition from without, no sooner bestowed than withdrawn.

Take the case of David Hume. In the dark days of logical [*sic*] positivism Hume's reputation ran high as the philosopher who first did away with causal necessity; he was thought to have shown that causation consists in nothing, objectively, but constant conjunction: things happen in regular sequences but nothing makes them happen that way. In reality, the cement of the universe consists in nothing over and above the dependable concatenation of separable events. But when positivism quietly expired, and natural necessity regained its lost respectability, Hume's standing correspondingly dipped. The neglected Locke began to seem like the philosopher with the better eye for metaphysical truth, while Hume started to look guilty of trying to deduce metaphysical conclusions from epistemological premises: "if no ideas then no reality."

Now here comes Galen Strawson to argue that Hume has been grievously misrepresented all along: for the real David Hume never denied the objective reality of causal necessity. He firmly believed in it. And so Hume's reputation is set to rise high again. He did not, after all, commit the mistake of

Reprinted with permission from the *London Review of Books* (November 23, 1989).

letting the ideational contents of our minds determine what the world might really contain—though he did indeed think there was a problem about our achieving an adequate grasp of the nature of objective necessary causal relations. Hume, then, is a sceptical realist about causal necessity, contrary to the widely received idealist interpretation; and sceptical realism is a view much favored in this postpositivist era. The positivists were right in their high estimate of Hume, but for exactly the wrong reasons.

J. L. Austin was a philosopher with a legendary reputation. Although he published little, he is revered, especially in Oxford, for his critical acumen, withering good sense, originality, and talent for hitting the nail on the head. He was made White's Professor in Oxford at the tender age of forty. His intellectual powers are said to have struck terror into the hearts of his contemporaries, to the point of deterring some of them from daring to put pen to paper, or mouth to thought. Indeed, it might fairly be said that Austin's reputation depends largely upon his reputation: one tends to hear more about his philosophical reputation than about his philosophical ideas. It therefore comes as a bit of a shock to read Geoffrey Warnock's study. The impression here conveyed is that Austin was almost pathologically incapable of getting anything right. Time and again Warnock has to correct obvious mistakes, apologize for unclarities, expose ground-floor misconceptions. It is all very puzzling. Even as Warnock attempts to celebrate his subject we see the man's reputation sink wanly over the horizon. He may have initiated some fruitful lines of inquiry, later developed by others, but he himself seems to have been unable to pursue these lines with any surefootedness or perspicacity. You begin to understand why he wrote so little. Funny things, reputations. Steer clear of them if you can.

Attend now to a typical causal sequence—say, Mike Tyson's fist colliding with his opponent's jaw and the opponent dropping to the canvas. The blow, we say, caused the fall. Now we can distinguish three views about what this causal connection involves. One claims that there is no kind of necessity relating the events to each other: all that occurs in reality is that one event is succeeded by another. A second view insists that a species of necessity underlies the savagery of the nexus: the opponent *had* to fall, given that his jaw was subject to the force unleashed on it (and the circumstantial conditions were as they were). However, this second view concedes, we cannot know or perceive the nature of this binding necessity: we can assert that it exists but we can have no proper conception of what it ultimately involves. A third view agrees that causal relations carry objective necessitation, but this view is more sanguine about our capacity to understand such necessitation; science can tell us what the nexus depends on, if it is not already clear to common sense. These three views of causation and our access to it may be labeled antirealist, sceptical realist, and naive realist, respectively.

Strawson contends, against the common antirealist interpretation, that Hume believes something like the second view. His main ground for attributing this view to Hume is that Hume repeatedly asserts the view, especially in the *Enquiry*. Thus: "experience only teaches us, how one event constantly follows another; without instructing us in the secret connection, which binds them together, and renders them inseparable"; "we are ignorant of those powers and forces, on which [the] regular course and succession of objects totally depends." Strawson adduces many such quotations, and disposes of rival interpretations of their purport: they are to be taken at face value, not as ironic or as occurring in suppressed *oratio obliqua*. He further contends that this agnostic position chimes better with Hume's strictly noncommittal scepticism about the world beyond our ideas: for such scepticism does not permit him actually to deny that there is necessity in nature. Similarly, Strawson argues, for the self and external objects: all we really know of them is contained in our ideas, which fall short of what we routinely take ourselves to know, and which fail to supply the basis for the kind of understanding claimed by certain rationalist philosophers of the period; but that does not imply that there is nothing more to these things than what is thus contained—quite the opposite. Causal necessity is something in which we do and may continue to believe: it is just that our ideas do not penetrate to its underlying real nature. What Hume objects to, on this interpretation, is not the objective existence of causal necessity: his objection is rather to the epistemological thesis, held by many philosophers of his day, that our minds furnish us with a full grasp of the nature of this necessity. We can reasonably assume that there is such a thing—Hume never doubts it—but we cannot arrive at an understanding of its inner reality.

And the reason we cannot embrace causal necessity in thought, for Hume, is that our ideas are derived from our impressions, and we have no impression from which we could read off the inner workings of objective causation. This thesis of Hume's creates an initial problem for Strawson's interpretation, to which he is acutely sensitive, since it is prima facie hard to see how Hume could consistently believe that something exists and yet deny that we can form any idea of it: how is it possible to formulate this existential thought if its components are not available to the thinking mind? Strawson registers the tension but argues that it can be relieved. The key is to distinguish merely referring to something from having a "positively contentful conception" of it: Hume allows that we have a "relative idea" of causation, which enables us to refer to it; what he denies is that we have any impression-based revelatory conception of the nature of that to which we refer. In this respect, his position mirrors that of Locke and Berkeley and Kant, who also had need of a category of concepts which by their own lights fall short of everything a proper hard-working concept should be: dummy concepts, as it were.

I find Strawson's case for the sceptical realist interpretation thoroughly convincing. The textual evidence for it is well-nigh overwhelming; its consonance with other elements in Hume's philosophy is striking; and the apparent clash with the theory of ideas is satisfactorily deflected. Hume emerges as a commonsense British Kantian. What is surprising is that a reader of the *Enquiry* could ever have run away with the antirealist interpretation. (It should be noted that Strawson does not claim to be alone in interpreting Hume correctly. As he remarks in his preface, others are onto the same interpretation, notably John Wright in his *The Sceptical Realism of David Hume.*) But, as I observed above, a philosopher's actual words are seldom sufficient to deter a reading that fits contemporary orthodoxy (cf. Wittgenstein). I would make only two criticisms of Strawson's otherwise admirable book. First, it is rather repetitive, as if the author feels that it is not enough simply to make his case once and well. I found that my level of credence had stabilized after a couple of restatements (or is it that I, like other philosophers, am easily persuaded that my intellectual heroes think the same things as I do?). Second, he does not appreciate further tension in Hume's overall position—namely, the tension between his tolerance of our natural beliefs and his radical scepticism. It is really not consistent to grant us permission to believe what we naturally do believe and at the same time to insist that we do not know any of the things we commonly take ourselves to know, since one cannot consistently continue to believe what one believes one cannot know. To believe is to hold oneself to know, so one cannot believe what one holds oneself not to know. One can, of course, combine belief in something with an admission that one does not know the nature of that thing, and this is clearly one part of Hume's general thesis: but it is another matter to try to hang on to one's beliefs while acknowledging scepticism with respect to what one claims to know. I have no right to believe in what I know I cannot know.

As to Hume himself, the obvious point of weakness, identified by Strawson, lies in his general theory of ideas. In effect, this theory takes perceptual confrontation as the model of what a good concept ought to be. Hume's concept police discriminate against any putative citizen of the mind that cannot produce sensuous credentials. This theory is doubly mistaken. In the first place, it dogmatically banishes concepts that don't enjoy a perceptual prototype, thus repudiating those of a more "intellective" kind. Secondly, and more damagingly, the theory is wrong even about those concepts for which it was expressly designed—namely, sensuous concepts. As Berkeley noticed, and Wittgenstein rammed home, this picture of concept possession by immediate ostensive confrontation is multiply flawed: no concept can be generated by mere confrontation with what it is a concept of. In fact, all concepts are much more like the kinds of concept Hume officially found defective. From this perspective, then, the concept of causal necessity is as healthy as any concept we have. And so there is nothing in what Hume says to prevent us from going one step farther than him and embracing naive realism about causality: there is causal necessity in the world and we *can* form an adequate conception of it. I therefore see no warrant for Strawson's making the following pessimistic concession to Hume: "It seems that there will always be a sense in which the nature of even the simplest causal interaction is entirely unintelligible to us." Which sense is that, once we have rejected, as Strawson does, Hume's restrictive and discriminatory theory of ideas? Some causal relations may well be unintelligible to us in principle, but why suppose that the unintelligibility is ubiquitous? Is snookerball causation really "entirely unintelligible"? Indeed, if every causal nexus is said to be unintelligible, then the point of declaring some to be so is blunted. One wonders what intelligibility would be if we could get it.

Geoffrey Warnock begins his study of Austin by remarking that "his reputation owed much to his certainly formidable personality," and that "the impression that he made as a philosopher upon those who knew him may be difficult to fully appreciate for those not included in that now diminishing number." Not being one of that number, I can only say that for me the difficulty is real. A certain jaunty contempt is never very far from the surface of his prose, a quality I can imagine intimidating some, but for the most part his arguments lack force and his doctrines are shallowly obscure. His studied casualness too often lapses into mere slapdashery. Warnock lists the defects Austin detected in the work of other philosophers: "carelessness; haste; a persistent tendency to invent and to rely on ill-defined and slippery technical terms; oversimplification; reckless and premature generalization; and perhaps above all, a predilection for ambitious either-or dichotomies." I am sure that Warnock intended no irony here, but the rest of his book is almost a case study in the diagnosis and correction of such faults in Austin himself. Was Austin peculiarly prone to these occupational hazards—and by Freudian projection tended to see them all around him? In any case, the following chapters consist largely of Warnock accusing Austin, evidently correctly, of precisely these failings. Did nobody dare venture these critical points at the time? Did Warnock himself not step in with the objections he now so effectively marshals? Did Austin listen? We are told that he advocated a cooperative approach in philosophy, in which patient criticism would lead to agreement and truth, but it is hard to believe that his own papers were the upshot of such collective efforts: there are just too many things wrong with them.

Take his suggestion that the wrongness of saying, "I know it is so, but I may be wrong," is parallel to the wrongness of saying, "I promise I will, but I may fail": that is, the suggestion that "I know" is, or is akin to, a performative verb. Calling this suggestion "really unprofitable and misguided," Warnock makes a number of simple objections to it. You can sincerely say, "I know," and not know, but you can't do the same with promising. You can say, "He promised to do it, but he won't," but you can't say, "He knows it is so, but it isn't." You can know something without saying, "I know," but you can't do the same with promising. There is in general no conventional or ritualistic setting in which you say, "I know," unlike promising. You do not, as a rule, in saying, "I know," do anything beyond saying so, unlike promising. The explanation of the original datum is just that knowledge implies truth and has nothing specifically to do with speech acts and what they lead audiences to expect. Contrary to Austin's thesis, "I know," unlike "I promise," is as descriptive as any first-person attribution. And, I would add, knowing is not an *act* at all, which precludes its being effected by the utterance of a performative verb. These objections are (a) elementary and (b) definitive. Ten minutes reflection should have made it clear that the assimilation is simply a mistake, prompted by the most superficial of similarities between the two verbs as they (sometimes) occur in the first person.

Austin's paper "Truth" defines truth as follows: "A statement is said to be true when the historic state of affairs to which it is correlated by the demonstrative conventions (the one to which it 'refers') is of a type with which the sentence used in making it is correlated by the descriptive conventions." Warnock struggles to clarify what Austin might have meant by the two kinds of "convention," but it remains unclear whether this is just a confused way of talking about indexicality in natural language, having little to do with truth in general. Certainly the account is hard to extend beyond simple indexical subject-predicate sentences: general statements, hypotheticals, mathematical statements, and analytic truths cannot be forced into the Austinian mould. Isn't this the very kind of overgeneralization on which he heaped scorn? In comparison with Tarski's semantic theory of truth, available at the time he was writing his paper, Austin's version of the correspondence theory looks at best quaint and at worse mired in obscurity and intractable difficulty.

The two chapters on action and ability find Austin frequently unclear, careless of important distinctions, and far too ready to dismiss defensible ideas for inadequate reasons. I mention two examples: his conflation of the question whether it is normally superfluous to append "intentionally" after a verb of action with the question whether it is true to append that adverb; and his not noticing that you can have an ability which you do not successfully exercise every time you try to. Not very difficult points, really.

We turn then, hopefully, to the final long chapter "Words and Deeds," which addresses itself to what is commonly regarded as Austin's most important and enduring work. And indeed his treatment of the performative aspect of speech has been fertile enough, giving rise to what has come to be called "speech act theory." The central idea to begin with is that uses of language are not exclusively "fact-stating": some utterances also enable us to perform actions of various sorts—promising, betting, bequeathing, naming, acquitting, and so forth. We do these things by uttering appropriate indicative sentences, but the sentences (Austin claimed) do not describe us as doing what we thereby do. (Why we cannot do something with language at the same time as describing ourselves as doing just that is never made clear.) So, it initially seems, Austin is directing us to distinguish the "constative" use of language from the performative use: there are two kinds of speech act to consider.

However, as Warnock is at pains to point out, this alleged dichotomy subsequently evaporates into the insistence that all uses of language have a performative aspect. It turns out, on close examination of Austin's text, that he has been roundly conflating at least three different definitions of "performative," and their demonstrable inequivalence ends up pulling the notion in opposite directions, eventually causing its disintegration. There is the notion

of a speech act uttered in a conventional setting, such as a marriage cere-
mony; there is the notion of a speech act that makes its own character explicit; and there is the notion of a speech act in which something is done,
which threatens trivially to include every speech act. It is thus quite unclear
what distinction Austin was endeavoring to capture with his original consta-
tive/performative dichotomy. Not surprisingly, therefore, he abandons in
midstream the attempt to characertize the nature of the distinction and
proceeds to analyze the structure of speech acts in general—distinguishing
the locutionary, illocutionary, and perlocutionary aspects of an utterance.
Here again Warnock is obliged to correct exaggerations, inconsistencies,
slips, confusions—but at least we are now engaged upon an adequately conceived project.

   I have not yet mentioned Austin's noted critique of Ayer in *Sense and
Sensibilia*. This work is almost entirely negative in intention, consisting in
generally convincing demonstrations that Ayer says many false and confused
things about the verb "to see." But what ought now to strike us is Austin's
own propensity, when engaged upon more constructive work, to fall into
comparable traps. As he himself acerbically remarks, discussing Ayer,
"[T]here is nothing so plain boring as the constant repetition of assertions
that are not true, and sometimes not even faintly sensible; if we can reduce
this a bit, it will be all to the good." Boring, yes, and irritating too—though at
least Ayer was trying to tackle hard and deep philosophical questions that
resist ready formulations. It seems to me that Austin, while for the most part
eschewing the traditional questions of philosophy, shows an equal proneness
to falsehood and confusion, and with less excuse.

   His personal charisma must have been powerful indeed, because he wrote
little of lasting value. Perhaps his greatest legacy was his early translation of
Frege's *Foundations of Arithmetic* (from which he seems to have learned little).
Warnock's book has the merit of providing us with a sober and not unsympathetic dismantling of a reputation that has long seemed inflated. Scrupulously courteous as he is to Austin, I cannot help feeling that he is well
aware of the perlocutionary effect his illocutionary acts are likely to have.

26

Sacks: Outpouchings

The Man Who Mistook His Wife for a Hat
by Oliver Sacks
Duckworth, 1985

It could be said that Oliver Sacks put neuropathology on the literary map. His first book, *Awakenings,* about the stunning effects of the drug L-dopa on patients afflicted with a form of Parkinsonism, attracted considerable critical acclaim from the literary world and "inspired" Harold Pinter's rather ponderous play *A Kind of Alaska.* Sack's second book, *A Leg to Stand On,* was similarly well received. He has published a number of short pieces in the *London Review of Books,* as well as in its elder American sibling, several of which are reprinted in the present collection, along with twelve previously unpublished pieces. (His book *Migraine* seems to have excited rather less popular interest, no doubt because it is a less popular kind of book.) Yet the scientists of the nervous system do not seem to have been similarly impressed. When I asked a colleague in neuroanatomy what he thought of Sack's work he said he had never heard of him, and the neuroscientists I consulted who *had* heard of him were not inclined to attach any scientific importance to his writings. Unanimity between the two cultures is nor perhaps to be expected, but in the present case the reason for this asymmetry of esteem lies deeper than mere difference of interest. The problem is that it is quite unclear what Sacks is doing. For whom is he writing? What kind of writing is it? Is it intended as sober science or fanciful fiction? What is its relation to an orthodox text of neuropathology? Can it really be taken seri-

Reprinted with permission from the *London Review of Books* (Januray 23, 1986).

ously? Literary people seem tolerant of such uncertainties, but those concerned to discover the literal truth will want them clarified.

Sacks's procedure is to describe as winningly as possible the case histories (or segments thereof) of various patients with whom he has had personal contact. These are, as it were, recreated before our eyes, like entries in a doctor's diary, rather than being set down once all the data are in. They have tension, surprise, realistic dialogue, resolution, tragic dénouements, touches of humor, epiphanies. The cases are divided into four categories: "Losses," "Excesses," "Transports," "The World of the Simple." Here are some samples from each category. The man who mistook his wife for a hat was a distinguished musician, learned and charming, who had, through damage to his visual cortex, lost the ability to recognize familiar things despite being quite capable of seeing them; he couldn't associate the visual appearance of things with their proper function or identity. Thus he mistook his foot for his shoe, his wife's head for his hat (he tried to put her head on his), and he would puzzle verbosely over ordinary things like gloves ("a continuous surface, infolded on itself. It appears to have five outpouchings, if this is the word"). These failures of recognition may have stemmed from a total loss of the concepts in question or from an inability to apply them to what is seen—it is unclear. Sacks characteristically throws no light on the question, though his data seem to suggest the latter alternative. Instead of approaching the matter in a coolly analytical frame of mind, he prefers to burble on about the "intuitive, personal, comprehensive and concrete" nature of judgment, suggesting that the patient has lost this capacity and then observing (inconsistently) that his judgment was "in all other spheres . . . prompt and normal."

The Lost Mariner, victim of alcoholically induced Korsakov's syndrome, can keep things in his memory only for a matter of seconds and has a retrograde amnesia stretching back thirty years. He has vivid memories of his life before the age of nineteen and thinks this to be his present age. He is shocked by his appearance in the mirror, with which Dr. Sacks brutally confronts him, and (we may presume) has often been so shocked in the last thirty years, each time having the shock erased within seconds. Naturally, his life was one of bewilderment and confusion. Witty Ticcy Ray suffers from Tourette's syndrome, which is characterized by an excess of nervous energy producing "tics, jerks, mannerisms, grimaces, noises, curses, involuntary imitations and compulsions of all sorts, with an odd elfin humor and a tendency to antic and outlandish kinds of play." Ray could not hold down a job (or the job could not hold him down) and his social behavior was found unacceptable, but he exploited his motor mania in jazz drumming and table tennis, at both of which (we are told) he excelled. Sacks put him on Haldol, which initially induced virtual catatonia but later leveled out, bringing him to near motor normality. Now he could keep a job and not upset his friends, but he felt that his tic-free self was less exciting than his old Tourettic self; he had from an early age built his life and personality around his affliction. The solution was to take Haldol during the working week but go cold turkey at the weekend, thus allowing his old manic and excitable self to reemerge. This odd inversion of the usual drug-taker's schedule apparently led to a more balanced and satisfying life for Ray.

A case of transportation is provided by Stephen D., a medical student constantly high on cocaine and amphetamines: he dreamt he was a dog with a dog's olfactory gift, and when he woke up he retained the heightened sense of smell. Now he could smell people's emotions, recognize his friends by their aroma, find his way around New York City with his nose. Three weeks later he reverted, with mixed feelings, to olfactory normal. He had known what it is like to be a dog. The Twins, retarded, misshapen, undersized, severely myopic, nevertheless have remarkable powers of computation, earning them regular television appearances. Say any date during the next forty thousand years and they will tell you instantly on what day of the week it falls. They can remember three-hundred-digit numbers, where most of us are taxed to the limit by seven. They can generate six-figure primes at will and are not defeated by the task of going up to ten figures. Yet their IQs are a mere sixty and they cannot even perform elementary addition and subtraction. They seemed, Sacks reports, to *see* numbers and to read off their properties without performing calculations. When they were separated "for their own good," they lost their mathematical powers and the enjoyment they derived from their exercise.

All this is very striking and remarkable, like strange tales from a fabulous foreign land. Sacks relates his case histories with great vividness and obvious compassion. The book is a fascinating read all right. But doubts assail one on almost every page. There is, first, the question of Sack's prose style. It has been lavishly praised by some critics ("beautifully written"). Lush, belletristic, edifying, competent—this is the best I could say for it. For the most part it is embarrassingly overlyrical, gushing, pretentious, and sentimental. Try saying this out loud with a straight face:

> "Watch Jimmie in chapel," they said, "and judge for yourelf."
> I did, and I was moved, profoundly moved and impressed, because I saw here an intensity and steadiness of attention and concentration that I had never seen before in him or conceived him capable of. I watched him kneel and take the Sacrament on his tongue, and could not doubt the fullness and totality of Communion, the perfect alignment of his spirit with the spirit of the Mass. Fully, intensely, quietly, in the quietude of absolute concentration and attention, he entered and partook of the Holy Communion. He was wholly held, absorbed, by a feeling. There was no forgetting, no Korsakov's then, nor did it seem possible or imaginable that there should be; for he was no longer at the mercy of a faulty and fallible mechanism—that of meaningless sequences and memory traces—but was absorbed in an act, an act of his whole being, which carried feeling and meaning in an organic continuity and unity, a continuity and unity so seamless it could not permit any break.

This passage is entirely typical of the kind of windy rhapsodizing with which Sacks embellishes the bare (and sufficiently eloquent) facts of each case.

There is a constant straining for cosmic significance, and with it a disturbingly self-regarding messianic fervor. A R. Luria is quoted with cloying reverence, and big names are dropped to no apparent effect save that of intellectual pretentiousness (Wittgenstein, Frege, Nietzsche, Schopenhauer, et al.). He is much too fond of the wistful ". . ." The result is that the patients and their plight are eclipsed by their doctor's desire for what he imagines to be a fine phrase.

More seriously, perhaps, there is the question of credibility. Sacks himself describes these pieces as "tales and fables" prompted by what he has observed in clinical practice. He says that he has changed "names and some circumstantial details . . . for reasons of personal and professional confidence, but my aim has been to preserve the essential 'feeling' of their lives." Is that *all* he has preserved? one wants to ask. A novelist could say the same yet would be making up more than mere names and "circumstantial details." What are we to make of the dialogue, for instance? There is no claim that his conversations with patients were tape-recorded, or that he wrote down what was said straight after, or indeed that such conversations ever took place. To what extent has Sacks invented stretches of dialogue for dramatic purposes? And was he really as ill informed about some of these cases as he seems to have been, or is it that he is feigning initial ignorance in order to create in the reader the thrill of discovery? Does he ever exaggerate the bizarre deficits and excesses he describes for greater literary effect? More fundamentally, did all of this really happen, and how does it stand in relation to Harold Pinter's play? Are questions of literal truth beside the point?

I myself suspect that the genre to which these "stories" belong is that of the dreaded "drama-documentary"—that art form which blends fact and fiction in a way that defies evaluation under either aesthetic or scientific criteria. Fictionalized fact cannot be criticized for being bad art, since it is intended as a report of fact. It is a genre in which you have no idea where you are and what you are supposed to be up to. It should be discouraged. Sacks wants his case histories to contribute toward a more humanistic neurology— no doubt a laudable aim—but neurology won't listen until it is told whether it is being offered data or drama. There is, of course, room for, and an honorable tradition in, medical (including psychiatric) case histories, but these are characteristically objective and impersonal in style, and the authors are quite clear that the circumstantial details have not been made up. There is a fine line between legitimate interpretation and overimaginative reading-into, and I am not convinced that Sacks has kept on the right side of it, or even intended to.

Putting aside the issue of genre, what positive value do these studies have? They certainly serve to remind us, especially the doctors among us, that patients are people too—that illness, however caused, and especially illness of the brain, has significance in the life of a person. This of course is a truism, but it seems necessary to keep on saying it in the face of the forces of "depersonalization." More theoretically, they compellingly demonstrate the fact, unwelcome as it is, that everything about the mind, from the sensory-motor periphery to the inner sense of self, is minutely controlled by the brain: if your brain lacks certain chemicals or gets locally damaged, your mind is apt to fall apart at the seams. What we call "the mind" is in fact made up of a great number of subcapacities, and each of these depends upon the functioning of the brain. It begins to seem a miracle that the system doesn't break down more often.

When it comes to theory, however, Sacks's studies yield little of consequence. He makes no effort to put his data into a systematic theoretical framework; indeed, the book contains remarkably little on the mechanisms of brain function. He offers us no philosophical account of the mind-brain relation, despite the importance of this question for his general theme of the dependence of mind on brain: is he a Cartesian dualist, an identity theorist, an epiphenomenalist, or what? His occasional references to Hume's theory of the self are naive at best. He seems to think that Hume regarded us as unconnected bundles of sensations possessed of no principle of unity: in fact, Hume claimed that the unity comes from precisely the sorts of connection that are missing in Sacks's pathological cases. It is therefore quite misleading of him to claim that Hume's theory fits those pathological cases but not us normals. Or is it that he is simply using Hume's theory as a loose literary metaphor? The problem of genre again.

It might be said that Sacks is not out to give a scientific or philosophical theory of the phenomena he reports; rather, he is providing the theorist with raw data to work with. But this is hard to square with Sacks's casual unconcern about the data assembled by other researchers. Uncomfortably often he appends a postscript in which it is observed that there is in fact a large (but uncited) literature on the syndrome he has just been describing. Then why publish further data of the same kind, unless he has made some new observations? The answer must be that he thinks he has, not new data, but new descriptions of old data—more dramatic descriptions. So, again, what he is doing is not science.

So I return to the question of what sort of book this is supposed to be. I fear that the answer must be this: it is a coffee-table book for the scientifically shy to dip into and amaze themselves and their friends. It has all the fascination—morbid and humanitarian—of a lurid text on medical pathology, with the bonus that it is easy reading. There is, of course, a place for coffee-table books—on the coffee table with the color-supplements—but they should not be confused with genuine science (or genuine literature). Above all, such writing should not be greeted by the nonscientific world as science at last Getting Somewhere, becoming Relevant, shedding its bogus Claims to Objectivity. This attitude is in its way as philistine as the obverse philistinism commonly attributed to scientists vis-à-vis the arts.

Sacks suggests that "classical neurology" needs to be supplemented with modes of description that address the person as a psychological being. This is a very familiar plaint, which was most vigorously urged in the sixties by

R. D. Laing and others in respect of medically based psychiatry. It is part of
the general question of the relationship between the psychological sciences
and the kind of understanding of people we find in novelists and biogra-
phers. This is a very hard question. The problem, not addressed by Sacks, is
how this integration is to be achieved—indeed, whether it can be achieved at
all. It seems that we have two distinct and distinctive modes of thinking here
which refuse to fit neatly together. To solve this problem we need to do some
hard thinking about the relationship between mind and brain, the nature of
science, and the viability of our ordinary notions of what a person is in the
face of the scientific facts. Pious pleas for neurology to "take account" of the
fact that human brains house human minds will not result in any progress
with these questions.

Perhaps a more radical thesis lurks in the background; if not of Sacks's
mind, then of the minds of his admirers. This is the idea that "classical
neurology" provides the wrong approach to the psychological disorders here
described; that it should be replaced, not supplemented. We must treat the
patient as a person (not as a machine) and forget about physical causes
altogether. This attitude (which I do not attribute to Sacks) makes a fundamental mistake. The proposal, in effect, is to treat Sacks's patients in the kind
of way psychoanalysis treats its patients. That is, we should address ourselves
to the psychological basis of the disorder and work on it, in collaboration with
the patient, in order to change his unhealthy psychic structure. This is a
mistake because the whole point of neuropathological disorders is that they
do not have psychological causes or an intelligible psychological history: they
have brute physical causes, such as head injury. Herein resides the peculiar
difficulty of bringing together neuropathology and a personal view of the
patient: for the person is prone to massive psychological changes the causes
of which are entirely impersonal. By all means let us remember that these
patients are people, but let us also not forget that their psychological problems do not lie at the personal level (as the problems addressed by psychoanalysis do). There is thus a clear sense in which these people *must* be treated
as machines—for the simple reason that the brain is a machine and hence is
prone to the breakdowns that are the lot of all machines. In this respect the
brain obeys the same laws as the body; and the mind wholly depends upon
the brain. No doubt this is a harsh and disturbing truth, amply and har-
rowingly demonstrated by the results of brain malfunction, but it is a truth
that cannot be dodged. There is thus no prospect of a fully personalized
neuropathology.

And what of the consequences of neuropathology for the immortality of
the soul? Pretty bleak, it would seem. For consider what becomes of the parts
of mind that are lost upon various kinds of brain damage. They can scarcely
be supposed to survive as separate bits, waiting for the other mental parts to
join them when the damage is complete; they must simply go out of existence. Suppose now the damage is progressive, so that the several components of mind are successively lost. What happens to the last bit? It can hardly

survive on its own, an incomplete yet immortal mental fragment. If parts of the mind depend for their existence upon parts of the brain, then the whole of the mind must so depend too. Hence the soul dies with the brain, which is to say it is mortal. This may be thought an irresistible conclusion anyway, of course, but it is gratifying to see it proved by philosophical neuropathology. Or is it that only the souls of those whose brains are destroyed *in one go* are immortal? This seems hardly fair.

27

Stroud: Not Knowing
What We Know

*The Significance of Philosophical
Scepticism*
by Barry Stroud
Oxford University Press, 1984

I cannot know that I am not dreaming now, because I could have experiences just like these in dreaming sleep and suppose myself to be awake. If I cannot know that I am not dreaming now, then I cannot know that I am now seated before a fire writing. Therefore I cannot know that I am now seated before a fire writing. So Descartes famously argued, thus raising the general problem of scepticism about the external world. The argument is apt to strike one as both preposterous and compelling. What is the source of its power? Where, if anywhere, does it go wrong? And what does it show about epistemology and philosophy in general?

These are the questions to which Barry Stroud's book is devoted. He begins by expounding the Cartesian argument with exemplary patience and care, making its steps as explicit as possible. His aim is to exhibit its strength and innocence of obvious fallacy. We can already appreciate that the argument is not going to admit of simple refutation, and that it gets at deep questions about the nature of knowledge and its relation to the world. Professor Stroud then goes on to consider a number of responses that have been made to this kind of scepticism, finding each of them in some respect inadequate.

J. L. Austin tried to convict the sceptic of misusing the word "know"; Stroud argues that Austin confused truth with appropriateness. G. E. Moore insisted that he knew he had two hands because he could hold them up and

Reprinted with permission from the *Times Literary Supplement* (February 22, 1985).

look at them; Stroud accuses Moore of dogmatically refusing to bend his mind to the sceptic's claims. Kant felt the power of scepticism and was driven to his problematic distinction between empirical and transcendental realism; Stroud points out that Kant's solution ends up limiting knowledge to the realm of the subjective. Carnap questioned the very meaningfulness of the sceptic's conclusion, on the ground that knowledge claims would be unverifiable if scepticism were true; Stroud takes scepticism to imperil the verifiability principle. Quine's "naturalized epistemology" avoids the whole issue by toughly dismissing traditional suprascientific epistemology; Stroud urges that Quine's own conception of knowledge invites the sceptical problems he wishes to ignore.

Stroud's criticism of these antisceptical efforts is insightful and convincing. Either the antisceptic concedes too little to his opponent and so fails to face up to the cogency of his argument (Austin, Moore, Quine), or he concedes too much and so fails to secure knowledge of the external world as we ordinarily understand it (Kant, Carnap). What emerges from Stroud's painstaking discussion is that scepticism derives its power from reflection upon the gulf between our sensory experience and the world that it is (we believe) experience of: this relationship is causal and contingent, yet knowledge seems to demand more than this—it craves a conceptual and necessary connection. Nor does this apparent demand issue from an unusual or equivocal interpretation of "know": it is our ordinary concept that seems to make this unsatisfiable demand. That, at any rate, appears to be the lesson of Stroud's book.

Though in many ways excellent, *The Significance of Philosophical Scepticism* is not without defect. The style, though mostly admirably clear, is often labored and repetitious: the same points are lengthily restated, and particular phrases recur with wearisome frequency. The book could easily have been much shorter. Its style is distinctly Moorean. As to content, I think there are some important areas of neglect. Chief among these, perhaps, is the absence of any systematically developed account of the concept of knowledge itself. Stroud relies upon a more or less intuitive grasp of the notion of knowledge and offers no real theory of the necessary and sufficient conditions of knowledge. It thus remains unclear what the sceptic's denial of knowledge rests upon—and indeed what it is precisely that he is denying.

It seems to me that there are at least three areas in which this lack vitiates Stroud's treatment of the sceptical argument. First, I do not think he gives enough weight to the idea that to know a proposition we do not need to know its logical consequences, even when we know what those consequences are. I might be able to know that I am seated before a fire writing without knowing that I am not dreaming—the reason being that the dream possibility is not in the class of possibilities "relevant" to the former knowledge claim. Stroud does, it is true, broach this idea, but he does not give it enough of a run for its money. Causal and information-theoretic analyses of knowledge, for example, do not require the would-be knower to rule out the dream possibility, and these analyses have much to be said in their favor.

Second, and connected, Stroud never considers whether the sceptic trades illicitly upon a conflation of knowing and knowing that you know. Maybe Descartes's argument shows that I do not know that I know that I am seated before a fire writing (perhaps because I cannot eliminate the dream possibility), but it does not immediately follow that I do not know this. Indeed, I would argue that the sceptic makes precisely this mistake—a mistake that a correct analysis of knowledge would reveal.

Third, Stroud tends to assimilate what seem distinct questions: whether we enjoy "direct perception" of the world around us, and whether we have knowledge of that world. This assimilation is rampant in the tradition with which Stroud is occupied, but its erroneousness becomes evident once we take a hard look at the concept of knowledge. In particular, the directness of our perceptions does not by itself undermine Cartesian scepticism (nor does their indirectness vindicate it).

Stroud does not pay close enough attention to the conceptual connections between knowledge and justification and certainty. He introduces the latter two concepts on occasions, but he does not defend the view that they are necessary to knowledge, and it is arguable that they are not. He does not discuss whether scepticism applies equally to all three concepts, nor why he takes knowledge to be the most important epistemic concept in sceptical contexts. Here it seems to me that Stroud has missed the opportunity to bring to bear modern conceptual analysis upon traditional philosophical questions. We need both.

Finally, Stroud restricts himself to scepticism about the external world; he says nothing of scepticism about other minds, induction, the past, and so on. No doubt he felt he had quite enough to chew on with the one scepticism, but I would think that a proper appreciation of the force and nature of scepticism needs to take these other kinds into account. Are there equally powerful sceptical arguments in them? Is scepticism structurally and diagnostically the same in all areas? Do the same kinds of response suggest themselves across the board? Not only would a comparative study of the different kinds help in assessing the general significance of scepticism—it might also enable us to understand better what is going on in the particular case Stroud has chosen to concentrate upon.

Despite these reservations, this is a book to be commended to both professional epistemologists and students: it is a serious and well-considered treatment of a topic that has only recently begun to receive the attention it deserves. If philosophical knowledge is possible then Stroud's book will create some.

28

Kripke: Naming and Necessity

Naming and Necessity
by Saul A. Kripke
Blackwell, 1980

Saul Kripke's brilliant and very influential article, "Naming and Necessity," appeared in 1972 in *Semantics of Natural Language* (edited by Davidson and Harman), having been transcribed from a series of unscripted lectures delivered at Princeton University in 1970. Now we have the record of those lectures in book form, accompanied by a new preface, in which the author dates the origin of his ideas from 1963–64.

As Kripke anticipates, those acquainted with the original article will be disappointed by the present publication, for the text is virtually unaltered and the preface is mainly given over to repeating points already contained in the earlier work for the benefit of readers for whom they were not crystal clear. It is not that Kripke thinks there are no genuine objections to take up—he admits to certain "substantive problems with the monograph"—but we are not told what these problems are, nor which passages he would (if he could) revise or expand. Indeed, he invites readers to judge for themselves which criticisms of his views are frivolous and which serious. It would have been interesting to know Kripke's own assessment of some of the many queries that have been raised over the past decade.

The concept of rigid designation is the main topic dealt with in the preface. Kripke begins by distinguishing the necessity of the identity relation from the idea of a rigidly designating expression (one that designates the same object in every possible world), and this in turn from the thesis that

Reprinted with permission from the *Times Higher Education Supplement* (June 13, 1980).

certain expressions of natural language—notably proper names—are rigid designators. He then devotes several pages to dismissing the obviously misguided objection that names cannot be rigid because they are ambiguous; the answer is that the question of rigidity makes sense only relative to a given disambiguation of the sentence at issue. A trickier question concerns the relation between the scope of designators in modal contexts and their rigidity. Here Kripke's reply to those who would interpret the latter notion in terms of the former is that the scope ambiguities alleged to attend names are spurious, since the small scope reading of the name is simply unavailable—and anyway the notion of rigidity applies in the case of simple sentences free of modal operators. Less satisfactory are his brief·remarks on the semantic difference between the rigidity of names and the rigidity of definite descriptions which express individual essences, for example, "the smallest prime." To mark the difference he introduces a distinction between rigidity *de jure* where the designator is "stipulated" to refer to a certain object, and rigidity *de facto* where it just "happens" that the referent uniquely satisfies the description in every possible world. This way of drawing the distinction certainly answers to an intuitive imparallelism between the two ways of referring rigidity, but clearly more needs to be said in explanation of the semantic difference.

Readers of the original article may well have come away with the impression that Kripke does not believe in the independent reality of possible worlds. In the preface he is anxious to remove the impression: he makes it clear that he wishes to take these entities perfectly seriously, at least on a certain innocuous understanding of them. A "possible world" is just an abstract *state* the world might have been in, to be compared with the alternative ways a pair of dice might fall, that is, with the "sample space" of probability theory. What is not entirely clear from Kripke's informal discussion is how precisely these possible states are to be conceived. Certainly the semantic interpretation of modal discourse will not, on this construal of the domain of possible worlds, much resemble (save formally) the kinds of model-theoretic structures standardly invoked for the interpretation of tense locutions or quantifiers generally. Perhaps the best (indeed the only) way to take this talk of possible states is to identify them with consistent sets of sentences or propositions; but there is nothing in Kripke's remarks to suggest that he regards his own view and that conception of possible worlds as equivalent. No doubt we will have to wait for Kripke's promised (or hoped-for) elaboration of these remarks to have the matter clarified.

Turning to the main text, let me identify some of the issues on which it would have been good to have Kripke's opinion. First, throughout *Naming and Necessity* Kripke makes heavy use of the notion of a priori knowledge without making any serious attempt to define that problematic notion. Requesting such a definition is not mere pedantry, for one of Kripke's more startling claims is that there are cases of contingent a priori truth; and it is conceivable that a harder look at the general notion of a priori knowledge will reveal Kripke's examples not to have that epistemic status. Indeed, the knowledge one acquires as a result of fixing the reference of a name seems to be based upon knowledge of one's own (linguistic) intentions, and so qualifies as a species of introspective knowledge, which should be classified as a posteriori. And it is noteworthy that in the preface Kripke prefers, neutrally, to characterize the knowledge a reference-stipulator possesses as acquired "in virtue of his very linguistic act": it is clear, however, that much knowledge so acquired (for example, my knowledge that I am speaking) is a posteriori.

Secondly, Kripke's so-called causal theory of reference still hovers rather uncertainly between a theory of how words latch onto the world and an insistence on the social character of names and certain other expressions. The latter interpretation probably best represents his considered view, but then there is the question how radically he diverges from the Fregean tradition he officially rejects. Does he not advocate simply a Fregean theory of *community* reference? The coefficient of confusion surrounding this topic might have been appreciably reduced had Kripke addressed himself to this question.

Thirdly, the Kripkean doctrine that has provoked the hottest debate is perhaps that of essentialism. Kripke does make very compelling appeal to our intuitions about what is essential and what accidental to a thing's identity, but we cannot rest content with such appeal: something must be said about why philosophers have always found the idea of objective necessity so profoundly problematic—and about what has to be done to render the idea finally acceptable. Kripke's contribution to this long-standing issue is really just the first stage of what ought to develop into a sustained philosophical inquiry into the metaphysics and epistemology of modality.

But the least complete and most contentious part of Kripke's discussion is the endeavor to revive Cartesian arguments against various forms of materialism. There have been several attempts to rebut Kripke's challenging arguments against identity theories of mind and body, none of which seems to have made an impact on his attitude toward those arguments. However, in one of his very rare additions to the main text he acknowledges the existence of one such objection to his claims, namely that there is no smooth generalization of his argument against identifying mental and physical *properties* to theories which identify only mental and physical *particulars*. About this line of objection Kripke makes the blunt and unhelpful remark, "The argument against token-token identification [in] the text *does* apply to these views." Exactly how the argument applies is left to the reader to work out for himself, if he can.

Despite the intense critical attention "Naming and Necessity" has enjoyed, it still stands up as an impressvie and enduring work of philosophy, outstanding in its sweep, clarity, and penetration. For that very reason one cannot but regret that its author has not taken the opportunity afforded by its republication to fill out and fortify his treatment of its various topics.

29

Ayer: Significantly Senseless

Wittgenstein
by A. J. Ayer
Weidenfeld and Nicolson, 1985

Outside the profession, Wittgenstein's fame as a twentieth-century philosopher is surpassed only by Russell's. Hardly a week goes by without our encountering Wittgenstein's name in one or other of the more popular organs of communication. There is some irony in this. For, unlike Russell, Wittgenstein maintained a ferocious aversion to publicity and wrote works of the utmost esotericism. Perhaps his present cult status in the extra-philosophical world stems, at least in part, precisely from this inaccessibility, thus doubling the irony. At any rate, a market surely exists for an exoteric study of Wittgenstein's notoriously recondite ideas.

It is this market for which A. J. Ayer's book is intended to cater: his avowed aim is to present Wittgenstein to interested readers who lack the benefit of a "considerable training in philosophy." If he succeeds in this laudable aim it will not be at the cost of vulgarization: though Ayer keeps his pills digestibly small, he does not stoop to sweeten them. In other words, the nonphilosopher will find it pretty tough going, despite the clarity of Ayer's style and his simplifications of Wittgenstein's doctrines. But it is not clear that a better job could have been done.

Ayer covers the entire span of Wittgenstein's career, as well as providing a biographical sketch and a chapter on Wittgenstein's influence on subsequent philosophy. We are taken at a fair clip through the rigors of the *Tractatus*, the exploratory transitional writings in which Wittgenstein's later themes begin

Reprinted with permission from the *Times Literary Supplement* (June 7, 1985).

to emerge, the work leading up to and including the *Investigations,* the last writings on knowledge and philosophical psychology, and even the remarks on magic and religion—and all this in a mere 150 pages. Nor does Ayer confine himself to exposition; he also criticizes Wittgenstein in the light of his own philosophical convictions. The discussion is generally clear and sympathetic, though Ayer lapses occasionally into simple announcements of agreement or disagreement without any real effort to expose the underlying issues. I would like to have seen more on *why* Wittgenstein put forward the views he did.

The chapter dealing with the *Tractatus* makes the important point that the early positivists, including Ayer himself, failed in their enthusiasm for that work to understand its central doctrine—the doctrine that ethics, aesthetics, and philosophy itself were strictly senseless. They took Wittgenstein to be denigrating and dismissing these systems of (so-called) thought, and elevating the claims of science to cognitive superiority. In fact, Wittgenstein assigned great importance to that about which he enjoined us to be silent: "senseless" was not for him a pejorative term. Ayer goes on to chide Wittgenstein for holding, inconsistently, that the propositions of philosophy can be both true and senseless. No doubt there is justice in this charge—for it is hard to see how a proposition can be true without corresponding to a state of affairs—but it is curious that Ayer omits to record that his own positivism suffered from the same affliction: the principle of verifiability was put forward as true, yet it must lack sense according to its own demands. The propositions of positivism thus had the same meaningless status, as, according to it, the disreputable propositions of metaphysics did. Had Ayer appreciated this parallel, he might have seen Wittgenstein's difficulty not merely as a kind of slip but as an inevitable consequence of a major philosophical tendency. Wittgenstein was simply more aware of this difficulty than those who took themselves to be following him, and he was bold enough to swallow the consequences. Any attempt to develop a criterion of meaningfulness with polemical edge is going to run up against this sort of problem.

Ayer's criticism of the *Investigations* focuses mainly on the "private language argument." The discussion here has some puzzling features. Ayer tells us more than once that he disagrees with Wittgenstein on this issue, but he also says that he has no wish to contest the claim that there could not be a language that was unintelligible to all except the speaker. Since this just *is* what Wittgenstein means by a private language, as Ayer notes at one point, it seems that the disagreement is not so great as Ayer supposes. Indeed, it is hard to see how Ayer *could* disagree with Wittgenstein here, since to do so would be to reject the verifiability principle when applied to what someone else means by their words. As the discussion progresses, it becomes clear that what Ayer is primarily opposed to is Wittgenstein's resistance to the idea of a private "ostensive definition" of sensation words. Ayer thinks that the speaker's memory can provide a satisfactory criterion of correctness for the use of such words, so that it is not necessary to suppose, for sensation words to be meaningful, that sensations have publicly observable manifestations. But then Ayer *does* after all seem to be allowing that there could be a private language in exactly the sense Wittgenstein denied and Ayer earlier acquiesced in.

On the question of private ostensive definition itself it seems to me that Ayer's discussion is vitiated by his failing to locate the question against the background of Wittgenstein's general account of ostensive training and of the conditions under which words acquire meaning. It is not a sufficient answer to Wittgenstein to say that I can now remember what I earlier meant by a sensation word; for this presupposes that I had earlier succeeded in meaning *anything*. Concentrating on the sensation while intoning the word to oneself is not enough to make the word *stand* for the sensation—a whole lot of linguistic "state setting" is needed before a word can be ostensively defined. I am not saying that Ayer is definitely wrong on this matter—only that it is more complicated than he acknowledges. In particular, more work would need to be done in elucidating Wittgenstein's dictum that "meaning is use" before his account of sensation language could be properly evaluated.

Ayer is on firmer ground in his criticism of Wittgenstein's views on knowledge and certainty. Wittgenstein held that it is a kind of nonsense to prefix any proposition about whose truth we could not be mistaken with the words "I know that," for example, "I am in pain." To this claim Ayer makes the entirely convincing (and familiar) reply that it confuses what it is nonmisleading to say with what it is true to say. You might well perplex your audience by saying, "I know that I am in pain," but you can nevertheless speak truly in so saying. Similarly for Moorean propositions like "I know that I have two hands."

As Ayer distinguishes the early Wittgenstein from the positivists, so he distinguishes the later Wittgenstein from the school of "ordinary language" philosophers, typified by J. L. Austin. Wittgenstein was always interested in the general nature of meaning, not just in drawing fine distinctions of meaning between words; his detailed investigations of the use of words were always directed at some general "theoretical" moral. And he always had a great respect for philosophical *error*.

Ayer ranks Wittgenstein second only to Russell among twentieth-century philosophers, despite his many disagreements with him. It is a considerable merit of this book that this judgment should seem to be not exaggerated.

30

Budd: Wittgenstein's Philosophy of Psychology

Wittgenstein's Philosophy of Psychology
by Malcolm Budd
Routledge, 1989

Sapiently gauging his distance, Malcolm Budd offers us a synoptic view of Wittgenstein's later thoughts on the mind. His treatment is selective yet representative. Seven dense chapters survey Wittgenstein's various surveys of meaning and understanding, sensations and sense impressions, the seeing of aspects, images, internal speech and calculation, thought and intention, and feelings, emotions, and bodily awareness. Budd's expositions are in every way exemplary. He is deeply sympathetic to his subject but by no means uncritical. I know of no other work on Wittgenstein that can match his for clarity, accuracy, concision, and penetration (and there are some fine books our there). He knows *exactly* what he is talking about and is able to convey this to the reader with unostentatious efficiency. His book would be perfect for students still trying to find their feet with Wittgenstein, but it can be heartily recommended to scholars who think they know their way around the Austrian's later thought. Here is a book on Wittgenstein that you can *trust.*

Beginning with a chapter on method, Budd emphasizes the prophylactic character of Wittgenstein's intentions: the notions of grammar, language game, and perspicuous representation are to be seen in a curative light. He brings out the consequent radical disjuncture Wittgenstein perceived between our ordinary mastery of psychological concepts and our bewilderment once we reflect upon this mastery: we go from genius to dolt simply by taking a downward glance at our concepts; we simultaneously grasp and do not

Reprinted with permission from the *Journal of Philosophy* (August 1992).

grasp what we mean. Budd is sensitive to the apparent paradox this presents
and does his best to explain how Wittgenstein lived with it. I feel that this
issue could stand further work: did Wittgenstein really have an adequate
account of the depth of error he attributed to our reflective understanding,
given that he took our ground-floor conceptual grasp to be essentially flawless?

Chapter 2 sets out Wittgenstein's position on meaning, rules, conscious
processes, mental mechanisms, capacities, reasons, and communication.
These topics have been hotly contested in recent philosophy, stimulated
largely by Saul Kripke's "community interpretation" of Wittgenstein's position. Budd shows definitively, I think, that this misrepresents the essence of
Wittgenstein's view; he stresses instead the contrast between inner and outer.
The main target of Wittgenstein's critique is the idea that meaning is a quality
of consciousness—something that happens *in* you.

Wittgenstein is surely right about this, but it does not follow that the
concepts of meaning and consciousness are unconnected, nor that the latter
is not a necessary condition of the former. Meaning can be (and be essentially) something we do consciously without thereby consisting in an intro-
spectible quality of consciousness. Wittgenstein seems not to have explored
other less direct ways in which meaning and consciousness might inter-
sect.

Budd's presentation of the private-language argument is impressively
clear and thorough. Since first-person ascriptions are criterionless, private
sensations could not afford the constraint on correct use that governs our
actual practice of ascribing behaviorally expressed sensations. The would-be
private linguist is thus bereft of any means of establishing a reference relation. Budd appears to accept this argument, while plausibly criticizing Witt-
gensein for extruding causality from his account of sensation concepts. I
would say that the introduction of a causal relation between sensations and
self-ascriptions provides one way of resisting the argument. We should, first,
remind ourselves of how surprising the conclusion of Wittgenstein's argument ought to seem. He invites us to believe that someone whose sensations
happen to have no behavioral expression is semantically impotent in respect
of those sensations. The subject has the sensations, she can speak a language
for public objects, but somehow she just cannot get her words to refer to her
sensations. Only if her body offers up potential criteria for others to detect
her sensations can she succeed in homing in semantically on those sensations.
Suppose the sensations are publicly undetectable up to time *t* and then acquire behavioral manifestations at *t*, only to revert to privacy ten minutes
later. According to Wittgenstein, the subject could not refer to her sensations
before *t*, though she can once her body starts to show their presence to
others; and when the behavioral manifestations go her sensation words lapse
back into mere empty sounds. Surely this is a remarkable result: it ties my
semantic abilities with respect to my own mental life to the epistemic powers
of others in detecting what it is I am experiencing.

The suspicion that some form of verificationism underlies Wittgenstein's argument is reinforced if we consider what a causal theory of reference might have to say about the possibility of a private lexicon, since such theories do not locate reference in the speaker's ability to *check* that he is referring correctly—only in the objective obtaining of causal relations between objects and uses (think, say, of Jerry Fodor's asymmetric dependence theory). Since Budd accepts that sensations cause self-ascriptions, he is not precluded from considering a theory of this kind. And if a causal theory can be applied to sensation words, we have this result: so long as the private objects bear the appropriate reference-conferring causal relations to first-person uses, that will be sufficient to underpin a semantic relation—no matter *how* private the sensations are. In other words, causal theories impose reference conditions that are inclusive enough to permit a private language (the same could be said of teleological theories). For such theories do not build in any necessity for anyone to be able to *verify* that words are being used as their semantics demands; it simply has to *be* the case that tokens of "pain" (say) appropriately covary with the occurrence of pains in the speaker. These theories may or may not be adequate, but we need to consider them if we are interested in whether the privacy of a sensation thwarts reference to that sensation.

Nor should we let the general mysteriousness of the reference relation induce us to suppose that reference is uniquely impossible where private objects are concerned, since that would be to pin the blame on the wrong thing. Maybe we cannot really explain reference in *any* context; it is just that this becomes more obvious when we strip reference down to its purest form. In any event, the private-language argument seems to me a good deal more questionable than it seems to Budd.

The chapter on aspect perception is a subtle and lucid discussion of the way in which Wittgenstein demonstrates the "polymorphous character" of the concept of seeing. Seeing an aspect is neither quite like seeing color and shape, but nor is it a case of interpreting what one strictly sees. The fact is that it lies between sensation and thought and cannot be assimilated to either. The phenomenon thus serves to expose the simplifying errors inherent in both empiricist and rationalist views of mind. Our mental concepts are much less monolithic than philosophers have supposed.

On the distinction between visualizing and seeing, Budd ably expounds Wittgenstein's idea that the difference consists essentially in subjection to the will. One's attitude in visualizing is active, while in seeing one is a passive observer. The difference is not a matter of experiential content or quality. This is held, plausibly, to explain what may appear anomalous: that one cannot see and visualize the same thing at the same time, though one can do this for different things—since one cannot be active and passive toward the same experiential content simultaneously.

Wittgenstein's opposition to the idea of an inner vehicle of thought is shown to be an instance of his wider point that nothing of an intrinsically nonrepresentational nature could ever be the basis of one's knowledge of the content of one's thought, so that the putative inner vehicle could play no epistemic role in an account of self-knowledge of intentional states. I would agree with this point but note that it does not follow that the inner vehicle might not be needed for other purposes. Indeed, given Budd's earlier insistence on the causal properties of sensations, he might regard with sympathy contemporary thinkers (like Fodor) who maintain that no account of intentional causation is possible without introducing an inner vehicle whose structure encodes the causal powers of thought.

The book concludes with a fresh discussion of the relation between emotion and proprioception, on the one hand, and somatic sensation, on the other. As we might expect by now, Wittgenstein's main target is the idea that bodily feelings are constitutive of emotion or proprioception. Such feelings *accompany* one's fear or one's awareness of the position of one's arm, but the concepts are not concepts *of* such feelings—rather as certain sensations accompany linguistic understanding without constituting it. Nor do we know our emotional state or bodily position by means of our awareness of the accompanying sensations. This explains something that might otherwise seem puzzling: how a horrible or agreeable emotion can be so much more powerful than the somatic perturbations that go with it. Affective tone is more a matter of the intentionality of the emotion than its bodily feel.

In the preface to his book, Budd makes a nice acknowledgment to me, adding that "he has not seen what I have written and is unlikely to agree with all of it." Well, now I have seen it and agree with far more of it than might be thought proper in a reviewer (and not merely because we are friends). The book is a model of Wittgenstein exegesis. Only on the soundness of the private-language argument do we seriously disagree: he thinks it works and I do not.

31

Searle: Contract with Reality

The Construction of Social Reality
by John Searle
The Free Press, 1995

When philosophers concern themselves with what fundamentally exists, they are apt to limit themselves to physical facts and mental facts, with perhaps a soupçon of the abstract thrown in. There are mountains and muons, beliefs and tickles, and maybe numbers and propositions. Then questions are raised about how these broad ontological categories are related, these questions constituting the core of traditional metaphysics. But this is to ignore at least one other broad category of facts: the social ones. We also have incomes and marriages and presidencies. How are facts about societies to be fitted into our general ontological framework? How, in particular, are they to be connected with mental and physical facts? What is, if you will forgive the expression, the ontology of civilization?

There is a reason that philosophers tend not to be powerfully exercised by questions of social ontology, and it is that social facts are less primitive than the other facts. Social facts depend for their existence on mental and physical facts, but the opposite is not the case. This is the basic intuition from which John Searle starts his inquiry: the ontological dependence of the social on the nonsocial. Searle's aim is to develop a theory that spells out the nature and consequences of this dependence.

WB

Consider money, a familiar social institution. What is it that constitutes something as money? How does it come to exist? What, as Searle puts it, is the structure of the fact of money? Clearly it is not a matter of the physical

Reprinted with permission from the *New Republic* (May 22, 1995).

features of those items with which we conduct our economic exchanges. It is the way we *use* those pieces of paper and those flat disks of metal. Searle builds his theory of money-creating human use around three basic concepts. First, collective intentionality is the possession by a group of agents of certain mental states, particularly beliefs and intentions. In a soccer game, for instance, *we* (the team) are attempting to score a goal, and what *I* do occurs within that collective intention. Second, functions are assigned to things when agents begin to treat them as having purposes, as when we assign to bits of metal and paper the function of acting as a medium of exchange. These functions are imposed on external reality; they do not exist antecedently to human interpretation. Third, constitutive rules are those rules that create, by human agreement or stipulation, a new sort of fact. Chess is constituted by its rules; it is not that the rules of chess regulate some prior independent activity.

The outlines of Searle's theory run as follows. Take a dollar bill and consider it only in its physical aspect, as an object obeying the laws of physics. By virtue of what does this merely physical thing acquire the character of a unit of exchange, a repository of value and so on? It does so because we, by collective intentionality, assign to it the status of acting as a medium of exchange and so on, where this new status cannot be performed by the dollar bill solely by dint of its physical properties. We lay down rules that constitute the physical object as having properties that go beyond anything in its physical nature. We thus confer new powers on the object, powers to buy and sell, to conserve wealth. We impose upon it a certain status, where this status represents our agreement to treat the object in ways that depend upon our having made that agreement.

This is the basis of our acceptance of the dollar bill in economic transactions. So we impose status functions on things against the background of our collective mentality. And so social reality comes into being. "The central span on the bridge from physics to society is collective intentionality, and the decisive movement on that bridge in the creation of social reality is the collective intentional imposition of function on entities that cannot perform those functions without that imposition." Money is money because we agree to treat it that way. In Searle's terminology, money is an observer-dependent fact. Thus money differs from mountains and screwdrivers, because mountains exist whether or not we believe in them and screwdrivers can perform their function by virtue of their physical features. For Searle, social institutions are distinguished by their inability to perform their function without a common acceptance of their legitimacy. In a sense, they depend on faith.

All this is explained with Searle's customary clarity and straightforwardness. The prose is spiky and simple. No stone is left unkicked. Polemical arrows thud into soft targets. Searle's book is almost pretentiously unpretentious, and the style is well suited to the project: a systematic and orderly dissection of our ordinary concepts of familiar things. Searle's aim is to make us see that social facts are unmysterious and yet remarkable. They are unmysterious in that they result completely from the raw materials and mechanisms that he identifies, which are themselves sufficiently perspicuous and anterior to what they are used to explain. And they are remarkable because what we fondly think of as civilization depends on the existence of these constructions, which are held in place by nothing other than a kind of groundless collective contract.

Society would collapse if people were to cease agreeing to assign appropriate functions to things like wedding ceremonies, dollar bills, English sentences. And since all of these assignments are essentially arbitrary, there is, in a sense, nothing stopping us from ceasing to accord them the status that we now accord them. Mountains will stay there no matter how much we might wish them away, but it would take nothing more than a collective decision to dismantle totally the institutional fabric of society.

This, Searle surmises, is the reason we tend to invest certain ceremonies with so much pomp and glitter: we recognize that it all comes down to one person agreeing with another, and we don't like the netless feeling that results. The emblems of authority are there to reassure us that it won't all come tumbling down around our ears. Human agreement is a fragile thing, and it is hard to accept that it is the only barrier that stands between us and chaos. Imagine what it would be like if people began to deny that the words you utter mean what you take them to mean, or if your diplomas were decreed invalid, or if people treated your dollar bills as bits of worthless paper. What if the institution of citizenship were to be abrogated? There would be nothing to fall back on, in observer-independent reality, to enforce the kinds of rights that we normally take for granted. These social institutions work, fundamentally, only because we say they do.

At the root of Searle's treatment of social facts is a distinction between brute facts and humanly constructed facts. There are two kinds of brute facts: the physical entities onto which we impose institutional functions, and the mental capacities that make this imposition possible. Neither sort of fact is itself humanly constructed. Rather, we construct social facts on the basis of such brute facts. Social reality thus presupposes a reality whose origin is not social. It cannot be, then, that reality in general is socially constructed; on the contrary, social reality is nonsocially constructed. There cannot be social facts without the logically prior existence of brute facts that are not the result of any social mechanism. Society is constructed on a bedrock of antecedent realities, both physical and mental, which are entirely objective in the sense that they are not products of human action or cognition. The raw materials of social construction are independent of all such construction.

Indeed, if we conjoin Searle's theory of society with the views about the mind that he has expressed elsewhere, we get, in effect, a reduction of social facts to physical and biological ones. For he maintains that states of consciousness, which are what intentionality depends on, are just biological properties of the brain, no different in principle from neural and biochemical properties. Thus collective intentionality, which is the main engine of social construction, is really a biological feature of the human species. Society is biology imposed outward. It is a property of the brain that has attached itself to external things, giving them functions they would not otherwise have had. Culture, then, is just one manifestation of our biological nature, and has no autonomous existence. And this is simply because the mind itself is a biological fact.

Searle is by no means oblivious to the polemical thrust of his analysis of society. Indeed, he revels in it with the kind of breezy gusto we have come to know and enjoy: "Derrida, as far as I can tell, does not have an argument. He simply declares that there is nothing, outside of texts (*Il n'y a pas de 'hors texte'*). And in any case, in a subsequent polemical response to some objections of mine, he apparently takes it all back. . . . What is one to do, then, in the face of weak or even nonexistent arguments for a conclusion that seems preposterous?" Searle's analysis, as he points out, supplies a kind of transcendental deduction of realism from the nature of social facts: there can be social facts only because there are already brute nonsocial facts that provide the basis for social construction. This inverts the way of thinking associated with so-called social constructionism, in which it is apparently maintained that *all* facts are somehow the product of social realities.

I agree completely with Searle that such views are absurd, that they have no respectable argumentative support, that in the end they always rest on an elementary confusion between reality and our representation of it. Of course the universe could exist without there being any human societies; it did for quite a while. (It is equally obvious that there could not exist human representations of the universe without humans.) I recommend, a little urgently, Searle's patient and devastating dissection of the social constructionist way of thinking: it doesn't take very long to read and it could do a great deal of good in many quarters.

Since his theory of society is premised on commonsense realism about the physical and mental worlds, Searle gives us an extra couple of chapters on these more basic metaphysical questions. The discussion here is more purely philosophical, especially in the chapter that sets out to rehabilitate what is known as the correspondence theory of truth. According to that theory, there are language-independent facts, such as the fact that snow is white, and we make statements corresponding to these facts, such as the statement *that* snow is white, and so truth consists in a relation between language and the world. This may seem obvious to the naive reader, but it has been denied by most twentieth-century philosophers. Searle's trick is to show that this banality conceals no logical solecisms. We can safely conclude, I think, that his theory of the social cannot be faulted at the underlying metaphysical level.

But that does not mean that it cannot be faulted at all. The theory offers a set of necessary and sufficient conditions for the existence of social facts, so we need to ask whether it succeeds in these analytical aims, if it is to give an adequate account of social concepts. As to whether the conditions are necessary, I think there are problems with the use of the notion of collective intentionality. First, it is not clear that we need to accept Searle's doctrine of primitively defined "we-intentions" in order to get social facts off the ground. There are cases in our experience in which shared and coordinated "I-intentions" will do the job. If I intend to treat certain pieces of paper as money and so do you and so does everybody else, then we shall have an institution of money; it is not necessary that the group of us has a collective intention expressible as "we intend to treat this as money." It may well be that "we-intentions" are irreducible, and that our social practices are generally backed by them, but it does not seem logically required for the assignment of status functions that such intentions be present.

Second, and more important, the requirement of full-blown intentionality looks too strong. Consider ants and bees. These are rightly described as social insects, but they do not have beliefs and intentions. What they have are dispositions and capacities that interact to produce socially coordinated behavior; and they form societies by virtue of these interactive dispositions. Searle might object that such societies don't generate functions for objects that go beyond their physical features, so that nothing *symbolic* results from ant or bee behavior, nothing analogous to money and marriage vows. But that seems wrong. Ants mark their territory by means of chemical signals that do not block others by sheer physical insurmountability; and this kind of symbolic territory-marking is regarded by Searle, in the human case, as paradigmatically social and institutional.

So status function can be assigned in the absence of ordinary intentionality. Famously, bees perform symbolic dances that convey the location of nectar to other bees. This is precisely a case of taking a physical phenomenon—a mere wiggle—and imposing upon it a function that goes beyond its physical features; the wiggle plays a social role in bee colonies. The point here is that the imposition of function, even representational function, does not necessarily depend on the agents having the kind of mind that we have, with our conscious intentions, contracts and rules. Social facts can arise from more primitive sorts of disposition, as they do in these nonhuman cases.

Neither does Searle provide properly sufficient conditions for sociality, and this for a simple logical reason. A social fact must, by definition, involve a group of individuals, not a single individual in isolation. Searle's actual examples are all of this kind, but his analysis does not itself secure that result. It might seem to him that it must since it uses the notion of collective intentionality, but in fact this does not deliver the intended result. The problem is that the imposed function might relate only to a single individual, despite its imposition by a group of individuals, and so will not give us a genuinely social fact. Conversely, a single individual could stipulate a function that relates to a social group, as when a king decrees a new coin legal tender in society at large.

Suppose we all decide that the full moon is to have the function of indicating to John Searle that it is time he trimmed his sideburns, and suppose he then duly trims them. This function is defined relative to a single individual

and its fulfillment does not involve anybody else; it is not that we have
decided that everyone should trim their sideburns at the full moon. What we
have here is an individualistic status function. The reason examples like this
are possible is simply that Searle's basic concept—assigning a function that
goes beyond the merely physical features of the object—does not itself im-
port any social element, at least on the natural understanding of "social."
Institutional it may be, but it is not thereby a group fact.

This suggests that Searle's book is misnamed, since what he is really
analyzing is the notion of stipulated or intention-dependent fact, not a social
fact in the usual sense. His primary contrast is between the natural objective
features of things and the features that we impose by human decision; but
that contrast does not logically coincide with the distinction between the
individual and the social. Robinson Crusoe can confer status functions on
things, but that does not ease his isolation.

The only way to get society into the picture is explicitly to build into
the notion of function the idea of a function that concerns a group of individuals. Since this will work only if the collective intentions that impose the
function match its scope, we need to suppose that the intentions themselves
have a content that relates to a social concept: there must be an intention that
a certain social institution shall come into being. But then, of course, we are
presupposing that we already have social concepts in play; we are not constructing them from other nonsocial concepts. What Searle is really explaining is how we convert our social concepts into social realities.

But these are the objections of the trained analytical philosopher. They
should not be taken to undermine the general shape of Searle's account. He
is right to observe that the social depends on the nonsocial, and that the
driving force of institutional facts is simply the human propensity to invest
more significance in things than their objective nature can bear. Human
creativity is at the root of social facts. There is a reality out there that does not
owe its existence and its nature to our creative acts, and what we then do is
create further realities by imposing meaning on otherwise meaningless
things. Thus we have language and money and weddings and academic
gowns and guest passes. The world bifurcates into the created and the uncre-
ated, though there cannot be the former without the latter.

But isn't all this obvious, even banal? Not banal enough, in our post-
poststructuralist intellectual life. I wonder if Searle would have written this
book were it not for the polemical purpose of refuting certain fashionable
doctrines to the effect that reality itself is a construction from human institutions; and yet, even if Searle's book may be low on primary philosophical
thrills, it is bursting with plain and necessary right-headedness. He has performed a genuine service in bringing his rigor to bear on the lazy and pernicious relativism latent in the idea that reality is just what we humans choose
it to be. *The Construction of Social Reality* might not exist if it were not for the
bad ideas of other people, but there are many important books about which
that may be said.

32

Dennett: Leftover Life to Live

Darwin's Dangerous Idea: Evolution and
the Meanings of Life
by Daniel C. Dennett
Allen Lane/Penguin, 1995

Purposive creatures, such as ourselves, tend to find purpose everywhere. It takes some mental discipline to banish it from our thoughts, even when we know very well it does not belong there. Random, mindless, mechanical processes are hard for us to keep in focus. And this is particularly difficult where the process leads to creatures with purposes—how can our purposes lack purpose?

But that is the way Darwin's theory of evolution by natural selection explains the history and existence of living things. There is no *point* to the long painful process whereby animal species come to exist; it is simply the unfolding of a purposeless sequence of mechanical steps. Yet even those who fully accept the theory are tempted by teleological descriptions of the process, supposing it to be *aiming* at something—complexity, mind, morality, self-annihilation, or what have you. Agency lurks somewhere behind the scenes, it is obscurely felt, directing the process to some predetermined end. To see why this is a mistake, we should note that the concept of natural selection itself applies also to the inanimate world; in fact, *everything* exists by virtue of natural selection. Mountains, snowflakes, tectonic plates, hydrogen atoms, planets, galaxies—all these exist because natural selection has operated in their favor. That is to say, the destructive forces of nature allow entities of these kinds to come to be and to endure. A particular mountain, say, comes to exist by virtue of the laws of nature, and it persists because nothing occurs

Reprinted with permission from the *Times Literary Supplement* (November 24, 1995).

to destroy it. Another mountain, a sandier one, may last less long, being more easily eroded into nonexistence by wind and water. This is primitive natural selection—the differential survival of individual things in the face of destructive forces. Plainly there is no *telos* here; it is just the forces of nature destroying some things while others endure—this depending on the physical constitution of the thing in relation to its environment. Welcome to efficient causation blindly executing its winnowing work.

According to Darwin's theory, the survival of animate things is just as unplanned and mechanical. Some organisms are destroyed more efficiently by nature than others. The notion of "selection" here has no purposive connotation; we could equally (and less misleadingly) speak of evolution by natural destruction. The survivors are just the organisms that are *left over* when nature has done its destructive work. They are selected, but they are not selected *for* anything. Of course, in both the animate and inanimate cases it is the structure of the entity that determines its talent for continued existence—the form of its matter is what enables the object to cling to existence. Matter comes in vastly different forms, and some forms persist in the presence of destructive forces more robustly than other forms. The forms of elementary particles seem particularly resistant to being selected out; they are the ultimate survivors. Some of the most robust of existents, the hardest to kill, are some of the simplest natural objects. Natural selection is simply the differential application of the forces of material disassembly, and particles are notably tough to break down.

Since the concept of natural selection is so universally applicable, it cannot be what distinguishes organic existence from other kinds. What marks plants and animals off are the *mechanisms* whereby they exist to be selected for or against. They reproduce, generating close copies of themselves, and genes are what account for this process of duplication. They also mutate, which provides variation in the body types that compete for survival. But it is still ultimately a question of which physical structures are most robust in warding off natural destruction. The output of the mechanisms is just a natural object like a mountain, which endures or does not, depending on the natural forces it encounters. There is no more teleology involved in the existence of one thing than the other. Nature no more aims to make cheetahs or humans than it aims to make mountains.

Daniel Dennett is keen to stress the purposelessness of natural selection, to rub our noses in our own contingency. It is a blind mechanical algorithm, he says, but not an algorithm *for* anything. Natural selection simply runs its algorithmic course, throwing up whatever material forms are least perishable, most replicable. There are no "skyhooks," only "cranes"—mechanistic processes which happen to lead to complex organisms like ourselves: "The theory of natural selection shows how every feature of the natural world can be the product of a blind, unforesightful, nonteleological, ultimately mechanical process of differential reproduction over long periods of time." His book is a detailed and lengthy defense of Darwinian orthodoxy. He has no fresh perspective to offer, and is content to follow the lead of Richard Dawkins, whom he quotes and cites frequently (as well as quoting and citing his own earlier works with numbing frequency). Dennett does not have the lucid economy and theoretical vision of Dawkins, or his professional expertise, but he does have depths of patience in criticizing the opposition and mulling over the history. Much of the ground covered is therefore very familiar, and one sometimes wonders whether it is necessary to retread it. But Dennett's style is lively, if sometimes rambling and self-indulgent, the scientific facts are well presented, and the argument not really losable.

There is a good discussion of Stephen J. Gould on "punctuated equilibrium," in which Dennett convincingly argues that no serious revision in Darwinian orthodoxy is required to explain the "jumpy facts" of the fossil record. He is also effective in assessing the significance of the indisputable point that not every feature of an organism has been directly selected for; there are by-products and substrates ("spandrels"), which exist simply because you cannot get the selected trait without having them along for the ride. Antiadaptationist thinking, in so far as it is prompted by this obvious truth, is at best an exaggeration. The book is weakest in the later, more philosophical chapters, where Dennett is defending not Darwin but his own views about the mind, which tend toward the behaviorist, eliminative and confused. Some of his swipes at Noam Chomsky, John Searle, Jerry Fodor, and other perceived adversaries make for unpleasant (and unilluminating) reading.

Dennett makes heavy use throughout the book of the notion of "design," and is quite happy to describe organisms as displaying "excellence," of some designs being "better" than others. He takes such talk to be integral to Darwinian theory. But these are dangerous locutions for a deep-dyed Darwinian, and I am not sure that Dennett escapes the teleological pitfalls they invite. For in no literal sense is an organism *designed* by evolution, any more than a mountain is designed by the natural forces that permit it to exist. Organisms have natural structures, to be sure, as do mountains; but it would be misleading to say that some mountains are "better designed" than others, because they persist under wind and rain more robustly than others. If mountains replicated by fission, with small variations in the results, we would have the analogue of organic replication; but in neither case should we speak of the succeeding entities as designed by the process that gives rise to them. According to Darwin's theory, properly understood, peacocks are no more designed than hydrogen atoms are—though both exemplify certain organized forms. We may marvel at the beauty and intricacy of both, we may even value more highly the peacock's form; but that is a matter of *our* response to the natural objects in question—it is not part of the content of Darwinian theory. At the very least, Dennett's terminology and rhetoric belie the very naturalized version of natural selection that he is officially promoting. It is as if he cannot help thinking, in spite of knowing better, that somehow the animate world is "special"—that it somehow bears the marks of intelligence and agency.

It is the same with the notion of adaptation: to say that a characteristic is adaptive is just to say that it is part of what enables the organism to persist, and perhaps that it is present because in the organism's ancestors it preserved existence. In this sense, though, the solidity of a rock is adaptive with respect to the forces of erosion. It is true that an animal may itself have purposes—to find food or a mate—and that its anatomy helps fulfil these purposes; but there is no further notion of adaptiveness that properly belongs with a rigorous Darwinism. "Survival of the fittest" can mean nothing other than relative durability in the face of entropic forces; nothing evaluative can legitimately be read into it (here is where the Social Darwinists went wrong). Mere rocks have "fitness" too, relative to blobs of jelly, in virtue of their physical structure. Nor do we need any richer notion of adaptiveness than this to get Darwin's theory going.

Once this purified version of Darwin is absorbed, we can ask whether it really explains everything that needs to be explained. We should not let ourselves be lulled into theoretical complacency by a failure to purge the theory of illicit teleological elements. This stricture is particularly relevant when it comes to accounting for the *complexity* of organic forms: we should not suppose that evolution is aiming for complexity, with us as the ultimate complex organism just waiting to get ourselves evolved. Why then, given the mechanisms at evolution's disposal, do complex forms emerge? Dennett is weak on this crucial question, but I suspect the trouble is not his alone, because there really is a puzzle about why organisms display the kind of complexity we observe. Put crudely, the puzzle is this: why aren't all organisms as simple as the simplest ones? This is not the question of how, *given* complex forms, we can show how they develop from simpler forms. That problem has a ready solution in the idea that evolution permits a series of gradual changes, over millions of years, that take us from simple to complex. The problem I am concerned with, however, is why there is a trend to complexity to begin with.

The key point to notice here is that complexity is *not* a prerequisite of successful persistence. Some of the simplest organisms are the most abundant and successful by any objective biological standard, and inanimate objects can obviously be both simple and robust. Moreover, complexity has its disadvantages: complex objects take more work to construct and so call for greater energy resources; they are also more vulnerable to breakdown and malfunction. If you want something to last, keep it simple. But this maxim of sensible engineering is everywhere flouted in the biological world; there seems to be a definite trend toward complexity—and it has increased with time. Why? What is the pay-off of complexity with respect to the simple desideratum of continued existence? We are accustomed to thinking that we complex beings naturally evolved from much simpler beings; but why are we not now evolving *toward* simpler beings—given that simpler organisms can be just as robust and cost less to produce? Why is evolution not "downward" instead of "upward"? True, we humans are prone to value complex things— they impress us more than simple things—but there is nothing in Darwin to predict that complexity should come to characterize the biological world. More precisely, there is nothing in the *concept* of natural selection that predicts complexity as the output of its operation. For natural selection does not *in general* produce complexity of structure in what is selected; it simply "produces" durability. Neither does the mere fact of replication predict complexity, since simplicity could be preserved across replication. Neither does mutation inevitably lead to it, or else viruses would be the most complex of things. Talk of species-specific environmental "niches," which somehow call forth complex forms to "occupy" them, is transparently *post hoc*. On the contrary, it seems quite consistent with the principles of Darwinian theory to suppose that evolution should display a simplification over time. If you think that evolution is inherently progressive, aiming all the while at complex organisms with minds and culture, you will not be puzzled by complexity; but once this teleological error has been firmly repudiated, complexity comes to seem puzzling.

In the face of the puzzle, we might be tempted to argue that all our judgments of complexity are subjective, so that there is nothing objective in nature that needs to be explained—I am no more complex, objectively, than a stone. This would defeat Paley's argument to theism from organic complexity right at the start, but it surely goes strongly against our intuitions and indeed against plausible objective measures of natural complexity (e.g., number of components). So this medicine is too strong. The problem then remains: the best survivor of all would be some hard little simple object that could not be broken down by the forces of nature; so why should relentless pressure toward ever greater durability produce such soft, friable, complex creatures as we see all around us? Just think how durable a diamond is compared to a human being! So there is something here that the Darwinian apparatus, as currently understood, cannot by itself explain. We know that the Darwinian machine produced complex organisms, but we do not know why it did.

There are other puzzles, too, that Dennett does not consider, perhaps because he is so keen to put current theory in the best possible light. Acknowledging these puzzles does not, however, involve giving up Darwin in favor of some form of creationism or other supernaturalism; it is simply to point to areas in which our explanations are weak or nonexistent, as is the case in every science. Consider then the puzzle of why there are no Lamarckian organisms. It is an established fact that organisms do not pass on acquired characteristics to their progeny by genetic means; there is no mechanism which links lifetime changes in phenotype to genetic variation. Notoriously, Lamarck was wrong to suppose that the blacksmith might pass his acquired brawny arm on to his son or daughter. But why have

Lamarckian organisms never evolved? Surely a mutation that made the genes responsive to changes of phenotype ("learning") would have selectional advantage, and there seems no *physical* impossibility in such a set-up. Wouldn't natural selection favor a physiological mechanism that allowed learned characteristics to be passed genetically to offspring? Yet no such organism has been recorded. Abstractly considered, one would have predicted that *all* organisms would be Lamarckian, since the genetic transmission of acquired traits is not ruled out conceptually and has clear advantages. It is puzzling why Lamarck's hypothesis is empirically false.

There is also the puzzle of consciousness and evolution: how and why did consciousness evolve? Why is it that animals are not all mindless zombies, programmed to behave without benefit of sentience? Is consciousness adaptive in a way zombiehood is not, or is it just a "spandrel," a mere side effect of something with a genuine function? And how could sentience possibly emerge from mere matter anyway? In reply to these old questions, Dennett says little or nothing, which is odd in a philosopher who has written a book called *Consciousness Explained* and who is supposed to be considering the explanatory adequacy of Darwinian theory. But maybe it is not so strange when one remembers that Dennett, in effect, thinks we are zombies anyway, so that there is no real phenomenon of consciousness to explain. But for anyone who rejects this eliminativist position, there is a puzzle here: consciousness seems like a dubious luxury, biologically, and yet it is found with great regularity in the animal kingdom. There must be something here we do not understand.

Dennett's discussion of culture borrows Dawkins's notion of the *meme*—units of information that propagate and spread, subject to natural selection, in a way analogous to genes. This is a form of evolution that is distinct from genetic evolution and can even work contrary to it. Memes enable us, as Dawkins says, to rebel against our genes, since their survival does not coincide with that of the genes. Dennett spells out the utility of this idea vividly, but he does not squarely confront the problem of how this can enable us to have moral values. The meme for altruism may indeed pass from person to person, duplicating itself and directing individual behavior; but given that it goes against the selfishness of the genes, how can it be a stable element of human nature? In a battle between memes and genes, the genes must always ultimately win, because they determine which bodies will survive—and memes need bodies too, notably brains in which to nest. Any meme that has effects contrary to the interests of the genes that produce the brain in which the meme resides will result in fewer copies of those genes, that is, will decrease reproductive advantage. So the altruism meme will be automatically selected against, in the sense that any organism that harbors it will be at a reproductive disadvantage compared to an organism innocent of it; thus genes for *not* being receptive to such a meme will be favored. Not only, then, is it puzzling how the altruism meme could have taken root; we can also predict that its days are numbered. The only way out of this pessimistic conclusion that I can see, though Dennett does not mention it, is to show how receptivity to the altruism meme might be a necessary by-product of something with a significant genetic advantage, so that selecting it out will remove a trait of overriding biological value. Thus it might be suggested that you cannot enjoy the benefits of general intelligence without being susceptible to occupation by the altruism meme. But these are issues Dennett fails to address in his rather unfocused and disappointing chapters on evolution and ethics. Once again, the issues are not as straightforward as he likes to suggest.

Dennett spends some time defending the analogy between genes and memes, and does so quite plausibly, but he does not take the next logical step and note that in fact genes *are* a type of meme. This is simply because a gene is best defined as a unit of *information,* so that what is passed on to offspring is itself a semantic vehicle, containing instructions for body construction. Some memes spread by intentional communication—the cultural ones—while others spread through biological reproduction—the ones embodied in DNA. The entire process of biological and cultural evolution is therefore information-driven. Culture and biology are united by the central mechanism of the copying of information from one site to another—whether genome or brain. Genes are selected according to whether the information they contain builds bodies that work as effective protective archives. We can thus think of genes as DNA-based memes enclosed in mobile biological libraries—animal bodies.

Dennett refers to Darwin's theory as a "dangerous idea" and as a "universal acid" that remorselessly eats through our cherished systems of belief. I am not convinced that it is as dangerous as he suggests. Of course, it undermines religious creationism, but it does not threaten anything that a secular humanist might independently value. It certainly does not decrease one's respect for the animal world, including its human members. Nor need it change the content of one's moral outlook—since you cannot deduce a moral *ought* from a biological *is.* It is really no more dangerous than our post-Copernican astronomical ideas. It is high time that we stopped treating Darwinism as a battleground in some religious or political war and see it for what it is—a profound and true empirical theory, abundantly confirmed, but with several areas in which there are problems still unresolved. By advertising Darwin's theory as a dangerous acid, Dennett does the theory a disservice; it is simply the sober truth and nothing to be afraid of. Dennett's hyperbolic style may well be found exciting by some, but there will be others who find the overheated rhetoric more off-putting than stimulating. He has given us a perfectly adequate exposition of Darwin, brimming with boyish enthusiasm, but many readers will find the controlled passion and crystalline purity of Richard Dawkins's writings more to their taste.

III

ETHICS

33

Singer: Eating Animals Is Wrong

Animal Liberation, 2nd edition
by Peter Singer
Cape, 1990

I have been persuaded of the rightness of the moral position advocated in Peter Singer's *Animal Liberation* for the past twenty years. There is, in my view, no moral justification whatever for the human exploitation of animals. I was convinced of this principally by reading the path-breaking book, *Animals, Men and Morals* (1971), edited by Stanley and Roslind Godlovitch and John Harris. Singer acknowledges his debt to this pivotal work as well as to personal contact with some of the contributors, and his own 1975 book, of which there is now a welcome second edition, is largely a sustained working-out of the moral perspective developed by these earlier thinkers. I have to declare that, in my opinion, the arguments Singer mounts, and the facts he marshals, constitute a definitive and unanswerable case for the thesis that our treatment of animals, in every department, is deeply and systematically immoral. Becoming a vegetarian is only the most minimal ethical response to the magnitude of the evil. What is needed is a complete revolution in the way we deal with other species. Do not expect, then, to find me in any way "balanced" on the question: this is not really an issue on which there are two sides. It's a won argument, as far as I'm concerned—in principle if not in practice.

If I had written that twenty years ago, I would have been accused either of shocking moral arrogance or of mild insanity. Even now I am sure that I shall be charged with exaggeration and hysterical extremism. Extrapolating from

Reprinted with permission from the *London Review of Books* (January 24, 1991).

the changes of moral outlook that have occurred in the last two decades, however, I predict that 2010 will most likely see me accused of euphemistic soft-pedaling. Why wasn't I more scorchingly critical of the countless animal abuses that scar the moral record of *Homo sapiens?* Why did I hold back from pressing the historical parallels with more widely conceded forms of violent oppression? Where was my moral rage? The reason, future reader, is that an air of moderation is prudent when your audience still thinks that eating the dead bodies of intensively reared animals is quite okay morally, really not such a bad thing at all. You have to sound as if you take this to be a matter for serious moral debate, even when you know very well that the opposition doesn't have an ethical leg to stand on. Abortion, capital punishment, drug legalization—these are genuinely debatable questions; not so the kinds of exploitation of animals that human beings take for granted. So, present reader, be warned: I am even more extreme than I sound.

Actually, the whole issue of the human use of animals has undergone a sea-change during the last two decades. From being disdained as the crackpot preserve of cat-crazed grannies and soppy misanthropes, animal liberation has become a respectable political movement, founded on an articulated moral system and capable of effecting real change in the treatment of animals. People don't look at you in the funny way they used to. They are now more shiftily defensive than smirkingly condescending. Animal sentience has taken its rightful place in human consciousness. Animals get on the News.

This is not to say that sticking up for animals isn't still a real family-splitter, friend-loser, and spouse-excluder. You are in a restaurant with some people you really get on with quite well. Noting that you are ordering a flesh-free dish, some sheepish meat-eater decides to interrogate you about your food preferences: she wants to know why you will have only your own blood inside you. You have been dreading this moment, familiar though it is: either you stand up for your principles and tell her, or you try to brush the question aside. Is she perhaps secretly sympathetic? Foolishly, you reply that you think it's morally wrong to raise animals for food in the conditions they are raised and anyway you don't see why their lives should be deemed less important than our palates. Silence. There then ensues a vituperative two-hour row, which follows a depressingly predictable course: the more the assembled diners see that they cannot refute your arguments, and the more their own rationalizations are swiftly and humiliatingly exploded, the angrier and more resentful they become. You, in turn, grow contemptuous of their moral myopia, their evasiveness, and conformity. You leave the restaurant with fewer friends than you went in with—and forget arranging a date with the initial interrogator.

May I then suggest that anyone who still thinks that our treatment of animals is basically in the moral clear, especially in the areas of experimentation and food production, sit down and study Peter Singer's book: *then* they can come and tell me why a vegetarian diet must have weakened my brain. Is it a deal? The basic argumentative strategy of the book is simple. First, Singer establishes that speciesism is a morally unacceptable standpoint. Secondly, he demonstrates that nothing could justify our actual treatment of animals except implicit adherence to the speciesist attitude. Therefore, our treatment of animals is morally wrong. Speciesism, for those who haven't heard, is the assumption that a mere difference of biological species is sufficient to warrant differential moral treatment, so that the suffering and death of animals of species other than our own is *ipso facto* of negligible moral weight. Speciesism stands opposed to the following principle, cogently defended by Singer: indistinguishable suffering should be accorded comparable moral weight, even when the sufferers belong to different species. Thus, speciesism makes moral equality turn upon biological taxonomy, irrespective of a creature's actual psychological capacities; rather as racism and sexism invoke mere racial or sexual difference (themselves biological distinctions) as a basis for moral discrimination. The speciesist is someone who wants to know what zoological kind a sentient being belongs to before he can decide whether it is right to cause it pain; and if he happens to be a human speciesist, he elevates the human species above all others—biological affinity to *him* is the decisive qualification for serious moral consideration.

Speciesism as a normative ethical principle is easily refuted. It is palpably absurd to tie moral concern to zoological classification instead of to the capacities and conditions it directly involves—pain, pleasure, freedom, confinement, life, death. Sentience is what matters when it comes to the badness of inflicting unnecessary suffering, not the genetic makeup or evolutionary history of the organism that does the suffering. If this is not self-evident, then consider the following hypothetical cases. Martians invade Earth and proceed to enslave and exploit human beings: they do to us all the things we now do to our fellow species on earth. Our lives accordingly become a hell of fear, imprisonment, pain and early death. We protest to the militarily superior Martians, who are clearly an intelligent and compassionate species: we point out that they could get on perfectly well without ruining our lives. They don't disagree with this and concede that we humans are sometimes a *bit* roughly handled. However, they insist, we have no good moral argument against their flagrant exploitation of our species, since we are not of the same biological kind, so that our suffering and death don't count for much as far as they are concerned. Their attitude toward us, they point out, is really no different from our attitude toward species other than our own—and they are, when all is said, appreciably cleverer than us. Thus, thanks to the speciesist principle, they needn't scruple about brutally killing our factory-farmed children for breakfast, instead of having cereal.

Another case: suppose that in a few million years monkeys have evolved to become as intelligent and civilized as we are now, while remaining of a distinct species from us. Meanwhile human beings have persisted with their monkey vivisection, oblivious to the psychological changes that have occurred in the monkey. Now the monkeys can protest about these human practices: they organize and sign petitions, picket and demonstrate; they even threaten gorilla war unless we set their conspecifics free. We dismiss their arguments for humane treatment with a lofty shrug: we are under no moral obligation to cease our painful and fatal experiments on them, since their species is not identical to ours, no matter that they are our equals in every respect we deem morally significant in our own species.

Or suppose that geneticists discover that there has been a mistake in biological science: we thought mankind a single species, but it turns out that there are genetic or evolutionary variations among us sufficient to warrant dividing us into two separate species. Despite appearances, then, you are not strictly of the same species as me, for your DNA differs crucially from mine in some subtle way. Would such a scientific discovery license a complete redrawing of ethical boundaries, so that I can now treat you the way I have always treated animals of other species? Am I henceforward entitled to ignore or minimize all our other similarities—particularly psychological ones— and use the fact of our different biological grouping to put you beyond my moral consideration? Would cannibalism, for example, become morally licit? Rhetorical questions, surely. Speciesism is therefore indefensible as a general moral principle.

Someone is now bound to object that these examples are unfair, since the species we exploit do not differ from us merely in respect of their biological grouping: they are generally less clever than we are, and have almost no musical appreciation. True enough, but the objector is both missing the point and tacitly conceding that the speciesist position is wrong. The essential point is that a *mere* difference of species is morally irrelevant in assessing the rightness of violating a given creature's interests; it is not, of course, being denied that differences of species can *correlate* with morally relevant differences. And now the antispeciesist argument is precisely that what we do to animals would not be done *unless* we made their species count in itself, since in other respects, particularly those having to do with sentience, animals do not differ from certain human beings whom we regard as infinitely more morally considerable. Thus, as Singer says, we take the permanently retarded child to be far more worthy of moral respect than the intellectually superior gorilla. In general, we do not rate the severity of an animal's pain equally with the like pain of a human being: somehow the fact that it is a dog's pain is supposed to make it less undesirable for that pain to occur— rather as my Martians justify the pain they cause us on the speciesist (and specious) ground that it is, after all, only *human* pain. The simple point here is that it is the pain in itself that is bad, not the fact that it is happening to one biological kind of individual rather than another. A creature's interests determine the duties we owe it, not its biological proximity to us.

Having argued against speciesism as an ethical principle, Singer goes on to detail the facts of animal life under human domination, focusing on animals as experimental tools and as sources of food. I do not think it is possible for a normal person to read these two chapters without wanting to weep, and without an accompanying feeling of impotent fury at the moral violations so richly documented. If you don't know the grim facts of animal experimentation and modern factory farming, you should scan these pages: you will never be the same again. Singer reports these facts soberly and unemotionally, generally sticking to the words of those who most directly carry out the practices we as a society permit and endorse: the scientists and the farmers.

The chapter "Tools for Research" is a litany of more or less pointless acts of gross speciesism: millions of animals, often monkeys and dogs, are routinely electrically shocked, irradiated, nerve-gassed, poisoned, maternally deprived, sliced, starved, force-fed, drowned, heated to death, frozen, crushed, shot, strangled, burned, drug-addicted and otherwise tortured and maimed. We may safely assume that none of this would be perpetrated on members of our own species, however comparable to the animal subjects they might be: except, of course, for the notorious (and instructive) examples of racially based human experimentation. Animals are simply assumed to be means to our ends, morally negligible in themselves, just so much apparatus.

The chapter on farming and meat production is scarcely less disturbing. Here illusions flourish and wishful thinking holds sway. Chickens: crammed together into massive windowless sheds, their environment artificially controlled so as to get more meat, they develop the "vices" of feather-pecking and cannibalism, so surgical "debeaking" is employed. Laying hens are confined to tiny cages in which they cannot even stretch their wings, and in which sloping wire floors give them severe foot trouble and thwart their nesting instincts. Pigs: highly intelligent, active, and social by nature, these animals are kept bored and frustrated, and take to biting their fellows' tails. Solution: cut their tails off—without anaesthetic of course. Stress-death from overcrowding is common. Foot deformity from slatted floors is standard. Veal calves: separated from their mothers, tethered by the neck, these animals are confined for their entire lives to a strawless stall in which they can hardly move, while they are fed an unnatural liquid diet expressly designed to produce anaemia. They chew the stall in an effort to satisfy their craving for roughage; they suffer chronic digestive problems; they lick anything metal to make up the iron deficiency; many of them perish before slaughter. And the sole purpose of this regime of torment is to produce pale soft flesh for well-off humans to bite into. The veal calf is perhaps the purest illustration of the orthodox human attitude toward food animals: nothing is to be spared the animal if it caters to some trivial taste on our part.

If speciesism is manifestly absurd as a moral principle, and if our entire relationship to other animals is riddled with speciesist bias, leading to systematic oppression and cruelty, why are we so ready to tolerate these unjustified moral asymmetries? Why don't we recognize what we are doing for what it is and then just stop doing it? What holds the evils of speciesism so firmly in place? At this stage of the debate this is the question that most needs to be addressed. Exposing the basis of animal exploitation may help dislodge the

ETHICS

evil, revealing it for what it is. What we have here, I suggest, is an old enemy bolstered by a peculiar feature of interspecies concern. The old enemy is the First Law of Power Relations: the more powerful will always tend to oppress the less powerful, if they can get away with it. Where there is vulnerability, you will find that vulnerability exploited and magnified. Violence is invariably the ultimate means of subordination. This law holds historically for races, children, women, . . . and animals. Domination and enslavement are regularly visited on the relatively helpless: and animals are just one more powerless group that has fallen victim to this law. Nor can they so much as speak out against their exploitation (though they are quite capable of making their feelings known to their exploiters). Of course, it is common to find some religious or other ideology invoked to legitimize this kind of naked exercise of power: but we are not now so easily duped by this ploy in cases other than that of animals—we are wise to the ways of "false consciousness." In the case of animals, people still feel in their bones that their exploited position is somehow written into the order of things, that this is what the universe intends—instead of recognizing it for good old-fashioned power-mongering. We do it because we can and we like it, and that's really the end of the matter. Conjoin this with the sadistic impulses that are never far away from the abuse of power, and you have a profoundly satisfying state of affairs for the human species: we get to fuck animals up royally and they can't so much as talk back to us—not even a stray rebel or terrorist to handle. Perfect! We can then flatter our vanity with the delicious thought of how much they have to sacrifice in order to gratify our trivial fancies. "I must be *very* important because my coat took ten tormented rare wild animals to make it. As I am lord of all creation, it is my God-given right to use animals in any fashion I see fit. Why, it's the next best thing to being God!"

The special feature of animal exploitation, which makes the law of power so ingrained in their case, is that the countervailing force of empathy is so much weaker here than elsewhere. Because other species live lives that differ in various respects from ours, and because they look different and make different noises, it is less natural for us to enter into their point of view and appreciate how things are for them. It takes an imaginative effort to see the world as a turtle does—indeed, to recognize that a turtle sees the world in any way. Just so, my invading Martians may have limited empathy when it comes to understanding how it is for us to be locked in tiny stalls, malnourished, experimented on, hunted, killed. Empathy is the chief foe of discriminative harm, and human empathy can be withheld from an exploited group if that group differs from us in some salient (though superficial) respect. In the case of animals, our capacity for empathy tends to be fitful and arbitrary, sentimentally selective where it is not barbarically absent. Here, the moral bridge of identification is apt to be shaky at best. Accordingly, if speciesism, as a reflexive attitude beyond rational critique, is to be effectively undermined, it will be necessary to extend and deepen our capacity for interspecific empathy: we need to be able to look upon animals with fresh eyes, unconditioned by the role in which we have historically placed them, thus to engage more fully with their distinctive "forms of life." And the key to this is not some willed increase in the amount of affection we feel for other species: it must come, rather, from a respect based upon impartial appreciation of their intrinsic nature. It is a cognitive change more than an affective one that we need. In my view, fully absorbing the idea that we are all contingent creatures of Darwinian evolution, subject to its laws and constraints, is the best way of attaining the right perspective on the lives of other animals: we are just one species among others, making our way in a not terribly sympathetic world. There is no sense in which other animals were made for us (*pace* Genesis). What distinguishes us from them is our ability to inject a moral dimension into these natural facts: and so not go right ahead and exploit whatever we can at whatever cost to our victim. Animals are not inherently our tools, and we have the moral capacity to recognize that they should not be reduced to that status. Instead, think of other species as existing independently of our species, and as having their own enormously long evolutionary history; then remember that they have a mode of sentience that goes with their biological nature, just as we do. Don't think of animals as convenient natural artifacts whose existence is exhausted by their relation to us: they are autonomous beings. We once gave up a geocentric conception of the universe, in which we sat at the cosmic centre; now we need to complete the Darwinian revolution and accept that the animal creation is not fundamentally anthropocentric. Speciesism will end only when this kind of informed modesty has been properly achieved.

Singer completes the argument of *Animal Liberation* with a telling chapter on the history of animal abuse and the gradual recognition that the law should prohibit at least some of the grosser forms of human cruelty. He deals also with all the counterarguments to his position that he has heard, however fatuous these may be. He concludes with a challenge to the reader: "throughout this book I have relied on rational argument. Unless you can refute the central argument of this book, you should now recognize that speciesism is wrong, and this means that, if you take morality seriously, you should try to eliminate speciesist practices from your own life, and oppose them elsewhere." I can only reiterate this challenge.

What does the future hold for animals? Twenty years ago I was very pessimistic about the possibility of fundamental change, because at that time even morally alive people found the very idea of animal rights merely quaint. Today this is a respectable part of the political agenda. It is nice to be regarded no longer as a naive eccentric, a squeamish sentimentalist with mystical leanings (me, mystical!). Perhaps the progress that has already been made, such as it is, will continue and accelerate, leading to radical improvements for animals. It is arguable that we are now in a transitional period, in which old prejudices and ideologies about the cosmic place of animals have crumbled, yet our moral reactions are lagging behind; that it is only a matter of time before we wake up ethically to what we already implicitly believe about the biological world and our position in it. Old habits and powerful vested interests will thus eventually succumb to moral common sense, and one of human kind's greatest tyrannies will collapse like so many others before. As a bonus, there will be enough food to feed the world's hungry, once plant protein is no longer wasted on fattening unnecessary food animals for the better-off. The deepest form of exploitation and institutionalized death in human history will have been eradicated, making other forms of oppression psychologically harder to bring about, because less built into our daily lives.

I suppose such a rosy future is not impossible, though in my experience we shouldn't bank on ordinary civilized adults to bring it about: we need to appeal to the natural moral instincts of the preindoctrinated. As Peter Singer remarks, children very frequently express their horror at the origin of their dinner and wish to become vegetarian; it can take a lot of adult cajoling or worse to wean them off their sound moral standpoint. Children are the natural friends of animals, and paying them more respect might be the best way to get animals liberated. Put more practically: animal activists should work to ensure that the facts of animal life under human dominion are taught in schools and made generally available to the young. Put speciesism on the curriculum. To parents I say: do you really want your children to blame you for keeping them in the dark about all the rotten things we do to animals? Wouldn't you prefer to be able to boast to your grandchildren that you were in the vanguard when animals were given their freedom?

34

Frey: Beyond the Moral Pale

Interests and Rights: The Case
against Animals
by R. G. Frey
Clarendon Press, 1980

In questioning received attitudes toward the moral status of animals, it is a common experience to find one's qualms reinforced by the jejune and sophistical character of the arguments put up in defense of our current practices. R. G. Frey's book is sure to have this unintended effect, and for that reason may not be without value. He is out to oppose the "philosophical orthodoxy"(!) that calls for radical changes in our treatment of animals, and does so by offering a series of transparent paralogisms directed against the proanimal writings of various contemporary philosophers.

Frey's target is the claim, due originally to Leonard Nelson, that since animals have interests and interests confer moral rights, animals have moral rights. He is sceptical of this claim on two counts: he does not believe in moral rights at all, and he denies that animals have interests. Since the first of these contentions is not specific to the case of animals, he proposes to concentrate on the second. His procedure is to examine a number of suggested bases for the possession of interests—having needs, beliefs, desires, emotions, being sentient, and having the capacity to suffer—and to deny either that animals have them, or that they confer interests. On each of these topics his arguments have the unmistakable hollow ring of the bottom of the barrel.

Some have suggested that sentience and the capacity to suffer give animals an interest in not being subjected to certain kinds of life. Frey's reply to this modest suggestion is that it is inconsistent with the motivation of those

Reprinted with permission from the *Times Literary Supplement* (August 1, 1980).

who make it, because it amounts to a new form of "discrimination"—now against the insentient world of plants and rocks. This complaint is absurd: *any* attempt to circumscribe (as we must) our moral obligations will involve, as a matter of logic, such "discrimination," on pain of treating everything— including numbers, electrons and regions of space—as of equal moral status. Nor is one committed to according *no* value to an entity just because one insists that it does not bear a certain *kind* of value. Another favorite tactic of Frey's is to accuse his opponents of having no "argument" for their views. Thus he wants it *demonstrated* that pain is (other things being equal) a bad thing, or else he feels free to deny it. He seems unaware that every argument has at least one premiss and that moral argument, like any other, must stop somewhere—preferably with something no rational man can honestly dispute. But Frey tells us that, on the contrary, we are "autonomous" in respect of arguments—nothing can *force* our assent. One wonders how he comes to believe anything (if he does).

Frey's central thesis is that interests require beliefs and animals do not have beliefs. The question whether genuine belief is possible in the absence of language is indeed difficult and vexed, but Frey's own reasons for a negative verdict verge on the ludicrous. He says we cannot attribute beliefs to animals because (a) a particular piece of behavioral evidence never conclusively establishes whether an animal has a given belief, and (b) the human observer cannot directly perceive the animal's belief. With the requirements pitched this high, not even professors of philosophy can be credited with beliefs. Nor does the appeal to speech help here, since it does not enable belief states to meet these unrealistically stringent conditions—speech is itself a kind of behavior requiring interpretation. Frey's argument for connecting belief and language seems to be that since a belief ascription embeds a sentence, what is believed is that that sentence is true. Not only is this a breathtaking non sequitur, but the conclusion is open to the textbook objection that the believer would have to speak the same language as the ascriber. (It should be noted that, as Frey disarmingly acknowledges, speechless children are similarly robbed of interests by the above considerations. This consequence obviously places the normative significance of the whole book in grave doubt, a fact of which he is sometimes half-aware.)

The treatment of animal wants is scarcely less flawed. Here Frey announces a dilemma: either the wants of animals are mere needs, in which case they do not differ essentially from the "needs" of inanimate objects, for example, that of a tractor for oil; or they are said to be genuine desires, but then desires require beliefs and animals have already been shown not to have beliefs. The first horn of this alleged dilemma turns upon a crude equivocation on the word "need": plainly the needs of a conscious creature (and even Frey allows animals consciousness) are such that their frustration has ill effects on the well-being of the creature, notably suffering, different in kind from the breakdown of a tractor. The second horn of the dilemma assumes that *all* desires involve belief in a lack. Speechless children are thereby rendered nonconative, as well as animals. Frey attempts to ease the implausibility of this by trying to link desire with self-consciousness, but he never explains why unreflective consciousness would not suffice.

Emotions are likewise denied to the speechless. Frey's case for this is wholly vitiated by exclusive concentration on the emotion of shame. Shame does indeed appear to be the kind of emotion that requires a complex substructure of belief, unavailable to the average dog; but what of anger, fear, and (perhaps) grief? What does Frey think is going on, psychologically, when a child or monkey displays behavior we naturally describe as emotional? And what does he make of the physiological facts about emotions in men and animals? If we are to insist upon a cognitive component to such mental phenomena, we might do better, if belief proper seems inappropriate, to invoke informational states of nonlinguistic creatures which function in ways *analogous* to the ways in which beliefs function: thus it has been suggested that a creature can be said to *register* a proposition without strictly believing it. At any rate, this is one of the many substantive issues whose proper treatment evidently exceeds Frey's philosophical sophistication.

His remarks on suffering and interests show the lengths to which he is prepared to go in prosecuting the "case against animals." His main point is that not everything we would describe as an interest is conceptually linked to the sensation of pain. But this misses the mark: the claim he needs to contest is that the capacity for suffering is necessary and sufficient to confer *certain kinds* of interest upon a being, in particular those that our current treatment of animals (e.g., in factory farms) typically infringe. In respect of the simple claim that animals have an interest in not feeling pain because pain is an intrinsically bad thing, Frey resorts to his fallback ploy of asking for a *proof* that unnecessary suffering is intrinsically bad. By his standards *no* moral position could be established

Recalling the subtitle of Frey's book, one is somewhat taken aback by his postscript: for he there admits that animals may be wronged, and indeed regards it as a serious question whether we do systematically wrong them. This is laudable, but sits ill with his announced intentions: what he has offered us is, in fact, a critique of a moral theory with which he disagrees, not a set of normative claims. Indeed, it could hardly be other than that, given his concessions about speechless children. The suspicion is encouraged that his concern is less with the substantive normative questions themselves than with adding to the philosophical literature that has already been generated. While this may somewhat excuse the casuistical quality of the book, it is surely deplorable to find practical issues of this moment treated with such moral disengagement.

35

Pluhar: Born Free

Beyond Prejudice: The Moral Significance
of Human and Nonhuman Animals
by Evelyn B. Pluhar
Duke University Press, 1995

Strange to say, not all human institutions owe their existence to sound moral reasoning—not even those that have proved themselves most durable. Monarchy, slavery, patriarchy, dictatorship, child labor: these practices were sustained by power and advantage, not by their invulnerability to moral criticism. Spurious moral defenses, often bizarrely ingenious, have grown up around these practices, enabling their beneficiaries to soothe their consciences or to ward off their critics, but few would now pretend that these exercises of power enjoy any defensible ethical rationale. The suggestion that slaves were *made* to be exploited, by God or nature, would not now be received as anything other than self-serving delusion. Enslaved persons have their inherent moral rights to life, liberty, and the pursuit of happiness, and the institution of slavery violates these rights. This may not have been obvious then, but it is a platitude now.

In recent decades, we have grown used to hearing a comparable claim made on behalf of animals. It is said that they, too, are the victims of unjust exploitation. We humans use them as means to our ends, without regard for their inalienable rights. We treat animals in ways that are contrary to their interests—as when we eat them, confine them, experiment on them, hunt them, wear their skins—and this is a plain violation of moral principle. We are, in effect, discriminating against animals on the basis of their species. Isn't this really just an exercise of brute power, devoid of moral foundation?

Reprinted with permission from the *New Republic* (April 8, 1996).

Isn't it disturbingly like slavery, except that we are exploiting members of other species? If so, the practices in question should be dismantled and animals accorded in law what their moral status requires. So the animal liberationist argument goes.

To these claims there is a natural answer, frequently offered. In the other examples of exploited groups, the victims are all persons, while animals are not—and persons are the only proper bearers of moral rights. Slavery is the exploitation of conscious, rational, moral beings, with a sense of the future and their own potential, and capable of protesting against their enslavement; but pigs and cows and chickens fall short of this standard, being at most sentient and conative. So there is no valid comparison to be made here: it is wrong to violate the rights of reflective articulate beings, but animals do not fall into this category. Thus there is nothing arbitrary about the difference in the ways that we treat members of our own species and members of other species.

This reply has persuaded many people that the case of animals lays no serious claim on their moral attention. But it is open to a fairly obvious retort. What about those members of the human species who fail to qualify as full persons in the intended sense—the very young, the senile, the mentally retarded, the brain-damaged? The mental faculties of such individuals are severely truncated relative to those of the typical human adult, but we do not exclude them from the moral community, doing to them what we routinely do to animals. Compare a normal chimpanzee to a severely retarded human child unable to take care of itself or to speak or to reason. Given that neither qualifies as a rational moral being, capable of asserting its rights, why do we allow vivisection of the chimp but not of the child? Surely, if moral significance attaches only to full persons, then the child should be granted no more protection than the chimp, or the pig awaiting slaughter.

Do we want to accept this? There is an obvious dilemma here: either give up the link between personhood and moral rights or regard animals *and* mentally limited humans as both lacking basic moral rights. For in neither case are we dealing with full personhood, which is the alleged touchstone of moral worth. Evelyn Pluhar's book is devoted to the evaluation of this argument for animal rights. Taking her cue from Peter Singer's use of the argument in *Animal Liberation,* she undertakes to state it as rigorously as possible and then to defend it against every objection she has heard of or can think of. Her book is exceptionally thorough, expertly reasoned, and entirely convincing.

The essence of Pluhar's case is that there is no way to protect what she calls "marginal humans" from moral exclusion that does not extend to nonhuman animals. Once it is acknowledged that full personhood is not a necessary condition for moral significance, as in the case of marginal humans, then we must grant the same moral status to animals, on the ground that no morally relevant distinction can be drawn between the two cases. Pluhar is absolutely determined to argue through every possible objection to the argument, even some of the sillier ones, so that no doubt can be left about its cogency. The upshot, after the dialectical dust has settled, is that there is a deep inconsistency in current moral attitudes—a double standard that cries out for rectification. The simple truth is that we unjustly discriminate against members of other species for transparently selfish reasons.

It is a commonplace reaction to Pluhar's argument that marginal humans are human, while other animals are not. This is the ground of the moral distinction that we habitually make. Such a "homocentrist" position takes the human species to define the boundaries of the moral community: you are morally considerable if, and only if, you are a member of the human species. It is important to see, as Pluhar emphasizes, that this is *not* a version of the full personhood view—that it is, indeed, incompatible with it, since not all humans are full persons. What is being claimed, rather, is that a biological criterion, not a psychological one, is decisive from a moral point of view.

There are many problems, however, with this "speciesist" defense. Isn't it really just a form of bigotry, analogous to claiming that the biological characteristics of skin color or sex are morally crucial? What if scientists made discoveries that caused them to redraw the boundaries of the species, so that in fact we featherless bipeds are composed of two distinct species with different evolutionary origins and DNA structures? Would each of us then be right to conclude that only the species that *we* belonged to had moral standing, so that the other humaniods could be treated as we now treat pigs and mice? Do intelligent extraterrestrials automatically lack moral significance because they are not of our biological kind? Is God beyond the moral pale because he is not biologically human? Would the truth of the Bible imply that Jesus Christ suffered no moral evil by being crucified, since he was not fully of our species (being immaculately conceived and so on)? How can morality depend upon biology, anyway? Surely my rights stem from the kind of life I am able to lead—from my status as a psychological being—not from whatever biological substrate happens to underlie this. If I find out that I am not human after all, having been deposited here by a UFO, do I then voluntarily give up all my rights to decent treatment? No, I do not: my biological type is a contingent fact about me, and it is neither here nor there when it comes to assessing my moral rights.

It might now be said that marginal humans differ morally from animals not because they are human, but because they are members of a species whose *typical* members are full persons. The retarded child is not a full person, but he or she is at least a member of a species characterized by such superior beings. Thus, whenever a species has typical members who are full persons, any member of the species enjoys moral standing, even if that particular member falls woefully short of the mark. This suggestion is not "speciesist" in the strict sense, and it seems to give marginal humans a moral foothold; but Pluhar shows that it will scarcely do as a sound moral principle.

The suggestion locates the basis of a being's moral rights not in the intrinsic nature of that being, but in its relation to other beings: the retarded human is not valuable by virtue of his individual traits, but only because of his relation to other more richly endowed humans. This implies that if these relations change, then so does his moral standing. The marginal human's moral worth depends precisely upon his being marginal. But now, if the human species manages so to pollute the earth that in time a typical member is no longer a full person, almost everyone having been chemically brain-damaged, then no human will enjoy moral significance—though each is at the level of marginal humans *now* accorded moral worth. Similarly, an individual dog would become morally significant if its species, but not it, were to develop into full canine persons, despite the fact that there has been no intrinsic change in that dog. But how can you change an individual's moral status simply by fiddling with what is true of other members of its species? Surely we treat individuals with consideration because of what is true of them, not because of the contingent fact that they share their kind with other individuals who differ from them.

All this, of course, is a contrived attempt to escape the obvious. What makes the marginal human morally considerable is not that her conspecifics are typically full persons; it is simply that she is herself a sentient individual with desires and conditions of well-being. The human infant, though not yet a rational moral agent, can yet experience pleasure and pain, can have its desires satisfied or thwarted, can have its life wrongfully taken. The prerational infant is a subject of consciousness, a goal-directed seeker of well-being, an avoider of harm. Marginal humans can be happy or unhappy, according to whether their needs and desires are satisfied, and this is what underlies their claim on our moral attention. But it is equally true that animals are sentient conative individuals with conditions of well-being, and in some cases there is no relevant distinction to be drawn between them and marginal humans in respect of their degree of sentience and goal-directedness. Put crudely, some animals are as smart as some humans. Only by ignoring the moral relevance of sentience can we draw a sharp dividing line between animals and the less fortunate members of our own species.

Pluhar explores these issues in detail, dealing with such objections as that the mistreatment of marginal humans has a worse effect on the moral character of the agent than the mistreatment of animals, or produces worse utilitarian consequences in the human population. She has no difficulty showing the weakness of these arguments. But she also wishes to find a positive rationale for the moral relevance of sentience. What precisely is it about sentience that makes it so morally crucial? This part of the book will be particularly interesting for old hands at this subject, because here she parts company with Peter Singer and proposes a novel way to conceive of the rights of animals.

It might seem that sentience matters because moral value depends solely upon the maximization of pleasure and the minimization of pain—the utilitarian position. Since sentient beings such as dogs and gorillas experience pleasure and pain, we should act so as to maximize utility in their case.

Utilitarianism thus morally unites animals, marginal humans, and full persons, since all are receptacles of pleasure and pain. But there are problems. Utilitarianism allows us to sacrifice an innocent if this will produce a greater balance of pleasure over pain in sentient beings as a group; it permits what we would normally take to be a violation of individual rights. This is no comfort, however, to the animal vivisection community: whereas utilitarianism in principle permits experimenting on animals for the benefit of humans, it also permits experimenting on humans—marginal and typical—for the benefit of other humans (and animals!). Many find this morally repugnant, and reasonably so. And the "replacement argument" of the utilitarians is no better. If our duty is simply to maximize pleasure and minimize pain, then there can be no objection to killing individuals so long as we replace them with other individuals who will function as new repositories of pleasurable experience. The net amount of pleasure will not be reduced if I produce a new sentient being to take up where the old one has involuntarily left off. Thus is the right to life abrogated by the utilitarian principle.

Pluhar is right to conclude that this is not a workable moral theory. We need a viewpoint that finds a place for individual rights, human and animal. What, then, will these rights depend upon? Not on the capacity to claim rights, or else marginal humans are, with animals, off the moral map. We must look instead to what it is that rights serve to protect. Building upon the ideas of Alan Gewirth, Pluhar defends the view that rights stem from the capacity to care about what happens to one—from desires and their satisfaction. The emphasis thus shifts from sentience to conation, from the passive reception of sensations to the active seeking of goals. One can only satisfy one's desires if one is alive and free to act in appropriate ways; so one values one's life and one's freedom because these are necessary conditions for satisfying one's desires. What is presupposed by the valuable is itself valuable. Hence life and freedom are valuable and require the protection that the ascription of rights affords.

Desires vary, of course, from individual to individual, and some sets of desires are more extensive than others, though the satisfaction of desires is no less important to an individual because his desires are more limited than the desires of someone else. A dog's desire to run free does not matter less to it than my desire to enjoy a ballet performance matters to me. A sentient conative being has the right to the freedom and the continued existence necessary for the satisfaction of its desires, whatever these may be. This is the ultimate basis of my right not to be imprisoned or eaten or experimented upon, and the same is true of a chimp's right to similar freedoms.

So sentience matters, not because it is the vehicle of pleasure and pain, but because it is concomitant with a goal-directed agent that requires freedom from interference in order to fulfill its purposes. The sentient conative subject cares about what will happen to it, and hence is of a kind to have basic moral rights. This point of view unifies (many) animals with normal and marginal humans in a nonarbitrary way: all are morally considerable in virtue of their nature as sentient conative beings. We cannot treat animals as we would not treat mentally comparable humans.

The consequences of adopting this perspective are large. The human practice of using animals to serve human ends, regardless of their interests, turns out to lack a cogent ethical basis. When our interests conflict with theirs we cannot simply override them on the grounds that animals fail to count as morally considerable. It is really just a form of prejudice to count their interests as somehow less intrinsically significant than ours, especially when it is a matter of their vital interests versus our trivial interests. They deserve the same moral respect that we accord to marginal humans. When wondering what to do about a conflict of interest, always ask yourself whether you would countenance some proposed way of resolving it in the case of marginal humans: that is the acid test for whether unfair discrimination is being practiced. Would you shoot retarded people because they are encroaching on your food supply or messing up your back yard? Would you kill and eat them because of the culinary pleasure to be derived? If your answer is no, then you should return a similar answer in respect of animals.

Evelyn Pluhar has pushed this debate to the next level, challenging her readers to refute her arguments or to change their attitudes. She is moved as much by a passion for reason as by the plight of animals; and indeed it is the sheer irrationality of conventional attitudes toward animals that strikes some of us as humanity's worst moral failing. It is bad enough to mistreat animals for blatantly selfish reasons, but to defend this mistreatment by means of transparently shoddy arguments is almost as objectionable. It is not just the welfare of animals that is at stake here. The integrity of human reason is also on the line. Where is our intellectual pride?

36

Held and Baier:
Mothers and Moralists

Feminist Morality: Transforming Culture,
Society, and Politics
by Virginia Held
University of Chicago Press, 1994

Moral Prejudices: Essays on Ethics
by Annette C. Baier
Harvard University Press, 1994

G. E. Moore wrote, in *Principia Ethica,* the classic work of analytic moral philosophy: "By far the most valuable things, which we know or can imagine, are certain states of consciousness, which may be roughly described as the pleasures of human intercourse and the enjoyment of beautiful objects. . . . [P]ersonal affections and aesthetic enjoyments include *all* the greatest, and *by far* the greatest goods we can imagine. . . ."* This celebration of human intimacy, in all its forms, was the element in Moore's book that most ignited the members of the Bloomsbury Group, male and female, heterosexual and homosexual. (Beauty was already on the list.) It is nothing other than the firm suggestion that love—personal love of particular others, not an abstract love of humanity—is the central moral value. This emphasis on love was not, by itself, a particularly novel suggestion (there was that other male moral theorist, Jesus). But adjoining it in secular form to a pure and rigorous system of analytic thought was felt to mark a major moral advance. And it reflected Moore's personality: searchingly critical, relentlessly clear, yet famously kind, simple, and pure. To many, that seemed like a good way to be; and nobody at the time was surprised or troubled by the fact that Moore was a man.

Reprinted with permission from the *New Republic* (October 3, 1994).
*G. E. Moore, *Principia Ethica,* Cambridge: Cambridge University Press, 1993, pp. 237–8.

David Hume, two hundred years earlier, had proclaimed that the foundation of morality is not reason, but emotion. Reason may direct the "passions" in moral contexts, but it is fundamentally their slave. Moral altruism toward others originates in a "natural sympathy" with which we are endowed, and it spreads outward from the family to more impersonal kinds of human relation. Our moral sense, said Hume, is governed by innate fellow feeling, not by the affectless cognition of abstract truths; and despite Kant's opposition to this view of morality, it became the dominant conception. In our century, indeed, "emotivism" came to be the received view. Moral philosophy has thus been awash with emotion for a considerable time, and those dispensing all this affect have been mainly men.

Bernard Williams, among living moral theorists, is noted for his opposition to the impersonal character of certain ethical theories, especially utilitarianism. Such theories invite us to act solely on the principle of maximizing the total of human happiness, without regard to our own personal relation to those being benefited or harmed. As Williams observes, this sort of moral reasoning confers no special status upon those with whom we are intimately involved—family, friends, neighbors. But such relations, argues Williams, carry their own moral value, which should not be swallowed up in some global calculation of the likely effects of my actions on people in general. I owe special duties to my intimates; and therefore impersonal moral theories distort the pattern of obligations that defines my moral space. Williams's maleness does not seem to have impeded him from appreciating this point, which seems appreciable by anyone with human intelligence.

I adduce these three moral theorists because they constitute something of an embarrassment for the historical and psychological theory put forward by some feminist moral philosophers, including Virginia Held and Annette C. Baier. That theory is simple: moral philosophy has been produced mainly by men, under conditions of patriarchy, and so it has neglected or rejected the moral insights that are the prerogative of women. Each of the three contributions cited (Moore's, Hume's, and Williams's) is routinely arrogated by feminist moral theorists to themselves, as somehow uniquely their province: the value of affection between people, the emphasis on moral emotion as a guide to judgment, the importance of the family and other intimates in shaping one's moral world.

Clearly, then, male moral philosophers have been able to overcome whatever malign intellectual effects stem from maleness and male domination. For it is a raw historical fact that it did not take feminism to make these ideas possible. Moreover, there is nothing distinctively feminist about these ideas, beyond the fact that they appeal to certain feminists. These philosophical notions are gender-neutral, available in principle to any reflective person; they are based on intellectual grounds that in no way owe their origins to anything specific to women. As in other areas of philosophy, you can have worthwhile ideas no matter what sex you are. You need only the brains and the patience.

Perhaps there are other conceptions that might be more plausibly attributed to a distinctively female point of view, conceptions that have been systematically overlooked in male-dominated moral philosophy. The suggestion is not, I think, absurd. After all, moral theory was largely developed in
conditions of male dominance, in which women seldom got the chance to
work out or to state their philosophical views; and the biological and psychological differences between men and women might make certain moral perspectives come more naturally to one sex than the other. Maybe the moral
faculty of women *is* innately better tuned to moral reality than the moral
faculty of men. Feminist physics and feminist logic sound instantly silly, but
maybe not feminist morality. It is a heady and exciting thought that we might
make large moral strides, theoretically and practically, by attending more
closely to the moral thinking of women.

One would like to think this might be true, what with the pressing need
for such strides. Thus it was with great expectations that I cracked open these
two books by professional female moral philosophers. My expectations were
swiftly dashed, or slowly eroded. It turns out that patriarchy has not been so
bad for moral philosophy, however bad it has been for female moral philosophers. From the reading of these books, I conclude that there is no untapped
pool of deep moral reflection that a feminist perspective enables us to re-
cover.

Virginia Held's book has grand aims. It sets out to overturn traditional
moral theory in favor of a type of moral thinking uniquely consonant with
female experience. Once again, Carol Gilligan's work on moral development
in girls and boys is the starting point. Roughly speaking, Gilligan's thesis is
that boys are more concerned with abstract principles of justice, while girls
tend to dwell on caring and personal concern. Held claims that this alleged
difference shows up in the kind of moral philosophy produced by men and
women. Men favor the model of impersonal contracts between equals;
women take the involuntary trust and dependence of the mother-child relationship as primary. Thus feminist morality is held to fill a gap left by male
philosophers, pointing toward a more complete and satisfactory morality
that will help solve our many social and individual woes. Instead of viewing
obligation as men view it, in terms of voluntary contracts between equal
strangers in competition for the goods of the world, we should think of
obligation on the model of the preordained emotional relationship that binds
mother and child, which is how women view it. Instead of demanding impartial justice between people, we should encourage motherly concern. An
"ethic of care" should replace an "ethic of justice."

It is hard to state this position without making it seem foolish; and indeed
I think that, upon examination, there is little to be said in its favor. Held's
method of persuasion proceeds by sectarian exaggeration, tendentious formulation, political tub-thumping, and a resolute unwillingness to consider
potential objections to her position. The style is numbingly academic, foggy,
and hope-for-the-best. One has the constant impression that this book was

generated in an isolated world of yea-saying comrades who considered it unsisterly to argue with the speaker. Some of Held's better points are familiar from the male tradition, though she avoids giving credit where credit is due. Thus the Humean emotivist tradition is scarcely alluded to, and Moore's famous emphasis on personal affection is not mentioned. Held contrives to give the impression that everything in moral philosophy that opposes Kantian rationalism is of recent, and feminist, origin.

Her main critical thesis is that the "male" theory of morality as a social contract runs into trouble when extended to family relations. At the level of actual moral psychology, as opposed to idealized theoretical modeling, this certainly seems to be correct. But it is a fair criticism only if contractarianism was designed to apply to family relations. Surely, however, the point of contractarian theories is to take up the moral slack left *after* family relations have done their obligation-producing work. We don't need a social contract with members of our family, because of the nature of family bonds; but when it comes to strangers, no such instinctive underpinning sways us. The point of contractual agreements is to ensure that we treat people outside of our circle of intimates in a proper and decent manner. A contract theorist could happily accept that the moral cement of the family does not consist in a voluntary agreement between equals. Held's criticism is beside the point.

Many of Held's moral and philosophical recommendations are not distinctively feminist in any clear sense, but there is one argument that does appear to qualify as feminist in content. This is Held's suggestion that all moral relations between people should be considered according to the paradigm of mothering:

> The relation between mothering person and child, hardly understandable in contractual terms, is a more fundamental relation and may be a more promising one on which to build our recommendations for the future than is any relation between rational contractors. We should look to the relation between mothering person and child for suggestions of how better to describe such society as we now have. And we should look to it especially for a view of a future more fit for our children than a global battleground for rational, egoistic entities trying, somehow, to restrain their antagonisms by fragile contracts.

There are a number of severe objections to such a view. For a start, it ignores fathering, which is equally beyond the reach of contract theory. Surely it is the parental relation that should be invoked, not just the mothering relation. Held wavers and hedges on this point, sometimes conceding that fathers can be "mothering persons," which is all well and good, morally and theoretically; but then we have lost any distinctively feminine contribution to ethical understanding. All that is being said is that the care of children—by a mother or a father—is something that needs to inform our wider ethical outlook, that the experience of parenting can be a source of moral insight. This is true, but trivial. And the fact is that fathers are virtually absent from Held's depiction of family life; they are mentioned only to be rebuked for not doing their bit in child care.

But is the relation of mothering (or fathering) really a helpful paradigm for social relations in general? How exactly is it supposed to apply to one's relations with friends, colleagues, strangers on the train? On this crucial question Held is reticent, though she writes rather revealingly that

> on the first occasion when I spoke about considering the relation between mothering person and child as the primary social relation, a young man in the audience asked who the mothers are and who the children are in society, by which he meant society outside the family. It was meant as a hostile question, but is actually a very good one. The difficulty so many persons have in imagining an answer may indicate how distorted are the traditional contractual conceptions.

Note the strange antithesis between a "hostile" question and a "good" one. Plainly the young man in question was offering a straightforward criticism of Held, rather than engaging in sycophancy and ego stroking. In fact, of course, the questioner hit the nail on the head. In relations with that vast majority of people who are neither one's mother nor one's child, who is to be the mother and who the child? Held vaguely suggests that we might shuttle from one role to the other as we deal with people at large. This is absurd: people do not want to be the child to my mother, whatever that would mean, and I have no desire to be the child of every mother-surrogate (that is, person) who comes my way. The mothering relation is a highly specific relation, with a particular psychology and a particular set of obligations. It is ludicrous to suggest that we should go around duplicating this relation in every social encounter of our lives. It would be condescending, fake, and comical.

Should I be able to discipline people who don't do as I tell them? Am I expected to buy everybody Christmas presents? Presumably Held's suggestion is not supposed to be taken so literally. But if it is not, then it quickly collapses into the bland (but worthy) injunction to treat everybody with kindness and concern. Held seems to be committing the following fallacious inference: mothers (ideally!) treat their children with kindness and consideration; it is good to treat people with kindness and consideration; therefore we should treat everybody as if we were their mothers. The problem, obviously, is that kindness and consideration are not the exclusive property of mothers, though it sometimes sounds as if Held thinks that they are. Once her argument is detached from motherhood specifically, it becomes indistinguishable from the entirely nonfeminist injunction to care about one's fellows and treat them well. I could not subscribe more whole-heartedly to that injunction, but in so doing I am clearly not proposing to recast traditional moral theory along feminist lines.

Actually, it strikes me as somewhat reactionary, from a feminist point of view, to give mothering the central role. If mothering is where real goodness

lies, then we are all under an obligation to be mothers, since we should strive
to be as good as possible; but since "ought" implies "can," only women fall
under this edict, and so all—and only—women are obliged to be mothers,
assuming that they are biologically capable. But this assigns to women the
patriarchal obligation of having children and bringing them up, with this
obligation morally trumping any other projects that they might entertain. I
doubt that Held would welcome this result of her position, but it follows
logically from what she is saying. Held's view is also reactionary, at least by
implication, in a more general way. Insofar as it selects the family as the focus
of our moral concern, it is only too likely to lead to indifference and worse
when it comes to those not related to us by blood ties, since family feeling
cannot be simply willed into existence. In order to extend our moral concern
beyond the field of our intimates, we need impersonal principles of justice
and consideration, or the despised apparatus of "male" moral thinking.

Held has some subsidiary concerns to which she thinks a feminist perspective will contribute. She has a chapter deploring the commercialization of
culture in capitalist countries such as the United States, and she suggests that
feminists will share her condemnation. Maybe, but again there is nothing
distinctively feminist about the complaint, right or wrong, that contemporary culture has been debased by the power of big economic interests. There
is also a rather tired and unconvincing chapter about violence and gender, in
which it is predictably maintained that men are responsible for violence and
war, while women are pacific and nurturing. The empirical grounds for this,
as always, are inconclusive, and Held certainly oversimplifies the attitudes of
men and women toward violence and its prevention. It is odd, too, to suggest
that the family is the place to look for a nonviolent culture when, as we know,
there is so much violence within families, and not all of it committed by men.
Families are as much a part of the problem as a part of the solution. But the
wickedness of women seems not to appear in her worldview, except, I suppose, as the result of male domination.

Held's ideal society would be dedicated, she says, to the "flourishing of
children," with that aim being accorded a higher priority than it is now. It is
hard to disagree with the sentiment behind this, but it should not be forgotten that the well-being of adults is also of importance. Children become
adults, after all, and their problems don't stop when they do. It is idiotic to
suppose that if children were given more attention, the ills of the world
would disappear. Indeed, from Held's point of view, it is not easy to see how
more mothering could be the solution to our problems, since she believes
that it is women, not men, who now shape the moral outlook of the young
during their development (the men being off at work and war). One can
readily imagine a dystopian future in which the young are catered to lavishly
while the old are left to rack and ruin.

And then there is a more strictly philosophical matter, which is Held's   NB
persistent denigration of the use of abstract rules in morality, viewing them
as somehow cut off from context and feeling. This is a tendentious carica-

ture. Abstract rules can be rules about feeling and action, and they can always be qualified to allow for variations of context. The rule that one should treat others as one would wish to be treated oneself is by no means an abstraction removed from concrete reality. Such rules play an indispensable moral role. A morality without them would be vulnerable to caprice, special pleading and sheer chaos. If general rules are somehow characteristic of male moral thinking (which I doubt), then men have made a contribution to morality of great moment, which it would be folly to repudiate on grounds of feminist ideology.

Annette C. Baier's book is more successful than Held's. She, too, writes from a feminist standpoint, but she is much less anxious to convert every insight into a victory for feminism. It must also be said that her book is clearly superior to Held's for intellectual substance and literary style. This is not because she is any less of a feminist than Held; she is just a more circumspect and wary philosopher. She knows what it takes to establish a philosophical position. Her discussions of trust, in particular, constitute a serious effort at understanding; and her treatment of Hume and Kant on the role of emotion and reason in ethics shows real scholarly ability.

But she, too, occasionally lapses into ideological bias and dubious rhetoric. Take her discussion of Hume. Unlike Held, Baier has the grace to acknowledge that many of Hume's central doctrines prefigure themes that are dear to contemporary feminist philosophers, and she discusses Hume with sensitivity and resourcefulness. There is no tendency here to disagree with Hume because he was a man. In a pair of essays called "Hume, the Women's Moral Theorist?" and "Hume, the Reflective Women's Epistemologist?" Baier contends that Hume's philosophy fits the kind of moral outlook that Gilligan claimed to find exemplified by females, suggesting that Hume is "an unwitting virtual woman." But surely it is a contortion to infer from Hume's moral theory that he has a female moral faculty, rather than inferring that his (and her) kind of position is intrinsically gender-neutral. By Baier's method, *any* good idea could be put down to femaleness. The attractions of Hume's thought are purely intellectual; they are not the consequences of some female essence that occasionally takes up residence in men's bodies. Hume's position avoids the nonnaturalism of more "cognitivist" positions, and it carries all the appeal of empiricist theories in general. That is why it was so strongly favored by logical positivism, a male bastion if ever there was one.

Baier's main theme is trust. Her plaint is that trust has not been accorded the place in moral theory that its importance warrants. Trust, she thinks, should be the central concept of ethics. She sees it as woven into virtually all human encounters, from the most warmly personal to the most austerely economic. She also appreciates its intense psychological significance for us, both as a source of well-being and as a possible source of emotional distress. We can't do without trust, but its abuse can be devastating. Trust is not the same as merely believing that someone will behave reliably, since that might depend upon a mutually known power to take revenge on violations of contract. Trust is faith in the good will and the good sense of others, a sort of leap in the dark. One of the things it seems to take at least a lifetime to learn is whom to trust, and when. Mistakes as to who is trustworthy are among the most emotionally costly that human beings can make.

The importance of trust is surely one of the few areas of moral agreement that we have. For this reason, any philosophical attempt to clarify the concept, and to enable us to do better at trusting and being trusted, can only be to the good. After reading Baier's hundred or so pages on the subject, however, I did not feel particularly enlightened. The problem is that it is very hard to say anything philosophically interesting about trust, despite its human significance. We are better educated in the ways of trust by works of literature and by experience than by quasi-conceptual investigations of its necessary and sufficient conditions. I suspect that this is the real reason behind the relative neglect of the topic in moral philosophy. It is not that trust is a concept of more interest to women than men, nor that it somehow conflicts with other moral ideas favored by men; it is simply difficult to do any good philosophy on the concept. Once trust has been freed from the narrow domain of contractual obligation, as Baier rightly says it should be, it is hard to come up with anything general and illuminating to say about it.

The most political chapter of Baier's book, called "Ethics in Many Different Voices," has some curious and disturbing moments. Here she is at her most self-consciously feminist. Speaking of the presence of women philosophers in academic institutions, she writes:

> We have shown ourselves capable of pandering to male fantasies as well as having our own alternative fantasies. In philosophy seminars, as in the boudoir, some will prove protective of fragile male egos, others will fulfill the worst nightmares of the castrating woman by putting some teeth into their philosophical grip on male moral theories. . . . [O]thers alternate their styles in disconcerting ways, or simply display that postmenopausal rise in assertiveness which should be no surprise, but often does disconcert those who suffer assaults from feisty old women who had been meeker and more diplomatic when younger.

Wow. I don't know what kind of seminars Baier has been attending, but my own female colleagues simply proceed by making their points as incisively and civilly as is appropriate. I have never felt that my ego was being protected by women, beyond what any tactful person would do, nor have I felt imperiled, in the seminar room or in the boudoir, by castrating teeth or postmenopausal predators. Is it really necessary to say that in philosophy we try to seek the truth, and that honest criticism, constructive and destructive, is part of that enterprise? Serious philosophers of either sex remember only that simple rule when wondering how to comport themselves in the seminar room.

Later in the same essay Baier raises the question of tenure for women. She tells us that women "tend to get into their writing stride as men of the same age are losing steam," so that we would do well not to insist on the same quantity of published work for young women as for young men. "Will enough women professionally survive their high estrogen years, will they be able to squeeze out enough articles while they are menstruating, gestating, and lactating?" Now *there* is a problem. Baier suggests, as a solution, that women might be allowed to delay their own tenure decisions until they are fifty. Apart from the obvious point that such a delay would remove most of the rationale for the tenure hurdle, this whole line of thought is dangerously close to the kind of reactionary stuff sometimes peddled by prefeminist men who want to keep the academy exclusively male. What Baier is saying, when you get right down to it, is that women are biologically incapable of performing as well as men during the first several decades of their academic life. This strikes me as false, and as an insult to women. But then I am a feminist who believes in the equal treatment of women and men, and also that feminist philosophy is not much better than feminist physics or feminist logic. Philosophically, it turns out to be a dead end.

37

Foot: Good Things

Virtues and Reasons: Philippa Foot
and Moral Theory
edited by Rosalind Hursthouse,
Gavin Lawrence, and Warren Quinn
Oxford, 1995

[handwritten margin note: which charity?]

Suppose I perform an action certified by morality as good—say, giving money to charity. I then do something good because it is good. We might say that this action had the moral property *goodness* and that in acknowledging this to be so I had a reason to perform it. Anyone else has an equal reason to perform the same action, which is good no matter who performs it. Thus, generalizing: morality is aptly seen as a set of principles that ascribe values to states of affairs and thereby provide reasons for bringing those states of affairs about. Morality says what we ought to do and insofar as we grasp its dictates we have the reasons it specifies: we know what we ought to do, and that we ought to do it is a reason for doing it.

This commonsense picture makes many philosophers squirm, and not because they are avowed moral nihilists. There are two main reasons. The first is that it seems to presuppose moral "cognitivism": the agent recognizes goodness as an objective property that may be instantiated by his actions. By ascribing it to an action, he comes to know an objective truth—that his action is (or will be) good. This makes some philosophers nervous, because it suggests a metaphysics they don't like the look of, whereby goodness becomes a "queer" property of things.

There is a second reason why the picture is found rebarbative: it entails that morality affords reasons for action that fail to take into account what the agent may himself desire or what may be in his interest. Once I see that

Reprinted with permission from the *London Review of Books* (July 18, 1995).

giving money to charity is good I have a reason to do it, but that reason holds
whether or not I want to give money to charity. I may not care about the
people who will be benefited, but there is still a reason for me to do it—that
they will be benefited. So moral reasons do not appear to depend on my
contingent desires. To many philosophers that is hard to take: how could
reasons not involve desires?

Philippa Foot is foremost among those who have jibbed at the notion of
reasons that are independent of desires. She doesn't believe in goodness as a
property that, once recognized, provides reasons for action. Morality itself
does not, for her, supply *any* reasons for action; reasons come in only when
agents have desires that happen to conform to morality's prescriptions:

> Moral judgments are, I say, hypothetical imperatives in the sense that they
> give reasons for acting only in conjunction with interests and desires. We
> cannot change that, though we could keep up the pretence that it is other-
> wise. To hang onto the illusion, and treat moral judgments as necessarily
> reason-giving, is something I would compare to a similar choice in matters
> of etiquette; and indeed we do find some who treat the consideration that
> something is "bad form" or "not done" as if it had a magical reason-giving
> force.*

That an action is morally good is thus not a reason why I should do it. I
have no more reason to refrain from murder on account of its badness than I
do to refrain from holding my fork in my right hand when in England,
where it isn't done. Reasons enter the picture only if I happen to desire to act
in accordance with the rule in question. Morality thus has no intrinsic rational authority over our wills. There is nothing contrary to reason about not
doing the right thing, and irrationality can only consist in not doing what will
best satisfy our desires (which may be egoistic or altruistic).

This doctrine is rightly seen as subversive and disturbing. The mere fact
that something is good is not, according to Foot, even a start at providing a
reason to do it; it is the wrong kind of consideration altogether. We get into
the realm of reasons only when we dig around in someone's actual desires
and decide that he happens to want to do various things, as it might be to
keep promises. Reasons are internal to the agent and variable across agents;
morality's apparent universality is a fiction. This is a radical view. Instead of
being able to say to the miscreant, "You should do such and such" and expect
this to supply him with a reason, we can only say, "If you look inside yourself,
you will see that you really want to do such and such." Rational persuasion
then comes to an end if he retorts, "Actually, I don't want to do such and
such, thank you very much."

Such a view puts Philippa Foot, the model of propriety, no sort of wild
woman, into the same camp as the most extreme moral nihilist. She does not
reject the content of ordinary morality or favor existential choice as the way

*Philippa Foot, *Virtues and Vices,* Berkeley: University of California Press, 1978, p. 29.

to kick-start a moral psychology; but she does hold that there is no sense in which to be moral is to be on the side of reason, that it is *ir*rational, indeed, to be guided by morality if your desires don't incline you that way. There is nothing unreasonable about someone who fully accepts that promise keeping is good, yet sees absolutely nothing in favor of doing it. If he desires to keep promises and fails to, then he is being unreasonable; not otherwise. For Foot, morality is practically inert.

It might be possible to hold a similar position in respect of logic. We normally think that an inference's being valid is a reason to make it, and its being invalid a reason not to make it. Asked for my reason for believing that *q,* I might say that it follows by modus ponens from *p* and "if *p* then *q*"—my reason is that this is a valid rule of inference. A Footian would say that this was a mistake. Validity itself is not a reason for forming one's beliefs in a certain way; rather, we need to determine whether the thinker desires to reason validly. If she does not, she is not being irrational in reasoning by invalid rules of inference, concluding that *p* from "*q* and not-*p,*" say. We may hope that people will desire to reason as logic says they should, but we can't accuse them of unreason if they fail to.

Such a view of logical reasoning will strike most people as radical and bizarre: they will incline to the view that logic supplies us with a set of reasons for forming our beliefs according to certain rules and not others. Yet Foot and those who think like her (including Bernard Williams) reject the analogous position with respect to morality. Assuming that they would not embrace the view that logical reasons depend on our desires, they must then hold that goodness and validity differ fundamentally when it comes to providing reasons. An opponent of their position, such as myself, will wonder how to justify this difference and why it should be thought necessary to deny the commonsense view of ethical reasons. If reasons do not *generally* have to depend on desires to be reasons, why must they in the special case of morality?

Virtues and Reasons collects together a group of distinguished contributors, who nod in the direction of the honoree and then talk about what interests them. Some of the book is about Foot's moral philosophy, but a lot of it isn't. The papers are of a predictably professional quality, though not very groundbreaking. I shall comment on a few of those that engage most directly with Foot's views on moral reason.

Warren Quinn's paper, "Putting Rationality in its Place," is the best in the volume, both in its clarity and in the correctness of its arguments. He undermines Foot's position in the most direct way possible, by arguing that desires considered in themselves cannot be reasons at all, only judgments of value can. Reasons have to be justificatory, since they show an action to be rational; they cannot be merely causal. But since only propositions can justify, reasons must be propositional. This shows that desires cannot be reasons, since desires are not propositions. So the desire theory needs to be reformulated to the effect that propositions *about* desires constitute reasons.

But which propositions about desires? There seem to be only two serious options: first, the proposition that I have the desire; second, the proposition that satisfying the desire would be a good thing in some way. The first possibility is surely inadequate: why should the mere fact that I have a desire be a reason to act on it? Quinn gives the example of a brute desire to turn on any radio I come across. Surely a reason should make it apparent that my action has some good attached to it. But the mere fact that I have the desire fails to deliver that. And what about desires it is not good to act on, say jumping off a high building when under the influence of vertigo? Isn't it really because satisfying a given desire is good that it is reasonable (when it is) to act on it?

So we move on to the second alternative: the proposition that if satisfying my desire is a good thing, this gives me a reason to act on it. But this explicitly assigns a value to something: to the satisfaction of a desire. So the desire theory is not an alternative to the theory that locates reasons in values themselves; it is simply a special case of that theory. We need an independent ascription of value for a desire to become a reason. The reason for acting on the desire is that some good will come of it. The desire causes the action, but its reasonableness depends on the non-causal property of goodness.

This shows that even for egoistic desires an ascription of value is needed if they are to become reasons. But then the obvious commonsense point to make about moral reasons is that they can function simply in virtue of moral values, or the recognition of such. My reason for giving money to charity was that I saw it as morally good; just as my reason for eating a banana would be that I saw it as prudentially good. If I am asked to justify these actions I do so in the same basic way: by showing that they have good results, morally or prudentially. I certainly don't justify them by simply recording the presence of an urge, though I might cite this as their cause; and if I do so this is really an elliptical form of the fuller proposition that it was a desire whose satisfaction would be a good thing. Even if *some* good attaches to the satisfaction of any desire at all, the point still stands—that it is this goodness that constitutes the reason for acting on it. Suppose we were to identify our desire with a particular brain state; can it then be seriously maintained that our reason for doing something—our justification—is simply that we are in this brain state? That might well be what causes us to act, but it is not in virtue of this that desires supply reasons—they do so only because they meet certain evaluative conditions. It is reasonable to act on our desires when and only when it is good to satisfy them. Thus values enter into reasons from the start. The upshot of Quinn's paper is that Foot's desire theory has misconceived the nature of reasons quite fundamentally, and in doing so has generated a pseudoproblem about moral reasons. Practical reason is concerned by its nature with values as such: they are its proper subject matter.

Gavin Lawrence arrives at a similar position, though at greater and more diffuse length. It is odd that he makes no mention of Quinn's work in view of the similarity between them and the fact that they were colleagues until

Warren's tragic early death by suicide as this volume was being prepared. (I became friends with Warren at UCLA in 1979: that a person of his charm, kindness, and integrity, as well as intellectual talents, should take his own life is the kind of thing to which it is impossible to become reconciled.) Lawrence makes the same good point about the foundational role of values in the operation of practical reason. It would have been interesting to know Foot's reaction to these arguments and it is a pity that she hasn't contributed replies to the papers in this volume.

Of the other contributions those by Simon Blackburn and John McDowell make an opposing pair. McDowell, writing with the preacherly obscurity that has come, regrettably, to characterize his work, offers to defend a new kind of moral naturalism that reaches back to Aristotle. His point seems to be that since the rise of science in the seventeenth century we have become steeped in a view of the natural world as comprising only the kinds of facts mentioned by the physical sciences, but that the Greeks would have found a place for a wider set, including facts involving moral values. The ideology surrounding science has made us tunnel-visioned, so that we suppose values to be grounded merely in subjective human responses.

So far, not so unreasonable. But, in opposition to this, McDowell argues for a view of nature that has "intelligible order" built into it: "the world of nature is internal to the space of *logos,* in which thought has its being," he intones. But what could this mean? How "internal"? The idea is in obvious danger of reducing either to a triviality or to an obvious falsehood (assuming we reject idealism, as McDowell wants us to). Either it means simply that thought succeeds in representing the world—our thoughts sometimes correspond to how things are; which is trivial. Or it means that nature contains thought itself, which is idealism or maybe panpsychism. It is of course true that objective reality must be such that thought can represent it, if it does represent it; but it surely doesn't follow that "the natural world is not constitutively independent of the structure of subjectivity," in the sense that there would be no such world if there were no such subjectivity. Kantian idealism does not follow from the correspondence theory of truth. McDowell is pushing for the idea (I use the phrase advisedly) that thought and nature share a common feature or structure, but it is notoriously hard to make sense of this without implying idealism. Hume said we spread our minds on the world; McDowell's view appears to be that the world is already spread with mind. Finding values in the world is then nothing but finding that our minds have got there before us. It is difficult to see what any of this could mean, unless it is a frank espousal of the Kantian doctrine that the world of our experience is really an experiential world, that is, idealism. McDowell's discussion of this central issue is so obscure, metaphorical, and undeveloped that one has no idea whether anything can be made to rest on it on behalf of moral realism.

Blackburn defends the opposite point of view: that values are reflections of human sentiment, are subjective to the core. You know where you are with Balckburn; at least you know where he wants you to be. His doctrine is that

238   ETHICS

"attitudes, or feelings, or the recognition of reasons for action contain some kind of key to the nature of ethics." Ethics is thus really a branch of human psychology, not a discourse about objective values. He sees Foot as moving away from such projectivist theories (as he calls them), notably in the gap that exists for her between ethical judgment and reasons for action. She is psychologistic about moral reasons but not (apparently) about moral truths, while Blackburn favors a psychologism about values, too. Foot's view is a kind of subjective-objective hybrid, while Blackburn's is the pure subjective article.

What is strange is that Blackburn simply assumes, as if it were not a substantive point, that moral reasons must be founded in contingent attitudes of caring on the part of the agent; yet surely he would not want to say this of reasons in logic or empirical discourse—where reasons exist even when nobody cares what they recommend. As it were, reasons don't care whether we care. What prompts this assumption, it seems, is that Blackburn thinks reasons must influence the will—must have motivational force. But this conflates a conceptual with a psychological question. Conceptually, an action's being good is a reason to do it; psychologically, I may be indifferent to goodness and its reason-giving power, and hence ignore what it tells me. So moral reasons can exist even though they move me not at all, on account of my wickedness or stupidity. Blackburn takes it for granted that ethics *must* somehow be a matter of human psychology, the only serious question being whether the right part of human psychology to invoke is beliefs or desires, cognition or conation. He simply does not allow space to the idea, defended in this volume by Quinn and Lawrence, that values might figure foundationally in the way ethics give us reasons for action. He cannot contemplate for ethics what he would presumably accept for logic: a gap between reasons and psychological dispositions.

What is the attraction of the projectivist position to start with? Blackburn rests his argument on considerations of metaphysical economy: why have values in the world in addition to value-free facts that impinge on people's sentiments? All the necessary explaining can be done in terms of the facts on which values supervene. This is a perilous argument, however, threatening to eliminate from the world everything that is supervenient on something else. Why not just make do with particles in space and their impact on our sensibility? Why indeed have sensibility at all, in view of its supervenience on the physical? Blackburn's opposition to objective moral facts can be generalized to alarming effect. He needs to tell us more about how to limit the strength of the argument; he also needs to say more about why explanatory utility should be the only criterion of the real.

The essential thing about morality, as G. E. Moore long ago recognized, is that it stands above the flux of feelings and desires and tendencies to act, because you can ask of any of these whether it is morally good. Goodness cannot be a mere projection from human sentiments because, as a matter of conceptual truth, it is always possible to ask of any given sentiment whether it is a good sentiment to have. No matter whether everyone agrees on what they feel approval for, it never follows that what they approve is really good. Judgments of value are logically independent of the existence of patterns of desire. You cannot deduce an ought from an is—even at this late stage of the twentieth century.

can't we also say of every statement that is claimed to be true — "But, is it really True?"

When one says "I Feel it is good that the vaccine has saved a million infants' lives" would we say "But, is it good For you to feel that way about that?"

38

Collingwood: Homage to Education

Essays in Political Philosophy
by R. G. Collingwood,
edited by David Boucher
Oxford, 1989

*The Social and Political Thought
of R. G. Collingwood*
by David Boucher
Cambridge, 1989

Robin Collingwood (1889–1943) was born seventeen years after Bertrand Russell and died twenty-seven years before him. Given the style and content of Collingwood's philosophical work, this fact ought to seem surprising. For there is no apparent mark of Russell's influence, nor of those who influenced him, upon Collingwood's own philosophical corpus. For better or worse, he stands apart—even aloof—from the British analytical tradition exemplified by Russell. Or perhaps for better *and* worse: better, because he thereby created a distinctive style of philosophy, in which history, not science (or formal logic), was the model and focus of interest; worse, because his own thought lacks some of the clarity and rigor and analytical depth of the "school" he opposed, or ignored. Not for him the dry deductions of Russell's *Principia Mathematica:* consciousness in history was what excited his interest.

Yet there exists a certain affinity between the political and social writings of the two men. Both seem to have been drawn to political writing more by extramural convulsions (i.e., wars) than by theoretical inclination, feeling it to be their duty to set the world straight on how it should run itself. Both display the same belief in the civilizing role of dispassionate reason, the importance of education, the dangers of submission to authority. There is the same tone of pained rebuke in their political admonitions, as if they

Reprinted with permission from the *London Review of Books* (August 16, 1990).

cannot quite believe what they are witnessing—civilization confronted by barbarity. They are men of the ivory tower compelled to look incredulously down on the swarming hordes below, and plead for order. Oddly enough, however, they seem reluctant to hail each other and join voices in the Battle against Confusion: there is no mention of Russell in either of the books here reviewed, and I do not recall Russell having a good word to say for Collingwood. Philosophically, each was on the wrong side, so far as the other was concerned; politically, they would have got on famously.

Like the boy Bertie, young Robin was educated at home, where he showed remarkable precocity. His father, who was John Ruskin's secretary, undertook the task of educating his son himself; Robin received from him a very wide and thorough education—in ancient and modern languages, history, science, music, art. In his *Autobiography* Collingwood reports having had a certain amount of trouble, at the age of eight, with understanding Kant's ethics, but this only determined him to become a philosopher when he grew up. (Russell had a similar experience with Euclid when he was a lad.) These halcyon days were abruptly put a stop to when Collingwood minor reached fourteen, at which time he was sent to Rugby School. He loathed it there. "I went to Rugby," he said, "where we thought winter a time for playing football—and summer a time for thinking about playing football." Liberation came in 1908 when he gained a classical scholarship to University College, Oxford. Four years later he was elected to a philosophy fellowship at Pembroke College.

He spent the rest of his professional life in Oxford, ascending to the Waynflete Chair in 1935, which lifted the teaching burden of thirty to forty hours a week which he had hitherto endured. But he was, David Boucher tells us, as intellectually isolated within his own university as he was from the broader philosophical currents represented by Russell. His chief influences came from quite elsewhere—notably, from the Italian idealists, Croce, Gentile, and de Ruggiero. Neither did Collingwood much care for the company of his Oxford colleagues, who included Bosanquet and Bradley; he even went so far as to remove himself to Didcot. He was pretty much ignored by the philosophical establishment during his lifetime, and in his obituary in the *New York Times* was noted more for his work in Roman archaeology than for any philosophical innovation. Nevertheless, he was a popular and effective teacher in Oxford, renowned for his clarity of presentation and for his exceptional speaking voice, which he had trained especially for the purpose of lecturing.

What distinguishes Collingwood from the run of philosophers is the breadth of his interests, and his desire to develop a philosophy that will find a place for all of them. Multilingual, polymathic, hydratalented, omniskilled— he didn't want to be tied down to one way of looking at things. In particular, he didn't want to be confined to the present: historical knowledge had to be integral to philosophy, as it was for Hegel. And he liked his influences to come from a different time or place, preferably filtered through an alien medium, made perspicuous by learning. The Italian philosophers of history fulfilled his archaeological predilections perfectly.

In *Essays in Political Philosophy,* a somewhat mixed collection of Collingwood's published and unpublished writings, we find discussions of economics, moral action, punishment, religion, liberalism, fascism, communism, education, war, sex, Plato, Marx, Freud. Some of these essays are dated, others slight, but there is plenty of interest here for readers other than the dedicated Collingwoodian. I found "Economics as a Philosophical Science" and "Punishment and Forgiveness" especially fresh and insightful, both essays demonstrating the benefits to be derived from patient and seemingly pedantic conceptual inquiry. Collingwood's relaxed incisiveness and moral acuity are here displayed in their sharpest and most engaging form.

Focusing on the essence of economic action, he brings out the conflict of interest inherent in any economic exchange, and argues that the idea of a just wage or a just price is incoherent, a confusion of the moral and the economic. "Indeed," he remarks, "a renunciation of purely economic aims is the essence, negatively defined, of the moral life." An economic action is defined as one person using another as the means to his own ends by permitting the other to use *him* as a means to the ends of that other.

Punishment is argued to be a binding moral duty which is not merely consistent with forgiveness but ultimately indistinguishable from it. This is because both attitudes or acts are directed, if they are properly conceived, at reforming the moral consciousness of the wrongdoer; they are intended to bring him back into the moral community. Characteristically, Collingwood observes that "the most perfect punishments involve no 'incidental' pains at all. The condemnation is expressed simply and quietly in words, and goes straight home." Theorists of punishment are advised to study this subtle essay.

An abiding concern of Collingwood's, stressed in David Boucher's sympathetic and thorough study, is that of education and its relation to politics. Education is held to be the province of both parent and politician, and it is defined as the process that creates and sustains civilization. Without proper education, Collingwood contends, liberal democracy cannot function or even survive. In an essay unsparingly entitled "Man Goes Mad," written circa 1936, he fulminates as follows:

> the conception of political life as permeating the whole community, of government as the political education of the people, is the only alternative to anarchy on the one hand and the rule of brute force on the other. The work of government is difficult enough in any case; it is only rendered possible if rulers can appeal, over the heads of criminals, to a body of public opinion sufficiently educated in politics to understand the wisdom of their acts. Authoritarian government, scorning the dialectic of political life in the name of efficiency, and imposing ready-made solutions on a passive people, is deliberately cutting off the branch on which it sits by de-educating its own subjects, creating round itself an atmosphere of ignorance and stupidity which ultimately will make its own work impossible, and make impossible even the rise of a better form of political life.

Contained in this passage is an important thesis of what Collingwood aptly calls philosophical politics: the thesis that there is an internal relation between liberal democracy and educational attainment. Let me spell out in my own way what I think Collingwood is getting at here.

Democratic states are constitutively committed to ensuring and furthering the intellectual health of the citizens who compose them: indeed, they are only possible at all if people reach a certain cognitive level. The reason is simple: rational government by the majority presupposes that the majority are rational—that they know what needs to be known, that they can think effectively, that they are not blinded by prejudice and confusion. This presupposition is, of course, built into the electoral laws of democratic states: children may not vote, nor may retarded people, nor may animals. Modern democracies are ruled, in effect, by an educational or intellectual élite—consisting of sane adult human beings who have gone to school. It is only a contingent fact that this élite constitutes the numerical majority: it would be possible in principle for the children in a society to outnumber the adults or for most adults to suffer serious mental retardation as a result of pollution. In such possible cases the minority of democratic rulers would be obliged, as they are now, to respect the interests of the politically disenfranchised majority of citizens, but the vote would belong only to those relatively few people who met the intellectual standards we now actually require. Superiority in point of adherence to democratic ideals consists not in majority rule as such but in the selection of a nonarbitrary subset of the population as those to be vested with political power—where cognitive competence is the operative criterion of selection. Thus the prime duty of a democratic state is the provision of sufficient mass education to satisfy its own preconditions.

Other duties of state are often urged: the facilitation of personal freedom, the maintenance of social order, the promotion of happiness, the defense of the state against the depredations of other states. Doubtless there are such duties, but they are not integral to the very concept of democracy; they are not essential to democracy *qua* democracy. Democracy is defined as that system of social decision-making in which political agency attaches generally to the citizens of a state (with the provisos just mentioned); but then it *follows*, as a theorem of philosophical politics, that rational political action requires a suitable degree of intellectual competence on the part of citizens at large—whether these citizens rule directly or through elected representatives. Democracy and education (in the widest sense) are thus as conceptually inseparable as individual rational action and knowledge of the world.

But now we must ask, as philosophical politicians, what education itself consists in. Plainly, it involves the transmission of knowledge from teacher to taught. But what exactly is knowledge? Here politics makes contact with epistemology, since it is an epistemic notion that, we now see, defines the prime duty of democracy. Setting aside certain irrelevant subtleties, the concept of knowledge is to be analyzed as follows: knowledge is true justified belief that has been arrived at by rational means. Accordingly, a democracy must aim to secure a state of mind in its citizens that satisfies certain epistemic conditions—namely, truth and rational justification; it must ensure that people's beliefs obey these epistemic norms, or else it is not securing knowledge. Thus the norms governing political action incorporate or embed norms appropriate to rational belief-formation. They may also, to be sure, incorporate moral or legal norms, but it is the epistemic norms that are *internal* to the idea of democracy. And given that the political is thus enmeshed in the epistemic, it is with the cognitive well-being of citizens that the state must be primarily or originally concerned. The educational system of schools and universities is one central element in this cognitive health service, but the state of the media of communication and of language itself is also a vital consideration.

It would be a mistake to suppose that the educational duties of the democratic state extended only to political education, leaving other kinds to their own devices. It is true that, according to the Collingwoodian thesis, political education is the only internally motivated duty of the state, since the agency of the state is (by definition) exclusively political. But brief reflection reveals that this educational end can be achieved only by means that include other kinds of education. For political knowledge clearly depends upon knowledge of many other kinds—knowledge of history, science, art, morals, and so on. Just consider the range of knowledge necessary to decide upon a sound political policy in respect of nuclear weapons. Political decisions require attention to the totality of knowledge, so the state must concern itself with knowledge in general.

How do we bring about the cognitive health required by democratic government? A basic requirement is to cultivate in the populace a respect for intellectual values, an intolerance of intellectual vices or shortcomings. The true enemy of democracy is the anti-intellectual, the brain-washer, the prejudice-pumper, since she undermines what alone makes democracy workable. The forces of cretinization are, and have always been, the biggest threat to the success of democracy as a way of allocating political power: this is a fundamental conceptual truth, as well as a lamentable fact of history. Those forces are, we know, many and various: intentional deception by leaders, more subtle forms of corporate propaganda, tabloid philistinism, manipulative advertising, narcotic television, ingrained prejudices—the usual suspects. Collingwood identifies a deeper problem: "It is much easier for any kind of man known to me to doze off into daydreams which are the first and most seemingly innocent stage of craziness. If labor-saving is what you want, give up all this trouble about thinking; go mad and have done with it. That is what the tyrant has to offer mankind—an end to the intolerable weariness of sanity." Democracy requires responsibility, which requires sanity, which is an achievement not a gift. Rational self-rule, individual or social, causes mental fatigue; it's less effort to be dictated to.

What Collingwood does not say, so I will say it for him, is that people do not really like the truth; they feel coerced by reason, bullied by fact. In a certain sense, this is not irrational, since a commitment to believe only what is true implies a willingness to detach your beliefs from your desires. You won't always get to believe exactly what you want to believe if you insist on believing only what is true. From the point of view of maximizing desire satisfaction, a commitment to truth is a poor strategy, at least in the short term, since truth is inherently indifferent to desire. Truth limits your freedom, in a way, because it reduces your belief options; it is quite capable of forcing your mind to go against its natural inclinations. This, I suspect, is the root psychological cause of the relativistic view of truth, for that view gives me license to believe whatever it pleases me to believe—the truth is always *my* truth. Objective nonrelative truth tends to be felt as inhuman, lacking in compassion. There is thus a basic endogenous obstacle to our reaching that level of cognitive health required for flawless conformity to epistemic norms; and if so, democracy itself comes into conflict with a deep fact about human nature— our reluctance, in a word, to follow the truth wherever it may lead. (Hence Plato's suggestion that philosophers be kings—they being specially trained or tuned to the truth.) One of the central aims of education, as a preparation for political democracy, should be to enable people to get on better terms with reason—to learn to live with the truth. And this will involve, as Collingwood stressed, an education that produces critical self-knowledge. It is a substantive, and neglected, and I would say unsolved, problem of educational theory to consider how this human accommodation with truth might be brought about. Certainly, twentieth-century man (and woman) is very far from meeting this essential condition for a well-functioning democracy. Indeed, I do not think that the urgency and importance of the task are at all widely appreciated. The cognitive health of modern democracies lags far behind their bodily health, yet this is scarcely even perceived as a serious *political* problem.

On one issue I think Collingwood oversteps the mark: he seems to have taken it to be a corollary of his conception of civilization that there is such a thing as "right imperialism." He cites the supposedly beneficial effects of the Roman domination of Europe, and he wonders what untold advances British imperialism might confer on Asia and Africa. That is, he thinks that an allegedly higher level of intellectual and political attainment on the part of one state can legitimate an imperialist policy with respect to another. Here he shows himself to be a man of his time (and of much earlier times) in a way that Russell, say, was not. It is true enough that if you instantiate a higher level of civilization than me then it would be a kindness for you to offer to improve my lot, but it does not follow that you have the right to force me to accept your tutelage against my will; and the same point holds for relations between more and less civilized states (assuming such a ranking to be feasible). Collingwood is making the mistake, natural to a don, of conceiving the relation of more to less civilized states on the model of the relation of adult teacher to child pupil—a common enough error. He is erroneously thinking of imperialism on the analogy of parental authority.

On most other points, however, he comes across as a political thinker of acute and balanced judgment—humane, sensible, unblinkered. He is not perhaps a major political theoretician, but his political philosophy deserves to enjoy the same rescue from neglect that his other philosophical contributions have enjoyed since his early death. These two volumes will do much to aid that process.

Putnam: In and Out of the Mind

Renewing Philosophy
by Hilary Putnam
Harvard, 1992

In a neglected passage in *The Problems of Philosophy* Bertrand Russell un-apologetically writes:

> *A priori* knowledge is not all of the logical kind we have been hitherto con-sidering. Perhaps the most important example of non-logical *a priori* knowl-edge is knowledge as to ethical value. . . . We judge, for example, that happiness is more desirable than misery, knowledge than ignorance, good-will than hatred, and so on. Such judgments must, in part at least, be imme-diate and *a priori*. Like our previous *a priori* judgments, they may be *elicited* by experience. . . . But it is fairly obvious that they cannot be *proved* by ex-perience. . . . Knowledge as to what is intrinsically of value is *a priori* in the same sense in which logic is *a priori*.*

Thus, for Russell, ethical knowledge enjoys the privileges and securities that the rationalists discerned in our knowledge of logic and mathematics: imme-diacy, certainty, necessity. It is a paradigm of what true knowledge should be like, and contrasts sharply, in Russell's epistemology, with the empirical knowledge we seek in science. There Russell finds only uncertainty, indirect-ness, questionable inference. We know the world of science merely "by de-scription," as a projection from what we are immediately "acquainted with," and we must rely on indirect, subjective "signs" if we are to venture any objective knowledge at all. The nature of the objects described by science is

Reprinted with permission from the *London Review of Books* (December 2, 1993).
*Oxford University Press, 1967, pp. 42–3.

inherently conjectural; even the space that contains them is beyond our faculties of direct awareness. Most disturbing of all, the basic principle of scientific inference—namely, induction—is incapable of empirical support, and subject to radical (and rational) scepticism. According to Russell's conception of human knowledge, then, ethics ranks a good deal higher than science on the scale of epistemic virtue; it occupies a place our faculties can reach. To compare ethical knowledge unfavorably with scientific knowledge would be absurd. Science is by no means the standard against which all other claims to knowledge are to be judged.

NB

Nor is this position merely eccentric or even obsolete: essentially the same structure emerges from the conception of human knowledge powerfully advocated by Noam Chomsky. Think of the human mind as a modular congeries of special-purpose facilities—organs for knowing—which are biologically based and innately specified. Then science, for Chomsky, is simply the result of a happy convergence between objective truth about the world and the particular epistemic organs we happen to possess. There is no sense in which these faculties were designed with scientific knowledge as their goal—in contrast with (say) our knowledge of language. Science is possible for us only because it is a remote by-product of some independently selected faculty; and it will encounter obstacles of principle where fact and faculty fail to match. We are not natural scientists, but rely on a kind of biological luck. This is why science is so hard to acquire and admits so much variation between individuals—in marked contrast to language.

Moreover, according to Chomsky, it is plausible to see our ethical faculty as analogous to our language faculty: we acquire ethical knowledge with very little explicit instruction, without great intellectual labor, and the end-result is remarkably uniform given the variety of ethical input we receive. The environment serves merely to trigger and specialize an innate schematism. Thus the ethical systems of different cultures or epochs are plausibly seen as analogous to the different languages people speak—an underlying universal structure gets differentiated into specific cultural products. So, while science must depend on faculties whose biological purpose is not itself science—or anything very close to science—ethics seems far more deeply embedded in our original mental design. Perhaps the innate system of commonsense psychology, installed to negotiate our social relations, contains the resources for generating the basic principles of ethics. But there is surely no prospect that knowledge of quantum physics or evolutionary theory will be found to stem thus directly from anything with a well-defined biological function. On the Chomskyan model, both science and ethics are natural products of contingent human psychology, constrained by its specific constitutive principles; but ethics looks to have the securer basis in our cognitive architecture. There is an element of luck to our possession of scientific knowledge that is absent in the case of our ethical knowledge.

really! I doubt it.

I have rehearsed the epistemological views of Russell and Chomsky in order to make the point that the ideology of scientism will have little attrac-

and for Chomsky it is a direct knowledge that involves no assessment of motives, states of mind, etc.

tion once such views are taken to heart. Science is no doubt an impressive intellectual structure, both theoretically and practically, but to single it out as uniquely virtuous from an epistemological point of view is unreflective and uncritical. There are other areas of human knowledge where our cognitive successes are no less impressive, though different in kind. Knowledge of language is as rich and remarkable as even the most recondite scientific knowledge, despite the fact that almost everyone can acquire it. We fail to notice this precisely because we are designed to develop the complexities of language without conscious effort. To suppose that linguistic knowledge, or ethical knowledge, is inferior to science simply because it proceeds by different principles, and from a distinct mental faculty, would be absurd; just as it would be absurd to brand knowledge of logic and mathematics as epistemically inferior to empirical knowledge simply because it is a priori. Idolatry of scientific knowledge stems from a defective and biased epistemology: indeed, science itself, particularly biology and cognitive psychology, already suggests that scientific knowledge is just one kind of cognitive system among others. Scientism isn't even scientific. *NB*

Hilary Putnam's book is offered as a polemic against scientism, particularly in philosophy and ethics, but he does not work from the sort of general perspective present in Russell and Chomsky—and which I would support. Instead, he engages in piecemeal discussions of some contemporary philosophers he takes to be guilty of the scientistic sin. He believes that scientism is rampant in current analytical philosophy, informing and deforming it, and that it must be rooted out and replaced with a new style of philosophizing, which will have the effect of restoring philosophy to its proper place in "the culture." *Renewing Philosophy* surveys a large number of topics and thinkers in a brief space, ranging all the way from Turing machines to democracy—with reference, relativism, materialism, deconstruction, religion, and the "absolute conception" in between. It reads as a series of glancing blows struck at people and positions Putnam now deplores, including his own earlier, insensitive scientistic self. Where once he was a metaphysical realist and machine functionalist, now he repudiates the idea of a "ready-made world" and disavows the computer model of mind. Notorious for his capacity to change his mind, he has come to see the whole analytic style of philosophy as mistaken. He tells us that during his earlier materialistic phase he kept his professional work and his religious feelings in separate mental compartments, but that he now wishes to bring them harmoniously together. Hence the need to "renew philosophy"—to find a way of philosophizing that does not reduce people to scientific specimens. The present book, based on his 1991 Gifford Lectures, and redolent of its declamatory origins, is unsatisfactory in a number of ways, not all having to do with the exiguity and unpersuasiveness of many of the arguments. Mainly, it remains quite unclear what Putnam is against and what he is for. Instead of careful formulation and qualification, we are treated far too often to a display of rhetoric and attitude, interspersed with pretty orthodox analytic philosophy.

The desire for intellectual redemption has produced a work of uncertain focus and empty exhortation.

The notion of scientism, never very clearly defined, is understood so broadly by Putnam that it appears to include any metaphysics of a systematic kind. In places the charge of scientism becomes interchangeable with the charge that analytic philosophy has become "a form of metaphysics." Putnam never quite says that all metaphysics of the kind characteristic of recent analytic philosophy is objectionably scientistic, but he implies as much—and gives no criterion to distinguish the good kind from the bad. This is surely a misuse of the term "scientism," but more important it excludes almost all of philosophical thought from Plato to the present. Can Putnam really mean this? Does he believe that traditional ontology and epistemology are tarred with the scientistic brush? Is Frege's work included? What about Russell's? Or Strawson's, or Davidson's or Kripke's or Dummett's? What of Leibniz and Spinoza and Kant and Hume and Plato and Aristotle? Is all this to be condemned as science fetishism? I rather fear he does mean this, at least in the sense that his words imply it. His positive recommendations, such as they are, leave no room for the activities of such thinkers. The problem is that Putnam vastly overstates his case, aided and abetted by an ill-defined use of polemical terms. We are told, repeatedly, that philosophy must be neither "metaphysical" nor "sceptical," but it is hard to take this literally, especially when Putnam's basis for saying it—the supposed errors of a handful of contemporary philosophers—fall so far short of the conclusion. Does he think there can be such a thing as nonscientistic metaphysics, and who (if anyone) does he think practices it? Let me offer Thomas Nagel as an example of the category in question: in what way is his work in metaphysics scientistic?

Putnam's constructive proposals for what good philosophy might be like are similarly underdescribed and jejune. Wittgenstein is cited as setting a good example, but there is no decent account of what this goodness is supposed to consist in. All we get are sentimental allusions to his "relentless honesty" and his "very real compassion" and his "effort to understand forms of life he himself did not share." The work of Wittgenstein's that is discussed is mainly that on the nature of religious belief—which comes to us only from notes taken at some lectures he gave in 1938. This is all the more curious because Wittgenstein did have an explicit metaphilosophy in which philosophy is distinguished from science; and he had definite views about what the philosopher can legitimately do—produce "perspicuous representations" of our ordinary concepts for therapeutic purposes. Putnam never aligns himself with either the negative or positive parts of Wittgenstein's metaphilosophical position, but he does not dissociate himself from them either. It would have been nice for the genuflection to have been accompanied by some statement about the rightness or wrongness of Wittgenstein's conception of the philosopher's task. As it is, Putnam has next to nothing substantive to say about how philosophy should proceed once scientism (in his dubiously broad sense) has been uprooted. All we are told is that Wittgenstein (along with John Dewey) illustrates the way "philosophical reflection which is completely honest can unsettle our prejudices and our pet convictions and our blind spots without flashy claims to deconstruct truth itself or the world itself." Surely he is a lot more interesting and singular than that. The reason Putnam has been reduced to this kind of vapid gesturing is that he has scattered his fire far too broadly: too much has been excluded as either scientistically "metaphysical" or wantonly "sceptical." This is not a renewal of philosophy but its death knell. Not that an attempt to terminate philosophy would necessarily be misguided: what is objectionable is to advertise it as a rebirth.

It is with some relief that one turns from the vague and portentous general themes of *Renewing Philosophy* to the more detailed discussion of particular theses by identifiable individuals. Here Putnam deploys the kind of analytic ingenuity that has made him so prominent, and which he now apparently would like to repudiate as merely playing the game of the philosophers he officially scorns. (He wishes he were Søren Kierkegaard but is condemned to be Hilary Putnam.) In the first chapter, on the prospects for artifical intelligence, he makes some fairly familiar, but telling, points about the obstacles in the way of simulating human reasoning, criticizing his own earlier advocacy of Turing-machine functionalism. The central difficulty is that nobody has any idea how to formalize human intelligence when it is operating abductively (i.e., constructing theory), because nobody understands the nature of this capacity when we exercise it. Functionalism is a theory with little to recommend it by way of intrinsic plausibility. But it does not follow that every theory of the mind must share this defect.

The next two chapters criticize teleological and causal accounts of intentionality, where the good old analytic topics of referential indeterminacy and the nature of causation and counterfactuals come in for the usual analytic philosopher's treatment. Some worthwhile points are made here, and they are sure to be pursued in the analytic journals. Can the teleological theory justify assigning *meat* as the referent of a dog's food-directed thought instead of some wider concept such as edible stuff of such and such meatlike appearance? Is Fodor right to claim that the counterfactuals "if cats didn't cause 'cat'-tokenings, then cat-pictures wouldn't" and "if cat-pictures didn't cause 'cat'-tokenings, then cats wouldn't" have different truth-values? These questions are pursued with Putnam's customary analytic brio, thereby reinforcing rather than undermining the interest of the kind of philosophy he has set himself against. If this is scientism, then at least it is interesting scientism.

Where matters turn murky is in Putnam's repeated claim that the notions of law, causation, and counterfactuality are intrinsically mind-dependent. His point appears to be that when assessing the truth-value of such statements we (commonly? invariably?) take into account the interests and intentions of the speaker, so that what we think of as the objective world is really tainted with mental and normative notions. Now it is vital here to distinguish two different claims, which Putnam is never pedantic enough to do: first, that there is a pragmatic component to what fixes the proposition expressed by statements of these kinds; second, that the truth conditions of the proposition so expressed themselves incorporate reference to states of mind possessed by the speaker. The second claim clearly does not follow from the first, as the example of tensed discourse readily shows. Putnam apparently wishes to make a claim of the second kind, so that the corresponding facts involve mental elements. Thus whether A caused B becomes partly dependent on human interests, as do counterfactual-supporting laws.

This thesis raises an obvious question, which Putnam does not get around to addressing: were there laws and causal relations and counterfactual dependencies before human minds came into existence? The naive answer would appear to be yes, but this is inconsistent with Putnam's avowed mentalism about the nomic structure of the external world. And, given that these notions are inextricably involved in the individuation of ordinary physical objects, it is hard to see how he can avoid the consequence that there were no atoms or stars or mountains before there were people. If not, what was there? Once idealism has begun, there is no stopping it. "To try to divide the world into a part that is independent of us and a part that is contributed by us is an old temptation," he remarks at one point, "but giving in to it leads to disaster every time." I don't know what disasters he has in mind, but I would find it pretty catastrophic if it turned out, on philosophical grounds alone, that the material universe did not predate human existence.

Putnam's diagnosis of lurking scientism is perhaps plausible in his discussion of Bernard Williams on ethics and science. Certainly Williams is keen to find a telling epistemological difference between the two, to the detriment of ethics; and he locates it in the way we explain convergence of opinion in each case. I think, with Putnam, that Williams greatly overplays the differences here—the Chomskyan perspective is a useful corrective. But Putnam's own position on the nature and availability of Williams's "absolute conception" seems uncompelling. First, he himself displays an unfortunate scientistic streak when discussing the objectivity of color, citing what he takes scientists to say as undermining the kind of subjectivist position often advocated by philosophers. He seems not to recognize that there is quite a large gap between scientific theories about color and the correct philosophical interpretation of these theories: here, as elsewhere, you cannot simply read the philosophy off the science. Odd, too, is his unpuzzled acceptance of mind independence with respect to secondary qualities, when he is so ready to find mentality where we might least expect it. Colors and tastes and smells are out there, he thinks, but physical causation and law are (partly) in here!

On the other hand, his denial that we can transcend our subjective peculiarities to develop a conception of the world available to beings with a different sensory perspective on it is never made convincing—indeed, I am not sure that the issue is ever properly formulated. Surely he would have to agree that physical theories identical to ours could be arrived at by intelligent beings who sensed the world differently from us; though of course their grasp of these theories would be conditioned by the structure of their intelligence. Realism does not require the myth of mind-free thought.

The final chapter of the book in which Dewey's work is set beside Wittgenstein's as a paragon of how philosophy should be done, can best be described as a well-meaning ramble through James, Sartre, Durkheim, Peirce, and Kierkegaard. The main substantive point appears to be that some beliefs and decisions involve faith as opposed to reason, so that you don't have to justify them. This is not the bright future of philosophical thought I want to be around to see. Is philosophy in a state of crisis? Yes, of course. It always has been. That is its nature—and we each have our theories as to why this is so. Does philosophy need renewal? Yes, assuredly, but that also is its natural condition.

Index